Depression

Constance Hammen
University of California, Los Angeles

Psychology Press
a member of the Taylor & Francis group

ABG 1309

Psychology Press Ltd., Publishers
27 Church Road
Hove
East Sussex, BN3 2FA
UK

British Library Cataloguing in Publication Data

A catalogue record for this book is available from the British Library

ISBN 0-86377-726-0 (hbk)
    0-86377-727-9 (pbk)

ISSN 1368-454X (Clinical Psychology: A Modular Course)

Front cover illustration:
Illustration of Depression, by Louise Williams/Science Photo Library

Cover design by Joyce Chester
Printed and bound in the UK by TJ International (Padstow) Ltd.

Contents

Series preface

Clinical Psychology: A Modular Course was designed to overcome the problems faced by the traditional text book in conveying what psychological disorders are really like. All the books in the series, written by leading scholars and practitioners in the field, can be read as stand-alone texts, but they will also integrate with the other modules to form a comprehensive resource in clinical psychology. Students of psychology, medicine, nursing and social work, as well as busy practitioners in many professions, often need an accessible but thorough introduction to how people experience anxiety, depression, addiction, or other disorders, how common they are, and who is most likely to suffer from them, as well as up-to-date research evidence on the causes and available treatments. The series will appeal to those who want to go deeper into the subject than the traditional textbook will allow, and base their examination answers, research, projects, assignments, or practical decisions on a clearer and more rounded appreciation of the clinical and research evidence.

Chris R. Brewin

Defining and diagnosing depression 1

Lew takes one look at me and says that he doesn't even need to ask how I'm doing. I pour it all out to him: I can't sleep. I can't eat. I can't read or talk or concentrate for more than several seconds. The force of gravity around me has tripled. It takes so much effort just to lift an arm or take a step. When I am not curled up in a ball on the couch, I pace. I rock desperately in my rocking chair. I wring my hands.

I try to go to my Saturday morning meditation group. I park the car but almost turn back two or three times before I get to the front door … I try to listen and add something, but I can hardly follow the conversation. I can't even fake it anymore. At the break I excuse myself with a lie that I have to get to Keara's softball game. I know that I can't make it through forty-five minutes of silent meditation. I come home crying. More empty tears to God about why this is still happening. Tears for an end to it. Tears for mercy.

The house is deserted. I search for things to do. It is all I can do just to empty the dishwasher and sweep the floor. Then I lie on the couch and stare into space, vacant and deadened. I have a haircut appointment that I am already dreading, even though it's three hours away. How will I keep up a conversation with my effusive hairdresser? It will be a monumental effort just to move my lips into a smile. My face is simultaneously waxy and frozen. The muscles have gone on strike.

Martha Manning (1994, p.104; pp.106-7), Undercurrents:
A therapist's reckoning with her own depression.

[By October] the fading evening light … had none of its autumnal loveliness, but ensnared me in a suffocating gloom … I felt an immense and aching solitude. I could no longer concentrate during those afternoon hours, which for years had been my working time …

Soon evident are the slowed-down responses, near paralysis, psychic energy throttled back close to zero. Ultimately, the body is affected and feels sapped, drained...I found myself eating only for subsistence [and] exhaustion combined with sleeplessness is a rare torture ... What I had begun to discover is that, mysteriously and in ways that are totally remote from normal experience, the gray drizzle of horror induced by depression takes on the quality of physical pain ... it is entirely natural that the victim begins to think ceaselessly of oblivion.

William Styron (1990), Darkness visible.

The words of these two modern writers capture vividly the experience of depression, but its themes have also been echoed in ancient texts of the Bible, Greek, Roman, and Chinese classics—as well as in Shakespearean plays and Russian novels. Depression is a universal, timeless, and ageless human affliction. Among those who first described the features of depression in modern clinical terms was Kraepelin (1921, p.76), the German scholar who helped establish a classification system for mental disorders:

Mood is sometimes dominated by a profound inward dejection and gloomy hopelessness, sometimes more by indefinite anxiety and restlessness. The patient's heart is heavy, nothing can permanently rouse his interest, nothing gives him pleasure ...

He feels solitary, indescribably unhappy, as a "creature disinherited of fate"; he is skeptical about God, and with a certain dull submission, which shuts out every comfort and every gleam of light, he drags himself with difficulty from one day to another. Everything has become disagreeable to him; everything wearies him, company, music, travel, his professional work. Everywhere he sees only the dark side and difficulties; the people round him are not so good and unselfish as he had thought; one disappointment and disillusionment follows another. Life appears to him aimless, he thinks that he is superfluous in the world, he cannot restrain himself any longer, the thought occurs to him to take his life without his knowing why. He has a feeling as if something had cracked in him.

While the personal experience of depression is profoundly painful, it is often misunderstood by others. The experience of depression often seems paradoxical: a new mother gets depressed after a much-wanted birth of a child; an executive slips into a depression following a successful effort to achieve a higher position; a widow seems more depressed when her dog dies than she did when her husband of many years died. Moreover, most individuals in Western societies are raised to expect to have considerable control over moods, and are exhorted not to let themselves suffer from depression. Thus, it is distressing to others when a loved one or friend does not "snap out" of depression, and the hopeless, helpless, and self-hating attitudes expressed by depressed individuals often seem illogical and irrational, as if the depressed person wilfully and perversely holds onto unreasonable moods and beliefs.

As this book hopes to explore, depression is neither uncommon nor particularly paradoxical—nor is it a failure of willpower and motivation. It is enormously impairing—and even deadly—and its effects on both the afflicted person and his or her family can be profoundly negative.

Phenomenology of depressive experiences

The term *depression* is used in everyday language to describe a range of experiences from a slightly noticeable and temporary mood decrease to a profoundly impaired and even life-threatening disorder. When used to describe a mood, the term conveys a temporary state of dysphoria that may last a few moments, hours, or even a few days. As such, it is usually a normal reaction to an upsetting event, or even an exaggerated description of a typical event ("This weather is depressing," or "I've gained a few pounds. How depressing!"). A young man might feel sad for a few days following a romantic disappointment, or a woman might be discouraged for a few days on being passed over for a job. Such experiences are not the topic of this book. Instead, the term "depression" as described in the book refers to a constellation of experiences including not only mood, but also physical, mental, and behavioural experiences that define more prolonged, impairing, and severe conditions that may be clinically diagnosable as a syndrome of depression.

The descriptions at the beginning of the chapter differ from one another, but they share features of the syndromes of depression. Each one has some features from the four different domains that define depressive disorders. Depressed people may differ from one another by the number, unique patterns, and severity of the symptoms. The four general domains are *affect*, *cognition*, *behaviour*, and *physical functioning*.

Affective symptoms.   Depression is one of several disorders generically called *affective disorders*, referring to the manifestations of abnormal affect, or mood, as a defining feature. Thus, depressed mood, sadness, feeling low, down in the dumps, or empty are typical. However, sometimes the most apparent mood is irritability (especially in depressed children). Moreover, not all depressed people manifest sadness or depression as such. Instead, they may report feeling loss of interest or pleasure, a feeling of "blah", listlessness, apathy. Nothing seems enjoyable—not even experiences that previously elicited positive feelings, including work and recreation, social interactions, sexual activity, and the like. Pastimes are no longer enjoyable; even pleasurable relationships with one's family and friends may no longer hold appeal or even be negative, and the individual may find it hard to think of things to do that might help to relieve the depression even temporarily. Even when he or she accomplishes an important task, there is little sense of satisfaction. Some severely depressed people have described the loss of pleasure as seeing the world in black, white, and grey with no colour. The experience of loss of interest or pleasure is one of the most common features of the depression syndrome, according to many studies of depressed adults and teenagers, from many different countries (reviewed in Klinger, 1993).

> George, a middle-aged man of apparent good health, has felt listless and bored for a few weeks. His favourite television programmes no longer interest him in the evenings, and on weekends he can't think of anything to do that he imagines would be pleasurable—in contrast to his formerly active and fun-seeking self. He says his pals are "boring" and his attitude about seeing his girlfriend is that she doesn't interest him anymore. Fortunately, she is astute enough to suspect that he became depressed ever since someone else got the promotion at work that he hoped for—though George himself would deny that he is depressed.

Cognitive symptoms.   Some have called depression a disorder of thinking, as much as it is a disorder of mood. Depressed people typically have negative thoughts about themselves, their worlds, and the future. They experience themselves as incompetent, worthless, and are relentlessly critical of their own acts and characteristics, and often feel guilty as they dwell on their perceived shortcomings. Low self-esteem is therefore a common attribute of depression. Individuals may feel helpless to manage their lives or resolve problems. They may view their lives and futures as bleak and unrewarding, feeling that change is not only pointless but essentially unattainable. Cognitions reflecting hopelessness about one's ability to control desired outcomes may be common, and the resulting despair may also give rise to thoughts of wanting to die or to take one's own life.

> Annette has been increasingly depressed since her boyfriend went off to the university. Although he keeps in touch with her, she is consumed with the thoughts that he is trying to meet other women, that she's not good enough to sustain his interest—and that indeed, why would anyone ever love her. At work she imagines that she is doing a poor job and expects to be fired—despite her boss's praise for her achievements. When her girlfriends ask her to go out with them she believes that they don't really want her company and are only feeling sorry for her that her boyfriend is away. As she becomes more and more depressed, she believes herself to be a horrible person; tasks at work seem more and more overwhelming so that she believes that she is incompetent and utterly helpless to figure out how to manage projects she used to do with ease.

The cognitive features of depression have been given particular emphasis by some investigators, who note that thinking in such grim and self-critical ways actually makes people more depressed or prolongs their depression. The negativistic thinking is commonly irrational and distorted, and represents very different interpretations of the self and the world during the depressed state than an individual would typically display when they weren't depressed. This observation gave rise to Aaron Beck's cognitive model of depression (Beck, 1967; 1976), that hypothesises an underlying vulnerability to depression due to tendencies to perceive the self, world, and future in negative ways. Somewhat similar models of depression emphasising self-esteem (Bernet, Ingram, & Johnson, 1993; Roberts & Monroe, 1994) and hopelessness (Abramson, Metalsky, & Alloy, 1989) are discussed in a later chapter.

In addition to negativistic thinking, depression is often marked by difficulties in mental processes involving concentration, decision making, and memory. The depressed person may find it enormously difficult to make even simple decisions, and significant decisions seem beyond one's capacity altogether. Depressed patients often report problems in concentrating, especially when reading or watching television, and memory may be impaired (Watts, 1993). Memory problems, in fact, often lead depressed people to worry further that their minds are failing, and in older depressed individuals what is actually a treatable memory deficit due to depression may be misinterpreted as a sign of irreversible dementia. As Watts (1993) notes, it is difficult to tell whether poor memory performances are due to cognitive impairment as such, or to depressive symptoms such as being slowed down or lack of confidence. Interestingly, according to Watts' review, some studies have shown that the memory deficits are less apparent for negative content material than for positive. It would appear that some of the mental problems of depression are due to distraction by irrelevant (depressive) thoughts, and others are due to slowed thinking and impaired concentration and memory.

Behavioural symptoms.   Because of their apathy and diminished motivation of depression, it is common for individuals to withdraw from social activities or reduce their typical behaviours. In severe depression, the individual might stay in bed for prolonged periods. Social interactions might be shunned because of loss of motivation and interest, and also because depressed people perceive, fairly accurately, that being around them may be aversive to others.

Actual changes in movements, called psychomotor changes, are often observed, taking the form of being either slowed down or agitated and restless. Some depressed individuals may talk and move more slowly, their faces showing little animation with their mouths and eyes seeming to droop as if weighted down. Their speech is marked by pauses, fewer words, monotone voice, and less eye contact (Cloitre, Katz, & Van Praag, 1993). Other depressed people display agitation, indicated by restlessness, hand movements, fidgeting and self-touching, and gesturing; Cloitre et al. (1993) note, however, that there is not increased speech in agitated depression.

Psychomotor agitation may be more commonly observed in depressed people who are also experiencing anxiety symptoms, while psychomotor slowing is thought to be more typical of "pure" depression. Interestingly, presence of psychomotor slowing has been found to be a good predictor of a positive response to antidepressant medication (Joyce & Paykel, 1989). Potential subtypes of depression based on symptom and etiological features will be discussed in more detail later.

Physical symptoms.   In addition to motor behaviour changes that are apparent in some depressed people, changes in appetite, sleep, and energy are also common. Reduced energy is a very frequent complaint (occurring in 93% of depressed patients in a study by Buchwald and Rudick-Davis, 1993). Depressed patients complain of listlessness, lethargy, feeling heavy and leaden, and lacking the physical stamina to undertake or complete tasks. Sleep changes are one of the hallmarks of depression, and can take several forms: difficulty falling asleep, staying asleep, or too much sleep. Depressed people sometimes experience what is called "early morning awakening," a problem of waking an hour or more before the regular awakening time, usually with difficulty falling back asleep. The Buchwald study found that 98% of depressed patients reported one or more sleep problems. Similarly, appetite changes may take the form of increased or decreased appetite with corresponding weight gain or loss. Some people eat more and others less when depressed—and such patterns seem to correspond with sleep (increased sleep and increased appetite).

Implications.   The multiplicity of symptoms of depression means that depressed people differ one from another in the manifestations of their disorder. Such differences may reflect variability in the severity of the depression, but may also suggest that there are different forms of depression that have different causes and treatments. The diagnostic systems in use today define several categories that cut across these variabilities, and that represent the major forms of the disorder that are the basis of most research and clinical categorisation.

Diagnosis of depression

The first diagnostic distinction to be made is the difference between *unipolar* depression and *bipolar* disorder. Unipolar depression, which is the focus of this book, includes only depressive conditions occurring in the absence of current or past mania or hypomania. *Mania* and *hypomania* (mild mania) are episodes of abnormal elevations of activity level, self-esteem, mood, and other features that are in many ways the opposite of depression. Individuals who have cycles of both depression and mania/hypomania are considered to have bipolar affective disorder, which is a chronic problem of recurrent symptoms, often marked not only by extreme mood swings but even by psychotic experiences including delusions and hallucinations. Even though their depressions may be indistinguishable from those of people who have only the severe unipolar form of the disorder, individuals with bipolar disorder are considered to have an etiologically different disorder with a different course, and to require different types of treatment. Thus, a researcher or clinician must carefully evaluate not only the current symptoms but also the past history of mood disorders, bearing in mind that research has found that about 10% or more of initially depressed people go on to develop bipolar episodes (Coryell et al., 1995).

> Ronald has just been hospitalised for severe depression and suicidality. Nearly unable to get out of bed, he is dishevelled, weeping, and moaning about wishing he were dead. The examining psychiatrist at the hospital determines, however, that in the months before the depression Ronald was extremely euphoric and overactive. He believed he had achieved a breakthrough in his business ideas, and had borrowed huge sums of money to finance new ventures that in retrospect had little chance of success. Sleeping only two or three hours a night, he had worked feverishly on his projects, jumping from one to another without completing any—and had talked incessantly to anyone he could find about how great his ideas were and how important he was about to become. Information from Ronald's family members revealed that he had experienced several such cycles of mania and depression since his early 20s. He was given a diagnosis of bipolar disorder, and treated with lithium as well as an antidepressant medication.

Bipolar I disorder includes a history of episodes of depression and mania, while depression with a history of hypomania is called Bipolar II disorder. The case above illustrates Bipolar I disorder, because of relatively clear patterns of severe mood disturbance, but Bipolar II is relatively more difficult to detect if the hypomania is more subtle or brief. An additional diagnostic problem is that sometimes there is no history of previous mania or hypomania but the person is nonetheless suffering from bipolar disorder. It has been demonstrated in longitudinal research that approximately 15% of individuals initially diagnosed with "unipolar" depression eventually "switch" to bipolar disorder with the eventual display of manic/hypomanic episodes. For instance, a large-scale 11-year follow-up of patients indicated that about 4% converted to Bipolar I disorder over time, and 8.6% converted to Bipolar II disorder (Akiskal et al., 1995; Coryell et al., 1995).

According to the *Diagnostic and statistical manual of mental disorders* (4th ed.) (*DSM-IV*; American Psychiatric Association, 1994), unipolar depressions basically take one of three forms: major depressive episode, dysthymic disorder, or "depression not otherwise specified" (including several forms of briefer or milder periods of depression). These conditions are briefly described.

Major depressive episode.   Table 1.1 displays the diagnostic criteria for major depressive disorder, according to *DSM-IV*; and Table 1.2 displays the very similar criteria in the *International classification of diseases and related health problems* (10th ed.) (*ICD-10*; World Health Organization, 1993). Acknowledging the heterogeneity of depressive presentations, these systems permit individual variability so long as essential features are shared. Note that individuals must show the symptoms all or most of the time for at least two weeks. Also, in order to be diagnosed, the episode must be clinically significant in terms of causing distress or impaired functioning in the person's typical social or occupational roles.

Dysthymic disorder.   In contrast to a distinct period of marked symptomatology, some individuals display milder but chronic symptoms. Dysthymic disorder would be diagnosed if symptoms persisted for at least two years (although there might be brief periods of normal mood lasting no more than 2 months). Additionally, in order to be diagnosed, dysthymic disorder must be seen to cause significant distress or disruption in the person's significant areas of functioning.

The subcategory of "early onset" dysthymia, referring to presence of the disorder before age 21, appears to mark an especially severe form of the disorder. In a study comparing early-onset dysthymic patients to patients with major depressive episode, the former had significantly higher rates of social and global maladjustment, personality and substance abuse disorders, and also higher rates of past major depressive episodes (Klein, Taylor, Dickstein, & Harding, 1988a).

When a person suffers from dysthymic disorder but has a major depressive episode superimposed on it, the condition is called "double depression." Double depression was observed in about 25% of depressed patients seen in a large study conducted by the National Institute of Mental Health (NIMH) (Keller et al., 1983). Double depression is particularly pernicious in its course and associated impairment (e.g. Klein, Taylor, Harding, & Dickstein, 1988b). Even in untreated community samples, the co-occurrence of major depression and dysthymic disorder is common, as indicated in interview surveys of both adults and adolescents (Lewinsohn, Rohde, Seeley, & Hops, 1991).

Table 1.1: Diagnostic criteria for depressive disorders.
Diagnostic and Statistical Manual (DSM-IV; **American Psychiatric Association, 1994)**

Major depressive episode

A   Five or more of the following symptoms during the same 2-week period; at least one of the symptoms is depressed mood or loss of interest or pleasure.

    a)   depressed mood most of the day, nearly every day (as indicated by subjective report or observation by others). Note: in children and adolescents, can be irritable mood

    b)   markedly diminished interest or pleasure in all or almost all activities most of the day, nearly every day (as indicated by subjective account or observation by others)

    c)   significant weight loss when not dieting or weight gain (e.g. a change of more than 5% body weight in a month), or decrease or increase in appetite nearly every day. Note: in children consider failure to make expected weight gains

    d)   insomnia or hypersomnia nearly every day

    e)   psychomotor agitation or retardation nearly every day (observable by others)

    f)   fatigue or loss of energy nearly every day

    g)   feelings of worthlessness or excessive or inappropriate guilt nearly every day

    h)   diminished ability to think or concentrate, or indecisiveness, nearly every day (either subjective or observed by others)

    i)   recurrent thoughts of death (not just fear of dying), recurrent suicidal ideation without a specific plan, or a suicide attempt or a specific plan for committing suicide

Dysthymic disorder

A   Depressed mood for most of the day, for more days than not, as indicated either by subjective account or observation by others, for at least 2 years. Note: in children and adolescents, mood can be irritable and duration must be at least 1 year.

B   Presence, while depressed, of two or more of the following:

    a)   poor appetite or overeating

    b)   insomnia or hypersomnia

    c)   low energy or fatigue

    d)   low self-esteem

    e)   poor concentration or difficulty making decisions

    f)   feelings of hopelessness

C   During the period of depression, the person has never been without symptoms in A or B for more than 2 months at a time. Also, the disturbance must not be better accounted for by chronic major depressive disorder (or major depressive disorder in partial remission)—i.e. no major depressive disorder in the first 2 years of the disturbance (1 year for children and adolescents)

Reproduced by permission of the American Psychiatric Association (American Psychiatric Association, 1994).

Table 1.2: Diagnostic criteria for depressive disorders:
International classification of diseases (ICD-10; **World Health Organization, 1993)**

Note: general diagnostic criteria and clinical features are specified, but the following are the more precisely-defined diagnostic criteria for research (for depressive episode and dysthymia)

Depressive episode

A   Symptoms must be present for at least 2 weeks; the person did not meet criteria for mania or hypomania at any time.

B
- a)   depressed mood most of the day and almost every day, uninfluenced by circumstances
- b)   loss of interest or pleasure in activities that are normally pleasurable
- c)   increased fatiguability or decreased energy

C
- a)   loss of confidence or self-esteem
- b)   unreasonable feelings of self-reproach or excessive and inappropriate guilt
- c)   recurrent thoughts of death or suicide, or any suicidal behaviour
- d)   complaints or evidence of diminished ability to think or concentrate, such as indecisiveness or vacillation
- e)   change in psychomotor activity, with agitation or retardation (either subjective or objective)
- f)   sleep disturbance of any type
- g)   change in appetite (decrease or increase) with corresponding weight change

Note: Depressive episodes may be diagnosed as: *Mild* (at least 2 from B plus at least 2 from C, for a total of at least 4); *Moderate* (at least 2 from B plus 3 or 4 from C, for a total of at least 6); *Severe* depressive episode without psychotic features (all 3 from B plus at least 4 from C, for a total of at least 9—no hallucinations, delusions, or depressive stupor).

Dysthymia

A   There must be a period of at least 2 years of constant or constantly recurring depressed mood; intervening periods of normal mood rarely last for longer than a few weeks; and there are no episodes of hypomania.

B   None, or very few, individual episodes within the 2-year period are sufficiently severe or long-lasting to meet criteria for recurrent mild depressive disorder.

C   During at least some of the periods of depression at least 3 of the following should be present:
- a)   reduced energy or activity
- b   insomnia
- c)   loss of self-confidence or feelings of inadequacy
- d)   difficulty in concentrating
- e)   frequent tearfulness
- f)   loss of interest in or enjoyment of sex and other pleasurable activities
- g)   feeling of hopelessness or despair
- h)   a perceived inability to cope with the routine responsibilities of everyday life
- i)   pessimism about the future or brooding over the past
- j)   social withdrawal
- k)   reduced talkativeness

Reproduced by permission of the World Health Organization. World Health Organization (1993). *The ICD-10 classification of mental and behavioural disorders: Diagnostic criteria for research.* Geneva: WHO.

These authors also determined that when individuals had histories of both disorders, the dysthymia was more likely to occur before the onset of major depression.

Other depression diagnoses. When depressive features are present that do not fit the criteria for major depressive episode or dysthymic disorder, they may fit one of several possible residual categories of "depression not otherwise specified." These include *premenstrual dysphoric disorder*, a controversial category awaiting further research confirmation of its validity; criteria include depressive symptoms occurring regularly in the end of the menstrual cycle prior to menses, and are sufficiently severe to cause impaired functioning. *Minor depressive disorder* includes at least 2 weeks of symptoms but with fewer than the 5 required for major depressive disorder. *Recurrent brief depression* refers to episodes lasting from 2 days to 2 weeks, occurring at least once a month for at least 12 months.

Diagnosis of depression in children and adolescents

Although the emphasis of the book is adult depression, there has been considerable interest in child and adolescent depression following the "discovery" that such conditions could be diagnosed in children using virtually the same criteria as for adults.

> Barney is a 10-year-old boy whose irritability and temper tantrums are evident both at home and at school. With little provocation he bursts into tears and yells and throws objects. At home he has been sleeping poorly, and has gained 10 pounds over the past couple of months from constant snacking. At school he seems to have difficulty concentrating and seems easily distracted. Increasingly shunned by his peers, he plays by himself—and at home, spends most of his time in his room watching television. The school psychologist talked with him, and she reports that he is a deeply unhappy child who expresses feelings of worthlessness and hopelessness—and even a wish that he would die. These experiences probably began about six months ago when his father—divorced from the mother for several years—remarried and moved to another town where he spends far less time with Barney.

This case illustrates three key issues about the diagnosis of depression in youngsters. One is that the same criteria used for adults can be applied and that the essential features of the depression syndrome are as recognisable in children as in adults (Carlson & Cantwell, 1980; Mitchell, McCauley, Burke, & Moss, 1988). Second, because children's externalising or disruptive behaviours attract more attention or are more readily expressed, compared to internal, subjective suffering, depression is sometimes overlooked. It may not be recognised, or it might not be assessed. Childhood depression has a high level of co-existing disorders, especially involving conduct problems and other disruptive behaviours; such patterns gave rise to the erroneous belief that depression is "masked." Third, there are a few features of the syndrome of depression, such as irritable mood, that are more likely to be typical of children than of adults, leading to age-specific modifications of the diagnostic criteria. Additionally, as we discuss later, certain features of depression are more typical at different ages.

Major depression, therefore, would be diagnosed with adult criteria as in Tables 1.1 and 1.2, but permitting irritability instead of depressed mood. Dysthymia in children must persist at least 1 year (in adults duration is at least 2 years). According to a recent study of dysthymic disorder in children, it differs from major depression primarily in the emphasis on gloomy thoughts and other negative affect, with fewer symptoms such as loss of interest, social withdrawal, fatigue, and reduced sleep and poor appetite (Kovacs, Akiskal, Gatsonis, & Parrone, 1994).

Developmental considerations should be taken into account when assessing for depression in children. For instance, irritability may be substituted for depressed mood because it is recognised both that irritability is a common expression of distress in depressed youngsters—as shown in the case of Barney—and that young depressed children may not express subjective negative affect. As an example of the frequency of irritability as a symptom of the syndrome of depression in youngsters, Goodyer and Cooper (1993) found that 80% of their sample of 11-16 year-old girls with major depressive episode reported irritability, while Ryan et al. (1987) observed irritability or anger in 83% of a child and adolescent clinic sample.

There may be other developmental differences in the kinds of symptoms most likely to be present in the depression syndrome. Young depressed children, especially preschoolers and preadolescents, are unlikely to report subjective dysphoria and hopelessness, but instead "look" depressed in facial expression and posture (e.g. Carlson & Kashani, 1988; Ryan et al., 1987). In adolescence, by contrast, depressed mood is commonly reported by more than 90% of those with major depression (e.g. Mitchell et al., 1988; Ryan et al., 1987). Also, younger depressed children are more likely to have physically unjustified or exaggerated somatic complaints (Kashani & Carlson, 1987; Ryan et al., 1987). In a community sample, depression symptoms were more associated with physical complaints among 12-year-olds than they were for 17-year-olds (Kashani, Rosenberg, & Reid, 1989). Younger children, as noted earlier, also show more irritability, uncooperativeness, apathy, and lack of interest (Kashani, Holcomb, & Orvaschel, 1986).

Two studies compared the symptoms of depressed youngsters and adults. Overall, several symptoms *increase* with age: loss of pleasure, psychomotor retardation, and diurnal variation, while several decrease with age: depressed appearance, physical complaints, and poor self-esteem (Carlson & Kashani, 1988). Comparing combined child-adolescent groups with a sample of adults, Mitchell et al. (1988) found similar differences for self-esteem, somatic complaints, diurnal variation, and also found that adult depressed patients report less guilt and more early morning awakening and weight loss than do depressed youngsters.

In addition to presentation of depressive symptoms, patterns of comorbid disorders are also likely to be somewhat different at different ages. For instance, depressed children (and young adolescents) are more likely than depressed older adolescents to display separation anxiety disorders, while adolescents report more eating disorders and substance use disorders (e.g. Fleming & Offord, 1990). Other kinds of anxiety disorders and disruptive behavioural disorders appear to co-exist with depression for both children and adolescents.

There are several other symptoms frequently seen in children and adolescents. Social withdrawal, for example, is commonly reported as a correlate of depressive symptoms in a community sample, occurring in 93-100% of groups of depressed girls ranging between 11 and 16 (Goodyer & Cooper, 1993), and in 76% of the Mitchell et al. (1988) sample. Excessive worrying and other anxiety symptoms are common, as are oppositional and conduct problems (e.g. Goodyer & Cooper, 1993; Mitchell et al., 1988). Indeed, the likelihood of comorbid anxiety and disruptive behaviour disorder diagnoses is very high (e.g. 60-70%), and we discuss the matter of comorbidity in greater detail later. Somatic symptoms and bodily complaints are also frequently associated with depression, as noted earlier, and problems with self-esteem—and in adolescent girls, distress over negative body image—are also common associated symptoms of depression (e.g. Allgood-Merten, Lewinsohn, & Hops, 1990; Petersen, Sarigiani, & Kennedy, 1991).

Suicidal thoughts and attempts are among the diagnostic criteria for major depression. Suicidal ideation is quite common in depressed youngsters, occurring in about two-thirds of preschoolers, preadolescents, and adolescents (Kashani & Carlson, 1987; Mitchell et al., 1988; Ryan et al., 1987). Actual suicidal attempts occurred in 39% of the preadolescent and adolescent samples of Mitchell et al. (1988), with 6-12% of the Ryan et al. (1987) child and adolescent samples making moderate or severe attempts. These rates appear to be higher among depressed youngsters than among depressed adults. Suicidality is not restricted to depressed youth, however, often occurring among those with substance use disorders and impulsive behaviour disorders, and may be greatly affected by social environmental factors (such as a friend's or publicised suicide) as well as by depression as such (e.g. Lewinsohn, Rohde, & Seeley, 1994). Indeed, the correlates and predictors of childhood, or especially adolescent, suicidality, represent an extensive body of work beyond the scope of this chapter, but see Berman and Jobes (1991).

Subtypes of depression

In addition to the more formal diagnostic subtypes of depression currently included in the *DSM-IV* that are defined by severity or duration, there is an enormous need to consider the possible qualitative distinctions in depressions. As indicated by the heterogeneity of expressions of the features of depression, some seem more "biological" in presentation while others are more "psychological". Also, the depressions may vary considerably in their possible etiological factors, including both biological and psychological origins. It is hardly surprising, therefore, that considerable effort has been devoted to the search for depression subtypes.

Unfortunately, the research on subtypes has been considerably confused by mixing severity, type of symptoms, and presumed etiology. Historically, research has focused on the neurotic-psychotic, reactive-endogenous, and endogenous-nonendogenous subtypes, but the terms *psychotic* and *endogenous* have variously referred to severity or qualitative distinctions, or to absence of precipitating stressors, often with different investigators using the same term with different operational criteria. A theme cutting across the search for subtypes has been the idea that there are "biological" (endogenous) depressions that are diseases arising in the absence of environmental precipitants vs. "psychological" depressions that stem from personality or situational factors. As Zimmerman, Coryell, Stangl, and Pfohl (1987) noted labels for "endogenous" depression have included vital severe, major incapacitating, psychotic, primary, retarded, melancholic, autonomous, and endogenomorphic, while "nonendogenous" depressions have been variously terms neurotic, reactive, characterologic, atypical, secondary, mild, psychogenic, situational, and nonmelancholic.

To date there is little evidence for a subtype of depression that is qualitatively distinct and that occurs independent of stress precipitants (Hammen, 1995). On the other hand, it does appear useful to identify depressions that are marked by a specific pattern of relatively more physical symptoms. This so-called *melancholic* depression was named thus to avoid the etiological implications of "endogenous" depression, and its features and correlates are described later. Also, there may be other subtypes of depression that future research will establish as etiologically distinct. Examples include "neurotic" depressions (Winokur, 1985; Zimmerman et al., 1987) characterised by young age, stormy life style, and personality disturbance; "autonomous" vs. "sociotropic" depressions based on vulnerability to specific types of stressors that either block independence and achievement or represent interpersonal loss or dependency, and that have distinct patterns of symptoms and response to treatment (e.g. Peselow et al., 1992). Another proposed subtype of "hopelessness" depression is hypothesised to have distinct etiological features leading to cognitions of hopelessness to change uncontrollable negative outcomes (Abramson, Metalsky, & Alloy, 1989; Rose, Abramson, Hodulik, Halberstadt, & Leff, 1994). Limited research bearing on some of these proposed etiological subtypes is reviewed in later chapters. Whether there will eventually be evidence of specific subtypes of depression with different symptoms, causes, and treatment implications is a matter for further research (e.g. Haslam & Beck, 1994), but remains an important theoretical and practical issue.

Diagnostic "specifiers". By using the term "specifiers" to define descriptively important distinctive features of a depressive episode, the *DSM-IV* avoids the implication that these are specific subtypes stemming from specific etiological features. Research may eventually reveal that these and other presentations of depression do have unique causes, but for now the main purpose of using the specifiers with *DSM-IV* diagnoses is to more precisely define patients groups for research or treatment purposes. The following are clinically-derived subgroups based on descriptive features.

Melancholic features include loss of pleasure in all or almost all activities, lack of reactivity to pleasurable stimuli such that even good events, funny stories, or enjoyable experiences do not elicit any (or only a small amount) of positive reaction. Also, depression is regularly worse in the morning than evening (diurnal variation), the person shows excessive or inappropriate guilt, early morning awakening, marked psychomotor change (retarded or agitated), significant loss of appetite and weight loss. The person with melancholia may also experience the depression as having a distinct quality that is different from the kind of sadness felt after the death of a loved one. The melancholic subtype of depression appears to predict a favourable response to antidepressant medications (e.g. Joyce & Paykel, 1989; Rush & Weissenburger, 1994), and therefore might have important treatment implications. It has also been found to correlate with certain abnormal biological functions that some have speculated are indicators of an underlying depressive "disease" (Rush & Weissenburger, 1994). Individuals who display the melancholic subtype tend to show similar features during subsequent episodes (Coryell et al., 1994).

Seasonal pattern depressions refer to those that have an apparent regular onset during certain times of the year, and which also disappear at a characteristic time of the year. In the Northern hemisphere, the most common pattern is Autumn or Winter depressions, clearing up in the Spring, although some individuals experience regular Summer depressions. The seasonal pattern has been observed in 15% of patients with recurrent mood disorders, including both unipolar and bipolar forms (Faedda et al., 1993). Qualitatively, such depressive episodes are especially marked by low energy, more sleeping, overeating and weight gain, and craving for carbohydrate foods (Jacobsen, Wehr, Sack, James, & Rosenthal, 1987).

> Ellen dreads the Fall. As the days become shorter and the weather cold and gloomy, her spirits sink. She becomes more and more lethargic, going to bed a bit earlier each night and having trouble getting up in the dark mornings. In contrast to her summer favourites of fruits and vegetables, she finds herself eating heavier foods, with a special interest in rich, thick sauces and oily meats and breads and pastries of any kind. Often, by December she slips into a depressive episode, marked by low energy and inactivity— with sleeping and eating representing her main enjoyments. Although she believes that she will never feel good again and sometimes finds herself wishing for death, she has learned that by March or April she begins to emerge from her gloom and return to her normal life.

Depression with psychotic features is usually a severe depression in terms of the general symptoms, and includes presence of either hallucinations or delusions. Typically, such hallucinations or delusions have a depressive theme, such as guilt due to the belief that one has caused a terrible misfortune, belief that one is deserving of punishment or is being punished (e.g. voices accusing one of sins or failures), nihilistic beliefs (delusions about the world ending or that one is going to be killed or is already dead), or bodily delusions (such as a belief that one is rotting away). Less often, depressed individuals may have delusions and hallucinations that are not related to depressive or destructive themes (e.g. belief that one's thoughts are being broadcast on the radio). Psychotic depression, even more than melancholic depressions, appear to be relatively stable over repeated episodes (Coryell et al., 1994; Sands & Harrow, 1994); that is, if a person has a psychotic depression their future episodes are also likely to show psychotic features.

Postpartum depression. Many, perhaps most, women develop mild symptoms such as crying, insomnia, poor appetite, and mood lability in the period 3-7 days after giving birth; called "baby blues"; these experiences are considered normal responses to the profound shifts in hormones. However, when a major depressive episode develops in the few weeks after delivery, it may be identified as major depression with postpartum onset. Generally speaking, the symptoms of postpartum depression are not different from symptoms of major depressive episode. Some studies have indicated that, if anything, postpartum depressions are generally milder than nonpostpartum depressions (e.g. Whiffen & Gotlib, 1993). O'Hara and colleagues (1990) did not find any higher rates of depression postpartum than among demographically similar nonchildbearing women. Moreover, several studies have indicated that postpartum status is probably not causally related to the depression. Instead, women who become depressed after childbirth are likely to have had previous emotional problems and vulnerabilities, with their depression likely the result of the stresses of having a child or marital difficulties (e.g. Gotlib, Whiffen, Wallace, & Mount, 1991; O'Hara, Schlechte, Lewis, & Varner, 1991). Women who do develop postpartum depression appear to be at increased risk for developing future depressive episodes, as indicated in a 4½ year follow-up (Philipps & O'Hara, 1991).

About one woman in 1000 has a psychotic postpartum depression. These severe episodes commonly involve delusions about the child ("He's the devil") that cause the woman to act in ways that endanger the child's life. Women who have had one such postpartum psychosis have an elevated risk for subsequent postpartum episodes with psychotic features. It should also be noted that such episodes are especially likely to occur among women with histories of bipolar disorder, but may also occur in unipolar depression.

Comorbidity in depression

In addition to the heterogeneity of the forms of depression, a further complication in understanding and treating depressive disorders is the problem of comorbidity. That is, depression is often accompanied by other disorders. In the recent US National Comorbidity Study, of all the community residents who met criteria for current major depressive episode, only 44% displayed "pure" depression, and the other 56% had depression plus at least one other diagnosis (Blazer, Kessler, McGonagle, & Swartz, 1994).

Depression is very often accompanied by concurrent or recent anxiety disorders (Sanderson, Beck, & Beck, 1990). Barlow (1988) reported that 39% of patients with agoraphobia, 35% of patients with panic disorder, and 17% of those with generalised anxiety disorder had concurrent major depression or dysthymia. The frequent co-occurrence of depression with anxiety once presented clinicians with the diagnostic task of deciding which was the "primary" disorder. However, ample research verified the fact that while some individuals have distinct episodes or periods of either depression or anxiety disorder, many people have current mixtures of both anxiety and depression symptoms (e.g. Blazer et al., 1988). Accordingly, the recent *DSM-IV* version contains a diagnostic category (anxiety "not otherwise specified") that is a mixed anxiety-depression constellation of symptoms.

Besides anxiety disorders, substance abuse, alcoholism and eating disorders are frequently accompanied by depressive disorders, in both clinical and community samples (e.g. Rohde, Lewinsohn, & Seeley, 1991; Sanderson et al., 1990). In the Rohde et al. (1991) community survey, for instance, 42% of depressed adolescents and 25% of depressed adults had at least one additional lifetime diagnosis.

Not only are other disorders highly likely to co-occur with depression, but also *personality disorders* are more the rule than the exception with depressed patients. Personality disorders refer to a set of 10 patterns of dysfunctional conduct and attitudes that started early in life, are persistent, and affect all areas of the person's functioning. An example included in the *DSM-IV* is narcissistic personality disorder marked by extreme self-centeredness and sense of entitlement to special favours. Depending on the study, rates of personality disorders among depressed people range between 23% and 87% (Shea,

Widiger, & Klein, 1992). In one of the largest clinical samples of depressed outpatients in treatment, the National Institute of Mental Health Treatment of Depression Collaborative Research Program, fully 74% of the more than 200 patients with major depression also met criteria for a personality disorder (Shea et al., 1990). Most studies have found that personality disorders in the "dramatic/erratic" cluster (such as borderline personality disorder), and in the "anxious/fearful" cluster (such as avoidant personality disorder) predominate (e.g. Shea et al, 1990).

> Antonia is in her 20s and has been brought to the psychiatric hospital by her desperate parents. She took a nonfatal overdose of pills ("Anything I could find in the medicine chest") following the break-up of her romantic relationship. She is currently extremely depressed in mood, crying and screaming about her loss. Her psychiatrist elicits a history of her adjustment, both from her parents and Antonia herself, and uncovers a complex history of drug use of various kinds since adolescence, poor performance in school while feeling "desperately unhappy". Her history includes frequent panic attacks in which she suddenly felt as if she was going to die, with pounding heart and shortness of breath for no apparent reason, and multiple brief and chaotic affairs with boys— one of which resulted in an unwanted pregnancy and subsequent abortion. Although she is clearly depressed, her depression is only one of several problems, some of which are chronic so that if her depression is treated the other difficulties will still be there.

Mixtures of disorders raise a number of important implications. One is that much research purporting to discuss "depression" might actually be about the comorbid disorders; since investigators commonly do not report co-existing diagnoses, it is difficult to tell how much the results are influenced by the correlated problems rather than the depressive disorder itself. A second issue is that depression comorbidity raises interesting and important questions about how the comorbid conditions came about: did one cause the other, did they stem from separate but correlated risk factors, is the comorbidity an artifact of the diagnostic system itself (Hammen & Compas, 1994)? Finally, a very important implication of comorbidity of depression is that it usually implies worse functioning and a worse course of disorder than "pure" depression (e.g. Lewinsohn, Rohde, & Seeley, 1995; Rohde et al., 1991). Lewinsohn et al. (1995) found that community adolescents with depression plus one or more other disorders were significantly more impaired in academic functioning, had higher rates of mental health treatment, and more suicide attempts.

The continuum of depression

Although most research on depression refers to clinically diagnosed conditions, we might ask whether mild, subclinical symptoms are also important to consider. The answer would be yes. While a very short-lived period of mild depressive experiences would have little significance for a person's life—and indeed would be a normal reaction to the inevitable disappointments and failures of daily living—increasing evidence suggests that recurrent or persistent mild symptoms might have important consequences. For one thing, such subclinical conditions often foretell the development of diagnosable disorders. A study of nearly 7000 representative US adults assessed their mood and other symptoms at one point in time, and then followed them up over a period of 16 years (Zonderman et al., 1993). Depressive symptoms predicted future psychiatric disorders that were significant enough to result in hospitalisation. Diagnoses included both depressive and nondepressive disorders, and higher levels of subclinical symptoms were more strongly related to eventual hospitalisation. Zonderman and colleagues (1993) speculate that depressive symptoms may be a marker of general risk for disorder, including presence of highly stressful environments, inadequate social supports, biological vulnerabilities, and personality predisposition to disorder and maladaptive functioning.

A large-scale epidemiological survey identified individuals with different levels of depression, including minor depression, and studied their functioning over a 1-year period (Broadhead, Blazer, George, & Tse, 1990). Not only did the majority of individuals with minor depression display persisting depression over the year, but 10% of those with minor depression went on to develop a major depressive episode. Thus, even among those with relatively mild symptoms, a substantial number have chronic symptoms or their mild symptoms are the precursors of more severe depression. In a similar study, over a 1-year period, more than 50% of new onset cases of major depression were associated with previous subclinical symptoms (Horwath, Johnson, Klerman, & Weissman, 1992). Or, to put the results another way, individuals with subclinical symptoms were 4.4 times more likely to develop major depression than were persons without such symptoms, and those with dysthymia were 5.5 times more likely than nondepressed persons to develop major depression.

Besides the possibility that mild symptoms may foretell significant disorder, they may also, like major depressive disorder, result in significantly impaired functioning in daily life—a topic discussed in Chapter 2.

Finally, what about *depressive personality*? Is there such a condition, and does it have implications for a person's adjustment? It has long been speculated in clinical lore that some individuals have stable personality traits that resemble pervasive and mild depressive symptoms. Efforts to measure depressive personality have identified 7 characteristics: quiet, introverted, passive; gloomy, pessimistic, incapable of fun; self-critical, self-derogatory; critical of others, hard to please; conscientious, responsible, self-disciplined; brooding and worrying; preoccupied with negative events, personal shortcomings, feelings of inadequacy (Klein & Miller, 1993). Klein and Miller gave screening tests to large numbers of college students, and interviewed selected students to determine whether or not they displayed these traits. A group of students with presumed depressive personality was compared with those who did not show these traits. Although there was overlap between depressive personality and presence of current or lifetime dysthymic disorder or major depression, the association was modest. Overall, 39% of those with depressive personality had no diagnosable depression. Moreover, even excluding those with a history of a depression diagnosis, those with the depressive personality traits were significantly more impaired in their personal and social functioning than students who did not have those traits. The results suggest support for a nonclinical form of depressive character that includes both risk for developing episodes or if no episodes, for impaired functioning.

Assessing depression

Both clinical description and research on depression rely on two types of methods: those that measure the severity of depressive experiences, and those that measure the presence of diagnosable conditions. This section briefly describes the most frequently used procedures, acknowledging that many more exist than will be discussed.

Diagnostic methods.   Applying the *DSM* or *ICD* criteria for major depression and dysthymia requires interviewing the individual (or an appropriate friend or relative). For research purposes it is highly desirable to use standardised interviews in which the relevant questions are asked in the same way each time by each interviewer. Such procedures ensure comparability and communicability across different studies purporting to investigate similar clinical conditions.

The Schedule for Affective Disorders and Schizophrenia (SADS) was developed by Endicott and Spitzer (1978) in an attempt to increase the reliability of interviewer-derived psychiatric diagnoses based on the *Research diagnostic criteria*, a forerunner of the current *Diagnostic and statistical manual*. Different versions cover lifetime history of disorders, current conditions, and changes in disorders occurring between assessments in a longitudinal study. The SADS covers not only depression, but also such diagnostic categories as schizophrenia, anxiety disorders, and substance use disorders. Trained clinical interviewers can administer the semi-structured procedure with adequate interrater reliability (e.g. Endicott & Spitzer, 1978).

For some years the SADS has served as the major instrument in the US for establishing depressive diagnoses. Recently, however, Spitzer and colleagues developed an updated version of the SADS, to cover the *DSM* criteria (Spitzer, Williams, Gibbon, & First, 1990). Called the Structured Clinical Interview for *DSM-IV* (SCID), it covers major diagnostic categories such as mood disorders, anxiety disorders, psychoses, eating disorders, somatoform disorders, and substance use disorders. It is similar in function to the SADS, and because it is more current, will likely replace the latter. (It should be noted, however, that a child version of the SADS, called the Kiddie-SADS (e.g. Puig-Antich, Chambers, & Tabrizi, 1983) continues to be widely used for juvenile populations). The semi-structured probes of the SCID are intended to cover both current and lifetime history of disorders, and clinical judgments are required so that it is assumed that interviewers have had clinical training. Field trials have indicated adequate reliability for major diagnoses. The following is an example of a probe for symptoms of major depressive episode (Spitzer et al., 1990):

> In the last month ... has there been a period of time when you were feeling depressed or down most of the day nearly every day? (What was that like?)
> IF YES: How long did it last? (As long as two weeks?)
> During this time ... did you lose or gain any weight? (How much?) (Were you trying to lose weight?)
> IF NO: How was your appetite? (What about compared to your usual appetite?). (Was that nearly every day?)

The Diagnostic Interview Schedule (DIS) was developed to be administered on a large scale, suitable for trained lay interviewers rather than clinicians (Robins, Helzer, Croughan, & Ratcliff, 1981). As a result of the need to be applied by interviewers with limited training, the DIS is highly structured and can be computer-scored to achieve diagnoses based on the *DSM-III* (now *DSM-III-R* or *DSM-IV*). Reliability coefficients comparing DIS-based diagnoses and clinician diagnoses were generally high. Interjudge reliability for major depressive disorder was high; however, the DIS tended to underestimate major depression (see also Anthony et al., 1985 for problems in the reliability of DIS diagnoses). A child and adolescent version of the lay-administered DIS has been developed for epidemiological surveys, and the test–retest reliability for diagnosing depression, while adequate in clinical samples, appears to be quite low in community samples (Jensen et al., 1995).

The Present State Examination (PSE; Wing, Cooper, & Sartorius, 1974) was developed in the UK around the same time as the SADS. Its standardised 140 items cover various symptoms of different disorders, and the interview has been widely used in international studies with a high degree of reliability (reviewed in Smith & Weissman, 1992). Diagnoses can be derived from the symptom profile, using the CATEGO computer program utilising *ICD-9* criteria.

Assessing severity of depression. Several methods are commonly used to evaluate the severity of current depression separate from diagnosis. One approach is interview-based, such as the Hamilton Rating Scale for Depression (HRSD; Hamilton, 1960). It remains the most frequently used interviewer-rated measure of depression, and contains 21 items covering mood, behavioural, somatic, and cognitive symptoms. By convention, only 17 of Hamilton's original 21 items are typically scored. The HRSD is most commonly administered by experienced clinicians, although a number of investigators have demonstrated that laypersons can be trained in a relatively short period of time to reach acceptable levels of administration. The HRSD has been shown to be sensitive to change in the severity of depressive symptomatology over time, and consequently, is useful as a measure of the efficacy of therapy. The Hamilton scale has been extensively reviewed by Shaw, Vallis, and McCabe (1985).

There are numerous self-report instruments designed to measure depression or depressed affect. In fact, Moran and Lambert (1983) listed over 30 self-administered scales for the measurement of depression that had been reported in the psychological literature. Of these, only a few have achieved widespread use. Among them, the Beck Depression Inventory (BDI) is probably the most frequently used self-report method of assessing depressive symptomatology. It was originally developed by Beck, Ward, Mendelson, Mock, and Erbaugh (1961) and consists of 21 items selected to represent the affective, cognitive, motivational, and physiological symptoms of depression, although it is well-known that the BDI emphasises subjective symptoms to the relative neglect of somatic symptoms. For each symptom question there is a graded series of four alternative statements, ranging from neutral (e.g. "I do not feel sad", "I don't feel disappointed in myself") to a maximum level of severity (e.g. "I am so sad or unhappy that I can't stand it", "I would kill myself if I had the chance"). The items are scored from 0 to 3, with the sum of the scores representing the total BDI score, which can range from 0 to 63. Generally, a total BDI score of 0 to 9 indicates a normal nondepressed state; 10 to 18 reflects a mild level of depression; 19 to 29 reflects moderate depression; and 30 to 63 indicates a severe level of depression (Beck, Steer, & Garbin, 1988).

It is important to note that the BDI, along with any other self-report questionnaire for depression, was not designed to yield a discrete diagnosis of depression; rather, it was constructed to measure depression as one single dimension of psychopathology that cuts across a wide variety of diagnostic categories (e.g. Kendall et al., 1987; Fechner-Bates, Coyne, & Schwenk, 1994). Its major focus, therefore, is on the depth or severity of depressive symptomatology, essentially defined by the combination of the number, frequency, and intensity of symptoms. High scores may not be specific to depression alone, and may be highly correlated with other measures of psychopathology (e.g. Gotlib, 1984). Beck, Steer, and Garbin (1988) recently reported that the BDI had been used in over 1000 research studies. Additionally, numerous studies of its psychometric properties have been reported, indicating that it is a generally useful and valid measure of the severity of depressive symptoms. A questionnaire for children and adolescents, modelled after the BDI, is the Children's Depression Inventory (CDI; Kovacs, 1983), consisting of 27 items scored from 0 to 3. It is widely used in research and treatment, and has good psychometric properties (e.g. reviewed in Gotlib & Hammen, 1992).

Summary

- Depression ranges from a normal sad mood lasting only moments to a profoundly impairing condition that may be life-threatening.
- To be clinically significant, depression involves changes in mood, cognitive functioning, behaviour, and bodily states and must persist over time and interfere with normal behaviour.

- A crucial distinction must be made between unipolar and bipolar depression, due to different causes, course, and treatment.
- Both children and adults may be diagnosed with major depressed episode or dysthymia.
- Depression presents many faces, may co-exist with other disorders, and there may be different underlying subtypes with different causes.
- Different instruments are available to measure depression diagnoses and severity of depressive symptoms.

Course and consequences of depression 2

While depression has sometimes been called the "common cold" of psychological disorders, such a label is misleading because it implies that suffering from depression is merely a bothersome but brief and mild inconvenience. Unfortunately, nothing could be farther from the truth. Depression may be so severe as to be lethal, and, for many if not most sufferers, it is a recurring or even chronic disorder. Moreover, its effects may be devastating to the individual—not only in suffering, but also in terms of the damaging effects on one's work and family and marital relations. Indeed, the consequences to the lives of depressed people might even contribute conditions that create the likelihood that depression will continue or recur. Therefore, in this chapter we explore the features of the course of depression, including its impairing consequences.

Course of depression

Age of onset of depression

Depression is increasingly recognised as a disorder of relatively young onset. In previous decades attention was often devoted to depressions arising in middle-age, called "involutional melancholia," but today's researchers observe that youth and early adulthood are the most typical periods of depression onset. Figure 2.1 presents data from a US epidemiological survey of several communities, asking those who ever met criteria for major depressive episode the age of their first such experience (Burke, Burke, Regier, & Rae, 1990). As indicated, frequencies are highest for both men and women before age 30, but women in particular have an enormous liability to depression onset in the ages between 15 and 19—a surge that will be discussed in a later chapter. Age of first onset drops markedly after age 30, although there may be a peak again in very old age (not shown).

A survey of depression onset in Los Angeles found that 25% of those with a history of major depressive episode reported an onset

FIG. 2.1.
Relative ages of
onset of first
major depression
for females and
males (Burke et
al., 1990).

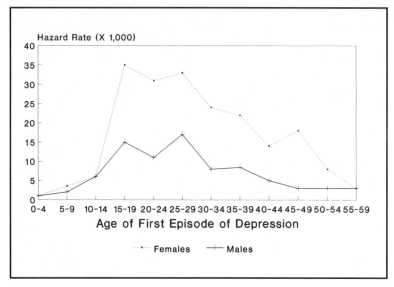

during childhood or adolescence, and 50% had onset by age 25. Women had earlier onsets than men did (Sorenson, Rutter, & Aneshensel, 1991). Somewhat similar findings were reported by Coryell, Endicott, and Keller (1992) who examined the relatives of patients with mood disorders. Of the never-ill relatives who were followed up for 6 years, those who developed a first episode of major depression were significantly likely to be younger than 40—a pattern true for both men and women.

Implications of age of onset.   One hypothesis that has been tested is that earlier age of onset reflects greater likelihood of familial transmission of the disorder. Several studies have reported an association between depression in close relatives and likelihood of early (childhood or adolescent) onset (e.g. Bland, Newman, & Orn, 1986; Hammen et al., 1992; Klein, Taylor, Dickstein, & Harding, 1988). Whether such patterns reflect heritability of a disease or psychological factors associated with being reared among depressed family members cannot be determined from these studies.

A second hypothesis is that early onset of the disorder predicts a more pernicious course. This could be due either to a more severe form of depression that begins earlier, or to depression disrupting learning and interfering with important adaptive skills that are needed to cope with adverse conditions. As a result, people are unable to deal with stresses and become depressed more readily. Evidence is somewhat mixed on whether younger onset of depression predicts more episodes or more impaired functioning. In large community surveys, Lewinsohn, Fenn, Stanton, and Franklin (1986) did not find that onset before age 40 predicted longer-lasting episodes, nor higher probability of relapse (Lewinsohn, Zeiss, & Duncan, 1989). However, Sorenson, Rutter, and Aneshensel (1991) did find that younger onset (especially adolescence and young adulthood) did predict greater numbers and worse severity of episodes, as did Bland et al. (1986) and Giles et al. (1989). Hammen et al. (1992), for example, found that earlier age of onset predicted more severe depression during a longitudinal follow-up—as mediated by chronic stress. That is, those with earlier onset (more of whom also had ill parents) experienced more chronic stress, which predicted more stressful life events that in turn predicted more severe depression. It was speculated that early onset disrupts healthy functioning and acquisition of problem-solving skills and healthy views of the self and others. Such limitations may contribute to chronic stressful conditions (or to failure to resolve them) and to the occurrence of stressful life events that the person cannot cope with effectively.

On the other hand, a study that specifically compared adolescent- and adult-onset depressed patients came to somewhat different conclusions. McGlashan (1989) compared the two groups of hospitalised patients during treatment and again an average of 15 years later. The groups did not differ in clinical features of their depression, but those with adolescent onset of unipolar depression had worse prehospitalisation psychosocial functioning and attainment in terms of education, work competence, and sexual adjustment. Most notably, over time, the younger-onset group did not differ on global functioning and work adjustment than did the adult-onset depressives— although they were less likely to have been married or have children. In view of the somewhat mixed picture of the fates of early- and later-developing depressions, more research is needed to clarify the sources of inconsistency.

Early onset of depression also includes childhood onset. Though relatively rare, childhood depression appears to predict high rates of recurrence and chronicity of depression, and considerable psychosocial impairment (Kovacs et al., 1984; see also Hammen & Rudolph, 1996, for a review of course and consequences of childhood depression).

Duration of depression

By definition, of course, major depressions must last at least two weeks to meet diagnostic criteria. Apart from this minimum, there is considerable variability in the length of depressive episodes. However, two duration features are noteworthy. One is that most people recover within 4 to 6 months. The other is that the vast majority of major depressions do vanish eventually, whether treated or not.

Several studies, based on both clinical and community samples, have supported the observation of recovery within 4 to 6 months. Keller, Shapiro, Lavori, and Wolfe (1982) found that 64% of patients had recovered within 6 months of entering their clinical study, while in a community study, Lewinsohn and colleagues (1986) found that 40% of major or minor depressions lasted less than 3 months. Most such studies have been limited by their relatively short follow-ups, however, and by the possibility that focus on a single episode may have identified depressions that might not have been typical. Therefore, a recent study based on the NIMH Collaborative Program on the Psychobiology of Depression is particularly useful, because it examined multiple depressive episodes in individuals over a 10-year period at various US sites (Coryell et al., 1994). Moreover, it included a 6-year follow-up of nonpatients, some of whom developed a major depression over the period of observation. Despite differences in patient status and location, the patterns of length of major depressive episode were remarkably consistent: 55% of patients and 57% of nonclinical subjects who developed depression recovered by 6 months; 73% and 69% respectively by 1 year and 83% and 87% by 2 years. Overall, 97% of both groups had recovered by the end of 6 years. Moreover, for those who had 2 episodes, the durations and likelihoods of recovery were highly consistent.

An important implication of these findings concerning duration is that no matter what the triggering event that instigates depression may be, once initiated there may be a fairly predictable course for the majority of individuals. Coryell et al. (1994) suggest that such patterns might reflect underlying biological processes and affective dysregulation—that is, once started, depressions reflect the inability of the body to return to a steady state in a rapid fashion as is typical of most nondepressive people.

Of course, not all individuals fully recover from major depression— and among those who do, there may be recurrences. Thus, in the next sections, we discuss recurrence/relapse and chronicity. *Relapse* is the term usually employed when individuals get worse following incomplete or only brief recovery (e.g. less than 2 months of being well), whereas *recurrence* usually means a new episode following a period of recovery lasting more than 2 months.

Recurrence or chronicity of depression

Research on the course of unipolar depression has increasingly characterised it as a recurring or even chronic (continuous) disorder. Although some individuals may experience a relatively painful but benign single episode of major depression, for the majority of those who have an episode, they will have more episodes. And for a substantial minority, their depressions persist for long periods or even indefinitely—varying in severity but never going away entirely.

As the earlier discussion of duration of major depressive episodes indicates, although the majority of individuals recover within 6 months, a substantial minority have persisting depression. For instance, in the Coryell et al. (1994) study, 27-31% of patients/ nonpatients were still depressed after one year. A community study of nonpatients similarly found that 24% had persisting depression when re-examined 1 year later (Sargent, Bruce, Florio, & Weissman, 1990). Similarly, an international study based on patients in 5 cities found that 22% had an episode that persisted for more than one year (Thornicroft & Sartorius, 1993). *Nonrecovery*, therefore, is a substantial problem for many depressed individuals.

Recurrent episodes.   Among patients seeking treatment for depression, longitudinal studies have reported that between 50% and 85% with one major depressive episode will have at least one additional episode (Keller, 1985). In a 20-year naturalistic study of unipolar depressed patients, Angst et al. (1973) estimated that the number of lifetime episodes is 5 or 6. Angst (1984) calculated that these individuals spend about 20% of their lives being in depressive episodes after the onset of the disorder. This figure is similar to that reported by Thornicroft and Sartorius (1993) in the World Health Organization international study: over 10 years, the mean total time spent in depressive episodes was 143 weeks (27.5% of the total time).

There is growing awareness that the period of a few months after recovery is associated with risk for recurrence of depression, and that over time the longer one goes without relapse the less likely one is to develop a new episode. In a review of research on when relapses occur, Belsher and Costello (1988) indicate that there is a 20% relapse rate within 2 months, increasing to about 30% at 6 months. Over time, the recurrence rate levels off at about 40% at 1 year, and about 50% at

2 years. Much of the relapse research has been conducted by Keller and his colleagues based on large samples studied through the National Institute of Mental Health. Keller (1988) reported that by 5 years, 76% of the patients had relapsed. A 10-year international study of depressed patients found that over the period, the mean number of episodes was 2.7 (Thornicroft & Sartorius, 1993).

Predictors of relapse.   One of the strongest findings in predicting the course of depression is that past depression predicts future depression. For instance, among patients with three or more prior episodes, the relapse rate may be as high as 40% within 11 to 15 weeks post recovery (Keller et al., 1982; 1983). Similarly, recurrent depressives who were withdrawn from medication were highly likely to relapse: 70% experienced a recurrence within 6 months, and less than 20% remained well at the end of 18 months of follow-up (Frank, Kupfer, & Perel, 1989). The phenomenon that past depression predicts future depression has been well-replicated in a variety of studies and populations (e.g. reviewed in Belsher & Costello, 1988).

In addition to past depressive episodes, predictors of relapse include clinical features, demographic factors, and psychosocial conditions. Among clinical features, for instance, is the occurrence of a major depressive episode superimposed on pre-existing dysthymic disorder—the condition called "double depression," which occurs in about a quarter of all depressed patients. Double depression appears to increase risk for recurrence of major depression. Keller et al. (1983), for instance, found that double depressives had a relapse rate of 50% within 1 year, compared with 35% for those with major depressive episode alone. Although double depressives appear to recover faster from major depression, they relapse faster and have an overall higher relapse rate (Keller, 1988). In addition to double depression, a predictor of relapse is presence of a history of some psychiatric disorder besides depression. Coryell, Endicott, and Keller (1991) found that nearly a half of nonpatients who had had previous depression plus a history of nondepressive disorder experienced a relapse during a 6-year follow-up.

Certain demographic characteristics also may increase one's chances of having a recurrence of depression, although research studies are somewhat inconsistent. Being female, for example, was found to be associated with a greater chance of having a recurrent episode (e.g. Lewinsohn, Zeiss, & Duncan, 1989), especially among young women (Lewinsohn et al., 1994). Characteristics of depression in women are discussed more fully in Chapter 3.

With respect to age of onset as a predictor of relapse, Lewinsohn et al. (1989) did not find that those with younger ages of first episode of depression were more likely to have a relapse, but Coryell et al. (1991) did find that onset before age 40 was a predictor of greater likelihood of recurrence of depression (consistent with Giles et al., 1989 studying a patient sample). The most recent Lewinsohn epidemiological survey of adolescents, however, appears to indicate that those with adolescent onset experience relatively high rates of recurrence even within a year's period (Lewinsohn, Clarke, Seeley, & Rohde, 1994).

Chronicity of depression. Depending on the level of severity of symptoms and whether they meet diagnostic criteria, it has been estimated that chronic depressive symptoms occur in at least 25% of cases (e.g. Depue & Monroe, 1986). Chronic depressions may take various forms ranging from dysthymia of childhood onset to failure to recover from an episode of major depression. In their longitudinal study of patients, Keller et al. (1986) found that about 20% of patients with major depressive episode failed to recover from a recurrent episode following initial recovery from the index episode. Over time, this led to a cumulative rate of 30% of chronicity in their sample. Eventually, some chronic depressives may recover but do so more slowly than nonchronic patients. Predictors of eventual recovery, not surprisingly, included better previous impairment of functioning and less severe depression (Coryell, Endicott, & Keller, 1990).

Investigators who have examined the correlates and predictors of chronicity of depression have generally studied treated samples. Clinical features of the course of disorder that have predicted increased likelihood of chronicity include *duration* of previous major depressive episode but not the *number* or the *severity* of episodes (Akiskal, 1982; Keller et al, 1986). Older age at relapse and low family income predicted chronicity (Keller et al., 1986). According to Akiskal (1982), chronicity is associated with family history of affective disorder, and his clinical studies suggested that a variety of adverse stressful conditions also predict continuing symptoms.

Klein et al. (1988) found that early-onset dysthymics tended to have significantly more episodes of major depression, poorer global functioning, more personality disorder and negative traits, and higher levels of chronic strain and perceived stress than did patients with nonchronic major depression. The authors interpret the findings to suggest that the chronic depression overlaps with character pathology, and with social maladjustment and chronic strain, and urge further research to explore the direction of effects in these related processes.

Important follow-up studies of the functioning and social context of treated depressed patients have been reported by Moos and colleagues. For instance, Billings and Moos (1985) obtained 1-year follow-up data on 424 patients who had been in treatment with an RDC diagnosis of major or minor depression. Approximately a third remitted, another third remitted partially, and a third were nonremitted. Social functioning and stressors returned to levels comparable to those of normal controls in the remitted group, while the nonremitted continued to show high levels of stressors and reduced social resources. At the 4-year follow-up, Swindle, Cronkite, and Moos (1989) found continuing improvement, although noting that most improvement occurred during the first year, and that previous symptom levels continued to be a strong predictor of subsequent symptoms. Stressors, coping, and resources were associated with symptom levels, while stable stressful conditions such as medical problems and family conflict consistently predicted poor long-term outcome.

Because the above studies were based largely on clinical samples, their generalisability is unknown (since the great majority of diagnosable conditions of depressed people go untreated). Thus, it is useful to turn to a large-scale community study of a large representative sample of community residents. As noted earlier, Sargeant, Bruce, Florio, and Weissman (1990) examined the 1-year outcomes of 423 individuals who received a diagnosis of major depressive episode at the initial interviews, and found that about 24% had persistent depression over the 1-year follow-up. It was not possible using the methods of the epidemiological survey to separate those who had chronic, unchanging, symptoms from those whose current depression represented a relapse after a period of recovery. Overall, women had higher rates of persistent depression (25.4%) than men did (17.1%) although the effect was not statistically significant. Women above the age of 30 were significantly more likely to have persistent depression than younger women, but for men age did not affect rates. The highest rates of persistence also varied by other demographic characteristics: women who were divorced, widowed, or separated, and women with lower levels of education, were most likely to have persistent depression. In terms of clinical predictors, indicators of more severe histories such as higher numbers of episodes and longer or more severe episodes, were associated with persistent depression.

Psychological predictors of persistent depression. Several of the later chapters of this book will review some of the personal and environmental features of the lives of those with chronic or recurrent depression. Topics such as marital, family, and interpersonal relations, stressful life events and circumstances, and individual psychological characteristics have all been the focus of considerable research. Most of the findings of such studies apply directly to recurrent or chronic depressions, since most depressions in patient and community samples concern not just the first experience with depression, but its persistence or recurrence. Thus, we defer until those chapters, a complete discussion of the factors that predict continuing depression.

Course of depression in children and adolescents

Further details concerning features of childhood depression are presented elsewhere (e.g. Hammen & Rudolph, 1995). In general, information on children and adolescents is less extensive than for adults, but generally suggests similar patterns of persistence or recurrence.

As noted earlier, the most common age of adult onset of major depression is 15 to 19—and therefore is adolescent onset. Among the relatively smaller numbers of childhood onset, treated samples of depressed children, the longitudinal studies of Kovacs and colleagues (Kovacs et al., 1984) found onset of both major depression and dysthymic disorder at around age 11. Similarly, depressed children of depressed parents also have early onsets (average age 12 to 13) compared to onsets in youngsters of nonpsychiatric patients (around age 16 to 17) (Weissman et al., 1987; see also Hammen, Burge, Burney, & Adrian, 1990). Earlier onset of depression, as with most disorders, appears to predict a more protracted or more severe course of disorder in children (e.g. Kovacs et al., 1984; although see McCauley et al., 1993).

Duration of major depressive episodes. Generally, research indicates that major depressions last 4 to 9 months, depending on the age and the nature of the sample. Keller et al. (1988) reported a median length of episode of 16 weeks in their mixed sample of community adolescents and offspring of depressed parents—a result very similar to the inpatient sample of Strober, Lampert, Schmidt, and Morrell (1993). In an adolescent community sample, however, Lewinsohn et al. (1993) reported a mean duration of 24 weeks. McCauley et al. (1993) reported a mean of 36 weeks in their combined inpatient and outpatient sample (similar to that observed by Kovacs et al., 1984).

Recovery and persistence of depression. Related to mean duration is the question of recovery. The great majority of child and adolescent depressives recover within a year, but a sizable minority remain depressed— around 20% after 1 year and about 5-10% after 2 years. Kovacs et al. (1984) reported that 41% of their outpatient sample was still depressed after 1 year, and 8% after 2 years. Interestingly, McCauley et al. (1993) found that girls were significantly more likely than boys to have long episodes, but the other studies either did not find, or did not examine, sex differences.

Recurrence of episodes is common among youth with major depression. Several studies of both inpatients and outpatients reported that approximately 20% had relapses within 1 year and about 40% within 2 years of recovery (Asarnow & Bates, 1988; Kovacs et al., 1984; Lewinsohn et al., 1993).

The issue of chronicity of depressive symptoms in children has been addressed less often than episodic course. Keller et al. (1988), for instance, found that 24% of the youngsters with major depression also suffered from dysthymic disorder—in effect, double depression, with the dysthymia preceding the major depressive episodes. Kovacs et al. (1984) also reported finding double depression, and such youngsters had a greater likelihood of relapse. Indeed, early-onset dysthymia is strongly predictive of further affective disorder, with 81% of dysthymic children estimated to develop major depressive disorder (Kovacs, Akiskal, Gatsonis, & Perrone, 1994); Kovacs and her colleagues argue that early-onset dysthymia is a risk factor for recurrent mood disorder. Ryan et al. (1987) followed a sample of child and adolescent depressed patients, and reported that nearly half of the sample had chronic major depression or fluctuating major depression with dysthymia over a 2-year course.

Studies of youth scoring high on self-report measures of depressive symptoms, typically indicating subclinical depression, suggest considerable stability of depressive symptoms over repeated testing (although of course, periodic rather than chronic elevations cannot be ruled out) (e.g. Garrison et al., 1990). Verhulst and van der Ende (1992) found that elevations of the anxious/depressed syndrome of the Child Behavior Check List were fairly stable over 4 testings in 6 years. Overall, 16% of the youngsters were high on all 4 testings.

The growing body of longitudinal data on clinical course certainly suggests that children who are diagnosed with depression are likely to experience recurrences within a few years. Less information is available, however, on the continuity between child/adolescent depression and adult depression. Indirect evidence of continuity comes from the community study of adult depressives by Lewinsohn et al. (1988) who found that more cases of major depression occurred in young women, and were actually recurrences presumably of adolescent-onset depressions. More direct evidence of continuity comes from longitudinal or follow-up studies. Kandel and Davies (1986) found that dysphoric feelings reported by adolescents predicted similar depressed feelings 9 years later in adulthood; women who reported such experiences in their teenage years were significantly more likely to be treated by mental health professionals. To date the longest and largest follow-up study of clinically depressed youngsters has been reported by Harrington et al. (1990). The investigators recontacted former depressed patients who had been treated for depression an average of 18 years earlier: 60% had experienced at least one recurrence of major depression during adulthood (and had elevated rates of other psychiatric disorders as well). Garber, Kriss, Koch, and Lindholm (1988) also reported on a follow-up of a small group of child patients, and found that the majority had experienced recurrence of major depression in the 8-year period since discharge.

Overall, these few studies of continuity indicate that occurrence of depression in childhood or adolescence portends future depression—in keeping with the maxim in adult depression that the best predictor of future depression is past depression. Also, the relatively few longitudinal studies of the course of depression in young samples also indicate a pernicious course.

Impaired functioning and consequences of depression

Moderate and severe depression obviously interfere with a person's ability to go to work, perform chores, and relate to family and friends. At depression's worst, the afflicted person may spend endless hours in bed or staring into space, or aimlessly pacing and brooding—often finding it difficult to perform even minimal tasks such as bathing or getting dressed. The negativism, hopelessness, and lack of motivation are often a source of wonder or even of frustration and impatience to others, and it is therefore not difficult to foretell the development of interpersonal conflicts added on to apparent problems in performing typical roles.

As the previous sections have indicated, for many depressed persons the course of their disorder includes repeated episodes or chronic symptoms. The accumulated impairment, therefore, may be quite substantial. Two long-term follow-up studies document the extent of social disability. The multi-site World Health Organization study mentioned previously (Thornicroft & Sartorius, 1993) assessed depressed patients' functioning after 10 years. Only a third of the patients showed normal functioning over most of the follow-up; 24%

were considered to have poor outcomes (illness interfered with normal functioning) for over half of the follow-up; and the remaining patients showed moderate functioning (impairment of normal functioning) for up to half of the follow-up period.

The other large-scale follow-up study, the NIMH Collaborative Program on the Psychobiology of Depression, followed 240 unipolar depressed patients for 5 years (Coryell et al., 1993). Compared with nondepressed persons matched for age and gender, the unipolar patients achieved significantly lower educational and income levels, and over time significantly fewer of the unipolar patients were employed and more of them had decreased occupational status. Fewer of the depressed persons were married, and those who were in relationships reported significantly worse relationships than did the comparison group. Interestingly, even among patients who sustained recovery from their depressions in the final 2 years of the follow-up, their psychosocial functioning in job, income, and marital quality was significantly worse than among comparison subjects. Taken together, these two studies indicate that depression is associated with significant impairment of functioning that may persist even when the person is not specifically in an episode of depression.

Research has documented at least three specific areas in which depression causes significantly impaired functioning: work, family, and marital/interpersonal relationships. These impairments are discussed briefly here, but will also be discussed more fully in later chapters concerning theories of the origins of depression.

Work. A study of disability associated with depression found that a person with a major depressive episode was nearly 5 times more likely to miss work in the past 3 months due to disability or illness than were nonsymptomatic individuals, and experienced a mean of 11 disability days during the period compared to 2 for nonsymptomatic people (Broadhead, Blazer, George, & Tse, 1990). Of course, such studies do not account for the fact that even if people do continue to go to work, the quality of their performance may also be affected.

Parent–child relations. Studies of family relationships have indicated significant impairment of the parental role when a person is depressed. For instance, studies of the effects on children of having a depressed mother uniformly indicate that the children are at risk for developing depression, or other disorders, themselves (Downey & Coyne, 1990; Hammen, 1991). Much of the negative effect appears to be attributable to the parent's difficulties in sustaining warm, responsive, supportive relations with their children. Instead, when observed in interactions with their youngsters, depressed mothers are frequently more critical, uninvolved, and unresponsive than non-depressed mothers (Gordon et al., 1989). Depressed mothers often wish to be good parents, and are troubled by their difficulties. Nonetheless, the depression takes an enormous toll on their energy, interest, patience, and mood—all of which doubtless impair their abilities to sustain positive, supportive, and attentive relationships with their children.

Marital relations.   Depression may also take a toll on marital rela- tionships. Sometimes poor marriages cause depression, but often it is the depression that causes marital problems. Studies have indicated a strong association between depression and presence of marital distress (reviewed in Gotlib & Hammen, 1992). The effects of depression are diverse, probably including irritability, withdrawal, dependency, and other symptoms. Also, of course, depressed spouses are often viewed as a great burden, causing worry, reducing the sharing of pleasurable activities, failing to respond to encouragement and support. Indeed, a survey of spouses of depressed individuals found these and numerous other complaints, and also discovered that fully 40% of the spouses were sufficiently distressed by the depressed person to warrant treatment themselves (Coyne, Kahn, & Gotlib, 1987).

Impairing effects of mild depression.   While severe depression's impairing consequences are readily apparent, it might be somewhat surprising to learn the extent to which even relatively mild depression also interferes with normal functioning. The Broadhead et al. (1990) study found that even those with mild depression missed more days of work than nondepressed people. Several recent large-scale studies have documented the toll that depression takes in everyday life. The Medical Outcomes Study identified over 11,000 patients who were being seen for various medical problems or depression in representative health care settings in different US locations (Wells et al., 1989). Patients who had depressive disorders or depressed symptoms were compared on self-reported measures of functioning with medical patients suffering from 1 of 8 chronic medical problems (including diabetes, hypertension, coronary artery disease, back problems, angina pectoris, arthritis, lung problems, or gastrointestinal disorder). Individuals with depression had significantly worse social functioning than patients with each of the 8 medical conditions; worse role functioning in major role than 6 of the medical conditions; and significantly more days in bed than 6 of the medical conditions. Even physical functioning was rated worse by depressed individuals than that of 4 groups of chronically medically ill patients. Further, the study indicated that those with depressive symptoms only—not with diagnosed depressive disorders—showed poor functioning. In a more recent Medical Outcomes Study that followed up patients over a 2-year period, depressed individuals improved but continued to show significantly more impaired functioning than the medically ill groups on measures of social functioning and emotional well-being (Hays et al., 1995). Again, even those with mild subclinical depression continued to report significantly more impaired functioning than the medical patients.

A large-scale community study of teenagers recently found that those who had elevated symptoms which were not, however, sufficient to attain a diagnosis of depression did not differ significantly from the diagnosed depressed sample on a variety of measures of psychosocial functioning (Gotlib, Lewinsohn, & Seeley, 1995). Such findings again suggest that even subclinical forms of depression are significantly impairing.

Finally, to underscore the importance of even mild depressive symptoms, investigators studied the association between depressive symptoms in community residents and use of services and evidence of impairment (Johnson, Weissman, & Klerman, 1992). Figure 2.2 shows the results of a survey of more than 18,000 representative adults in 5 US cities, comparing those with no depression, mild symptoms, or diagnoses of major depression or dysthymic disorder. There was a signific-

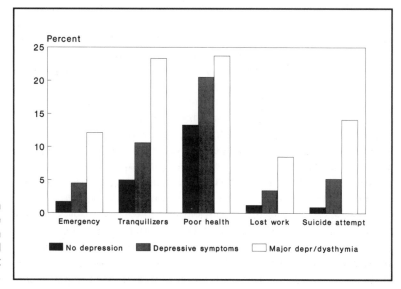

FIG. 2.2. Percentage with adverse outcome by depression status (adapted from Johnson et al., 1992).

antly higher rate of negative outcome for those with mild symptoms compared with no symptoms on each variable: use of emergency services for an emotional problem, use of minor tranquillisers, reported poor physical health, absence from work for more than 1 week due to emotional problems, and suicide attempts. Since mild symptoms of depression are fairly common in the general population, they would appear to account for a sizable portion of the community's costs for provision of services and costs due to economic loss and poor health.

Depression and mortality. Depression is one of the few psychological disorders that can be said to be fatal. Of all of the consequences, suicide is, of course, the starkest consequence of the individuals' feelings of hopelessness and debility. While there are many contributors to suicide that may unrelated to depression, the disorder in general and its symptoms of hopelessness in particular are especially predictive of suicide. Indeed, suicidal thoughts are a symptom of the syndrome of depression. Diagnosable depressive disorders have been implicated in 40-60% of instances of suicide (Clark & Fawcett, 1992; Fowler, Rich, & Young, 1986; Henriksson et al., 1993). It has been estimated, moreover, that about 10-15% of individuals with a diagnosis of major depressive disorder eventually kill themselves (Clark & Fawcett, 1992; Maris, Berman, Maltsberger, & Yufit, 1992).

The decision to commit suicide and the actions taken toward that goal may be consequences of negativistic thinking that is characteristic of depression, such as a sense of futility, a view that the future is bleak and that bad conditions are unchangeable, that there is nothing one can do to relieve the pain of depressive feelings, and the belief that one is worthless and that others would be better off without one. Such attitudes, when assessed on a scale measuring "hopelessness," have been found to be associated with a greater likelihood of eventual suicide in outpatients (Beck et al., 1990). Clinicians and researchers have learned that it is extremely difficult to accurately predict who will commit suicide among those who are depressed, who may threaten suicidal action, or who have made prior attempts (Goldstein, Black, Nasrallah, & Winokur, 1991). However, because expressions of a wish to die and feelings of hopelessness may precede actual suicide, it is always important to take such communications seriously.

Depression may also have lethal consequences in other ways besides suicide. Depression is associated with increased mortality due to accidents and medical problems. One community study followed individuals for 16 years, and found that those who had been characterised as depressed were more likely to have died. Men, in particular, were vulnerable to the effects of depression, and had a 1.5 times higher rate of death than nondepressed men even after controlling for the effects of age and medical status (Murphy et al., 1987). A recent study of individuals who were followed after experiencing a heart attack (myocardial infarct) indicated that those who were depressed after their heart attacks were more likely to die during the follow-up period (Frasure-Smith, Lesperance, & Talajie, 1993). Depression might interfere with seeking treatment or following medical regimens, or might actually contribute to accidents. Depression might also suppress the body's immune functioning, according to various studies in the field of psychoneuroimmunology (e.g. Evans et al., 1992; Schleifer et al., 1989). A large-scale study of European workers who had both depression and chronic medical problems found that when the depression improved over time, physical functioning also improved as measured by fewer days spent in bed and less restriction on work and social life (Von Korff, Ormel, Katon, & Lin, 1992).

Implications. Taken together, the picture that emerges of depression is one of a disorder that may have such negative consequences that it actually contributes to conditions that prolong it or increase the likelihood that it will recur. As we shall see in later chapters, many psychological factors are thought to cause depression, such as stressful life events, interpersonal difficulties, and negative attitudes about the self and others. It is possible that depression makes some of these same factors actually worse—more negative self-concept, more stressful events and circumstances and interpersonal difficulties. Thus, depression may perpetuate itself.

Summary

- Depression typically begins in late adolescence or early adulthood, and the younger it starts the worse course there may be.
- Fortunately, most depressive episodes clear up in 4-6 months even if not treated.
- However, most people who have had one episode will have another, and sometimes multiple recurrences, with about 25% developing chronic depression.
- The strongest predictor of depression is past depression; for both children and adults, more depression predicts more depression.
- Depression—even mild persistent depression—takes a severe toll on work, parental, and marital relationships.
- The consequences of depression in terms of impaired functioning can set the stage for further depression in a self-perpetuating cycle.

Who is affected by depression? 3

In this chapter we explore three issues. First, how common is depression and how many people are affected? Second, are some segments of the population more prone to depression than others? The third issue is why some groups are more depression-prone than others, and what might be the implications for understanding depression.

Prevalence of depression

One of the greatest challenges of depression is that it is so frequent, afflicting large segments of the population. When considering how frequent depression may be, it is helpful to consider two measures, one concerning how many depressed people there are at a given time and the other indicating how many people experience significant depression in their lifetimes.

The most useful method of counting the frequency of depression is a survey of representative adult community members who are systematically interviewed using standard criteria for diagnosing depressive disorder. The achievement of such standardised procedures is a relatively recent development, based on interview methods and diagnostic criteria first established in the 1970s. These surveys have used roughly comparable procedures such as the *Research Diagnostic Criteria* eventually leading to the *Diagnostic and statistical manual* (*DSM*) in the US, the World Health Organization *International classification of diseases* (*ICD*), and the Present State Examination (PSE) developed in the UK. About a dozen such epidemiological surveys of more than 500 adults in each have been conducted in various locations throughout the world (Smith & Weissman, 1992).

Current depression

Major depressive disorder is a universal phenomenon, occurring with some frequency in every country sampled. According to a review by Smith and Weissman (1992), the rates of current depression in various European countries ranged between 4.6% and 7.4%. In various US cities, rates based on the *DSM* criteria for major depression within the past 6 months were somewhat lower, ranging between 1.5% and 2.8%. However, the most *recent* US survey, called the National Comorbidity Study, sampled from every state instead of just a few locations, included people between the ages of 15 and 54, and used an interview procedure jointly developed by the World Health Organization and the US Alcohol, Drug Abuse, and Mental Health Administration. According to this survey, the rate of current depression was 4.9% (Blazer, Kessler, McGonagle, & Swartz, 1994). Interestingly, unlike other surveys, the National Comorbidity Survey determined the experience of "pure depression" as well as depression co-existing with other diagnostic conditions, and reported that more than half of the individuals with current major depressive episodes also experienced another psychiatric condition (Blazer et al., 1994).

Taken together, these epidemiological surveys indicate that in most countries sampled, at any given moment about 1 person in 20 is significantly depressed. These figures do not, of course, include additional numbers of individuals who might be experiencing chronic, low-grade depression, or acute depressive symptoms that fall short of diagnostic criteria for major depressive episode. For instance, dysthymic disorder may be estimated to affect between an additional 2% to 4% of the population, based on studies of North American cities, Italy, Taiwan, and Korea (Smith & Weissman, 1992).

Lifetime diagnoses of major depression

Not only is depression fairly common at any given moment, but its lifetime prevalence is also high. In older surveys of US locations, the rate was 4.4%, but ranged between about 1% in Taiwan to 9% in Canada and nearly 13% in New Zealand. The recent US Comorbidity Survey indicates a lifetime rate of 17% (Blazer et al., 1994). The variability in these figures is noteworthy, and is discussed further below.

Overall, the rate of 17% lifetime, since it is based on the most recent methods, warrants attention. It suggests that in some populations, major depression is quite common. Given its impairing properties as discussed in Chapters 1 and 2, depression is a public health issue of considerable magnitude.

Age and depression

For many years, depression was considered a disorder of middle age or older. However, as we explored in Chapter 2 on age of onset of depression, it is now apparent that the common age of onset of depression is in youth or early adulthood. Thus, it is not surprising to observe that the proportions of people with major depression are higher among younger individuals. US data on major depression by decade of age based on epidemiological data indicate the highest rate of current depression (6.1%) among the youngest group, and the lowest rate (3.6%) among the oldest group (Burke, Burke, Regier, & Rae, 1990).

Increasing rates of depression among the young

Not only are the rates of onset and current depression highest among those in their late teens and early 20s, but several studies have now suggested an intriguing possibility: depression is on the increase among the young. Klerman and Weissman (1989) were among the first to note that rates of depressive disorder were relatively higher in those born more recently. That is, when individuals of all ages are interviewed concerning the experience of major depression in their lifetimes, more of the younger people were reporting depression. A US study comparing rates of depression in those born between 1953 and 1966 with the cohorts born between 1937 and 1952, and 1917 to 1936 found a sizeable increase in each young group over the older ones—and a substantial increase in onsets between the ages of 15 and 19 for the youngest group (Burke, Burke, Rae, & Regier, 1991).

The "birth cohort effect" has now been substantiated in an international study. The Cross National Collaborative Group (1992) employed standardised methods of assessing retrospective reports of depression in various US cities, Paris, Beirut, Alberta (Canada), Puerto Rico, Munich, New Zealand, Taiwan, and Florence, Italy. Respondents were classified by decade of birth, and in all but the Florence study, rates of major depression were highest by age 25 among those born since 1955. Thus, the apparent increase in depression in more recent birth cohorts of young people is not limited to the US.

Interestingly, the trend toward more depression in younger people seems to be continuing even in children and adolescents. Ryan and colleagues (1992) evaluated siblings of preadolescent depressed and normal children, and found that the rates of depression were higher in siblings born more recently than in older siblings—among both depressed and normal groups. Also, the adolescent community study in Oregon has also recently found a significant age-cohort effect, at least for the young women, even among those between the restricted ages of 14 and 19 (Lewinsohn, Rohde, Seeley, & Fischer, 1993). Those born between 1972 and 1975 were significantly more likely to show major depression than those born between 1968 and 1971.

What could account for this alarming trend toward more depression among the young? Various explanations have been considered, including both methodological artifacts and psychosocial causes. For instance, it might be argued that younger people are over-reporting depression because they are more knowledgeable about depression, and more willing to acknowledge it. Thus, perhaps the increased rates are simply reflecting a lower threshold for counting depressive experiences. Arguing against such an artifact, however, Klerman and Weissman (1989) observed that objective measures of distress such as suicides and hospitalisation are also increasing for young people. Another argument is that older people have forgotten their previous depressions, and that the apparent increase in depression is really a memory artifact. However, studies of recall of depressive experiences among those known to have been depressed do not display significant evidence that memory for more distant depressive experiences is impaired (Klerman & Weissman, 1989).

Since methodological problems are probably not accounting for much of the dramatic birth cohort differences in depression, investigators have turned to more psychological explanations. It has been suggested that changing cultural trends such as breakdown in the family and increasing social mobility create potential sources of depression. Furthermore, such changes—less family stability and moving away from friends—might also reduce the available resources for helping individuals cope with stressful situations that cause depression. It has also been speculated that today's young people perceive that their worlds provide them with high expectations and goals but with reduced opportunities to achieve those goals. In later chapters we review various theories of the causes of depression that explore the role of stress, family and interpersonal relations, social support, and beliefs about the self and the future as they pertain to depression. Clearly, for any theory of depression to be credible, it must be capable of helping to account for the increasing rates of depression in young people.

In addition to the search for the origins of depression among the young, it will also be important for researchers to consider the implications of youthful depression. As we indicated in previous chapters, the consequences of depression may be considerable impairment and the chance of recurrent or even chronic disorder. When depression interferes with normal development as in children and adolescents, and when it impedes achievement of stable family and occupational adjustment, it can certainly set the stage for continuing depression. Thus, youth depression may be particularly disabling and pernicious in terms of its future course and its potential influence on the lives of the affected person and those around him or her.

Depression in children and adolescents

Except for the National Comorbidity Study that included ages 15 and above, other epidemiological surveys have excluded children and youth. Estimates of their depression, therefore, have been based on limited surveys. These few surveys were recently summarised by Angold and Costello (1993), and despite considerable variability due to different samples and methods, major depression in youngsters generally falls in the 6% to 8% range (in a 6 to 12 month period). However, the overall finding obscures important differences between preadolescent and adolescent age groups: younger than about age 12, depression is fairly rare—affecting 2% to 3% of the population (e.g. Angold & Costello, 1993). Adolescents, on the other hand, have higher rates. Depression in preschool age children apparently occurs in less than 1% (Kashani & Carlson, 1987), but data on young children are sparse.

One of the most recent large-scale surveys of adolescents in the community has yielded startlingly high rates of major depression (Lewinsohn et al., 1993). In an Oregon community based on interviews of nearly 2000 youngsters 14 to 18 years old, 3% currently met criteria for major depression or dysthymia, but a total of 20% reported lifetime depression, meaning that many were not presently depressed but had been so in the past.

The high rates of depression in those so young raise an important issue about the relation of age to depression.

Depression in older adults

Depression among the elderly, while apparently not as common as among younger groups, raises its own unique issues. For one thing, demographic trends clearly indicate that the numbers of older adults are increasing, because of the aging of the post-WWII baby boom and also stemming from greater longevity of elders due to improved health care in most nations. There is also some suggestion that depression levels increase in old age. Although generally the rates of major depression are not as high among older adults as they are in younger groups, there is some indication that rates increase in old age (Burke, Burke, Regier, & Rae, 1990). Wallace and O'Hara (1992) studied changes in depressive symptoms in a rural sample of people age 65 and over, retesting them 3 and 6 years later. They found significant increases over time in depressive symptoms—especially among the very old, age 85 and above—suggesting that late life may be a time of increased depression risk.

Depression among the older segments of the population has often been misunderstood. Sometimes its manifestations as problems of memory and loss of energy and other bodily symptoms are misinterpreted as senescence, an irreversible decline in mental and physical capabilities. Thus, treatable depression might be misdiagnosed as a largely untreatable problem.

Another important aspect of elderly depression is that it can be quite literally life threatening. Rates of suicide are highest among older white males and among some cultures such as the Chinese, among older females (e.g. Group for the Advancement of Psychiatry, 1989; Rockett & Smith, 1989). Particularly if depression is caused by or accompanied by social isolation and poor health, it readily leads to hopelessness and suicidality (Clark & Fawcett, 1992; McIntosh, 1992). Moreover, because depression appears to compromise the functioning of the immune system, it might impair the body's resistance to disease. Among older people who become increasingly afflicted with ailments, reduced immune functioning due to depression might predict a more severe or fatal course of illness.

Finally, we note that the apparently lower rates of depression among older individuals shown in many epidemiological surveys might themselves be methodological artifacts. Just as depressive symptoms in children might show somewhat different manifestations that require adapting the diagnostic criteria, it is possible that adaptations are also needed to validly capture depressive experiences among older people.

Gender differences in depression

In addition to age differences in who is affected by depression, one of the most noteworthy characteristics of depression is that it is far more common among women than men. Across different methods of study and in different countries of the world, studies repeatedly report roughly a 2:1 rate of depression for women compared to men. The most valid studies for examining sex differences are community surveys, since rates based on treatment-seeking might be biased by women's known tendency to admit to and seek help for emotional problems. Such epidemiological surveys of communities are clear: whether in the US, New Zealand, Taiwan, or Seoul, or any other location that has been surveyed, the excess of women meeting criteria for depressive disorders is readily apparent and has remained fairly stable for years (e.g. Weissman & Olfson, 1995; see Fig. 3.1). For example, among US adults aged 15 to 54, the overall current rate of depression of about 5% needs to be qualified to indicate 3.8% for men and about 6% for women. Similarly, lifetime rates in this survey are 12.7% for men and 21.3% for women (Blazer et al., 1994).

In addition to higher rates of depressive disorders in women than men, there are also indications that women's course of depression is different from men's. For example, women may have earlier onsets than men do (e.g. Sorenson, Rutter, & Aneshensel, 1991). Women appear to have a greater likelihood of recurrent depression. In a sample of community adults, being female was associated with a greater likelihood of having a recurrent episode (Lewinsohn, Zeiss, & Duncan, 1989); however, Coryell, Endicott, and Keller (1991) did not find gender differences in relapse rates. More recently, in an adolescent sample, Lewinsohn et al. (1994) found that young women with prior depressive episodes are the most likely to have recurrences. In a 1-year follow-up, nearly 22% of young women with a prior depressive episode had a recurrence, compared with only 10% of previously depressed young men. There is also some indication that women's depression are longer lasting and more likely to be chronic. Sargeant, Bruce, Florio, and Weissman (1990), in their large-scale community survey, found that women's rates of persisting depression over a 1-year period were higher (25.4%) than were men's rates of persisting depression (17.1%).

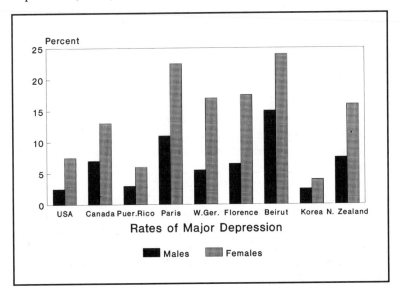

FIG. 3.1. Comparative rates of major depression for males and females (from Weissman & Olfson, 1995. Reprinted by permission of the Association for the Advancement of Science).

Gender differences in children and adolescents. Interestingly, among children, boys and girls do not differ in rates of depression (or in some studies, boys actually have higher rates than girls of depression as well as of most other disorders) (e.g. Angold & Rutter, 1992; Costello et al., 1988; Fleming, Offord, & Boyle, 1989). However, by adolescence the gender gap is quite apparent and approaches adult rates by early adolescence (e.g. Fleming & Offord, 1990). For instance, a prevalence of 7.6% for girls aged 14 to 16 compared with 1.6% for boys of the same age was reported by Cohen et al. (1993). While there is some disagreement about when the gender differences emerge, most studies agree that it is in early-to-middle adolescence (approximately 12–14; Angold & Rutter, 1992; Cooper & Goodyer, 1993; Petersen, Sarigiani, & Kennedy, 1991).

Why do more women show depression than men? And why do the differences emerge in early adolescence?

Why more depression in women?

Numerous efforts have been devoted to explaining sex differences in depression (e.g. Nolen-Hoeksema, 1987; 1990; Weissman & Klerman, 1977), but reach no definitive conclusions and instead point to multiple possible factors. The differences appear in virtually every culture studied, and in nearly every age group except preadolescent children. Some have argued that the gender effects may be partly due to "artifacts" of sex role differences rather than "actual" differences. To some extent it is likely that the excess of depression in women may stem partly from perceptions that depression represents emotional "weakness" and is therefore shunned by males as unacceptable behaviour. Males may experience depression but express their symptoms differently (e.g. by emphasising physical complaints or work difficulties rather than subjective distress, possibly leading to different diagnostic outcomes—or, by excessive use of alcohol and drugs to obscure depressive feelings). Apart from such so-called artifactual sources of gender effects, however, the major explanations have focused on biological and psychosocial differences between men and women.

Biological differences. To some degree there may be biological factors related to hormonal differences between the sexes, although as we note further in Chapter 4, depressions thought to be associated with hormonal fluctuations tend to be brief and normal (postpartum blues), or extremely rare (postpartum psychosis), or controversial as to their existence (premenstrual syndrome). Nor are there studies clearly linking female hormonal levels to major depressive disorders (e.g. reviewed in Nolen-Hoeksema, 1990). Thus, the biological effects due to hormones do not seem to account for the large gender effects.

Stress exposure. There are numerous variants of the idea that women experience greater stress than men do, and it is the stress (or stress interacting with some predisposing vulnerability) that causes depression. One version is that in general, women's lives are more stressful due to diminished opportunity and lower status than males—that women are poorer, have less power to control their own destinies, have lower status jobs or roles, have less access to sources of acclaim and reward than men do. It has also been hypothesised that women may be at risk for depression to the extent that their lives include "dual roles" such as worker and parent that might be in conflict, or hold dual roles that may be more demanding than those of men (e.g. spouse and worker). Support for the negative effects of dual roles for women was reported by Aneshensel, Frerichs, and Clark (1981) based on a large epidemiological survey. They found that among people who were both married and employed, women were more depressed than men—but among unmarried respondents, working men and women did not differ.

Apart from role-related stress that might lead to depression, there is additional evidence that women are exposed to greater levels of stress than men are. In a large survey of adult twin pairs, female subjects reported significantly more events overall than did men (Kendler et al., 1993). Their frequencies of negative events in the past year exceeded those of men in all content categories, with statistically significant differences in 6 of the 9 categories: interpersonal difficulties, financial, marital, and work problems, as well as events happening to others in their networks. Similar findings have been reported for adolescent women (e.g. Allgood-Merten, Lewinsohn, & Hops, 1990). Women may also be more affected by the stressors that happen to others than men are, to the extent that women tend to be more embedded in family and social networks than men are. As noted above in the Kendler et al. (1993) study, women reported more illness/accidents and crises happening to family members and close friends than men did. Eckenrode and Gore (1981) found that when negative events happened to friends and relatives, women experienced vicarious stress reactions resulting in symptoms. As Belle (1990) observed, this process might be even more problematic for poor women because they may be more dependent on their social networks for material and emotional support but also find that the networks exact a high cost in shared or vicarious stress experiences.

Analyses of women's potentially greater stress exposure and consequent depression must also consider the experience of sexual victimisation (both childhood molestation and adult sexual assault), which is much higher in women than men, and is well-known to be associated with later depressive experiences (e.g. Brown & Anderson, 1991; Winfield, George, Swartz, & Blazer, 1990). Women also experience relatively higher rates of other stressors that are known to be associated with depression: poverty (Belle, 1990; Bruce, Takeuchi, & Leaf, 1991); single parent status (Weissman, Leaf, & Bruce, 1987); teenage pregnancy (Troutman & Cutrona, 1990).

Coping factors. Some investigators have suggested that instead of, or in addition to, stress factors that promote depression, women might experience fewer of the coping resources necessary to combat stress and depression, than men do. Certainly, disadvantaged women exposed to chronic adversities simultaneously experience the reduction of coping resources. That is, they have less financial and material help, fewer stable marital relationships. Although disadvantaged women may have family and social networks, emotional support might itself be reduced if friends and family in their lives are taxed by their own adversities associated with disadvantaged status (e.g. Belle, 1990).

Women may also have characteristic ways of coping with depression that might actually intensify the dysphoria. Nolen-Hoeksema (1991) has proposed that when experiencing emotional distress, women display a response style that emphasises rumination, self-focus, and over-analysis of the problems and of their own emotions. They brood, weep, talk to their friends, and write in their diaries about their feelings and problems. In contrast, men use more distraction and problem resolution. They ignore the problems, or they do chores or play sports—or drink alcohol. Ruminative responses tend to intensify negative, self-focused thinking and to interfere with active problem solving—hence deepening or prolonging the symptoms of depression. Taking problem-solving steps or distracting oneself by activity, by contrast, might help to reduce and shorten the depressive experiences. Nolen-Hoeksema argues that sex role socialisation sets the stage for gender differences in coping styles, with boys being discouraged from showing emotionality and being encouraged to learn to take action, while girls are given license to express emotions and even encouraged to analyse them and discuss them with others. A series of studies has demonstrated support for these hypotheses, including gender differences in coping style and the association of ruminative coping with depression (e.g. Nolen-Hoeksema, Morrow, & Fredrickson, 1993; reviewed in Nolen-Hoeksema & Girgus, 1994).

Why do gender differences emerge in early adolescence?

As with adult gender differences, there have been numerous approaches to explaining the emergence of sex differences in adolescence. Nolen-Hoeksema and Girgus (1994) proposed three separate models to explain the effect: a) boys and girls have the same causal factors but such factors become more prevalent for girls in adolescence; b) factors leading to depression are different for boys and girls, and girls' factors become prevalent in adolescence; c) gender differences in personality characteristics that serve as diatheses for depression are present before adolescence, and interact with adolescent challenges which may be greater for girls, to cause greater depression in young women.

In analysing the validity of each of the models, a number of topics have been examined. For instance, one popular argument is that pubertal hormones set the stage for development of depression. Several studies have investigated the role of pubertal status on depression in adolescents, and generally conclude that depression emerges in young women independent of whether or not they have achieved puberty (e.g. Angold & Rutter, 1992). Brooks-Gunn and Warren (1989) found no correlations between depression symptoms and levels of several different hormones in a sample of 10-14 year-olds. Other research has suggested that it is not hormonal pubertal status as such, but rather the meaning of pubertal changes in the context in which they occur. For instance, Petersen, Sarigiani, and Kennedy (1991) found that girls who reached puberty at the same time as they changed school environments (e.g. from elementary [primary] to junior high [secondary]) were more likely to be depressed than girls for whom the changes did not coincide. Boys, on the other hand, did not show the same pattern. The researchers interpret the results to indicate that early pubertal change is stressful and unwanted for girls, and moving to a school environment that exposes them to older boys may accentuate their dysphoria. Boys, however, typically welcome pubertal changes—but also because they mature later than girls, they do not usually have both school and pubertal changes occurring at the same time. This line of reasoning is also supported by research that indicates that negative body image is associated with girls' depression.

Allgood-Merten et al. (1990) found that adolescent girls had more negative body image than did boys, and the association between stressors and depression was mediated by negative body image in the girls but not the boys. Overall, these and related studies suggest that pubertal changes negatively affect girls' body image, which in turn makes them more vulnerable to depressive reactions to stressors.

The role of stressors may also be important in the development in adolescence of gender differences in stressors. As with adult women, adolescent girls appear to have higher rates of stressors than do boys (Allgood-Merten et al., 1990; see also review by Compas, 1987). Included among stressors for young women is their heightened exposure to sexual abuse. Cutler and Nolen-Hoeksema (1991) reviewed the extensive research literature on the association between sexual victimisation and depressive symptoms and disorders. They note that childhood and adolescent sexual abuse are far more common in women than men, and appear to increase substantially in early adolescence. They suggest that such experiences may create a high risk for young women's low self-esteem and depression.

In addition to girls' increased exposure to major stressful experiences in early adolescence, Nolen-Hoeksema and Girgus (1994) review research suggesting that girls are also exposed during this time to various defeating and demoralising expectations about their roles. Emphasis on "feminine" pursuits and behaviours may place considerable demands on the young women to conform to expectations and restrict their ambitions and independence, compared to expectations for boys. Girls, for example, may be "punished" for competence and assertiveness, and rewarded for conforming to roles that might be stereotypically feminine but potentially less satisfying or more stressful. However, Nolen-Hoeksema and Girgus (1994) argue that a resulting sense of defeat and distress may not necessarily produce depression, unless it interacts with passive, less instrumental coping styles. Nolen-Hoeksema (1990) has argued that a ruminative coping style is especially characteristic of females; it involves a focus on internal distress and passive rumination about problems to the relative neglect of taking action to solve the problem or to distract themselves. Studies of adolescents have shown that they endorse such coping strategies more than boys do, and experience greater depressive reactions to their stressors than boys (e.g. Compas & Grant, 1993; Girgus, Nolen-Hoeksema, & Seligman, 1989).

In evaluating all the possible sources of the emergence of gender differences in adolescence, Nolen-Hoeksema and Girgus (1994) conclude that the interactive model best fits the data. That is, before adolescence, girls develop more risk factors than boys do, and in adolescence they experience more social and biological challenges that lead to the experience of depression.

Depression and other social-demographic factors

Although depression is a universal disorder with substantial current and lifetime rates in most cultures, variability by social and racial factors may provide additional clues about risks for depression.

Ethnicity and cultural differences. Cross-cultural differences, where they do exist, are most pronounced between Western and non-Western cultures. As summarised by Smith and Weissman (1992), for example, the lifetime rates of major depression are somewhat lower in Taiwan (e.g. around 1%) and Seoul, Korea (3.4%) than in the US (5.6%) or New Zealand (12.6%). However, cross-national data are relatively scarce and caution is needed in drawing firm conclusions that Western rates are actually higher. Even more notably, the methods for ascertaining depression in different cultures may not be fully comparable. The expression of depressive symptoms, for example, may vary by culture, so that the same measurement instruments may not be equally appropriate. One important cultural difference is the extent to which individuals distinguish between emotional and somatic experiences. The Western mind does make a distinction between mind and body that most of the non-Western world would find strange (Kleinman, 1991; Manson, 1991). Accordingly, depressive symptoms are more likely to be expressed as bodily complaints than subjective, self-oriented distress in many cultures. This pattern might be misinterpreted if only Western-based diagnostic tools were used.

Within the US, where fairly extensive studies have been conducted on ethnic subgroups, the general conclusion of the earlier epidemiological studies was that few differences are noteworthy (Smith & Weissman, 1992). White and African-American groups do not differ substantially in the more recent National Comorbidity Study (Blazer et al., 1994), although African-American rates are somewhat lower in that study. While women's rates of current depression did not differ, Black males had much lower rates (1.2%) than white males (4%). Also, Hispanics in this sample had higher rates than both whites and African-Americans—especially Hispanic women. A recent report of an African-American population, however, found that their rates of major depression were slightly higher than those in the general community (Brown, Ahmed, Gary, & Milburn, 1995); the discrepancy between this study and the National Comorbidity study might be that the former specifically surveyed African-Americans at all income and education levels, and included groups sometimes underrepresented in large surveys.

Urban/rural settings.   In the few studies that have examined differences in depression between rural and urban community residents, urban areas generally have higher rates of depression (e.g. Smith & Weissman, 1992). However, the recent National Comorbidity Study failed to find urban–rural differences (Blazer et al., 1994).

Social status factors.   In general, depression increases with lower social status. Lower income level is generally associated with more depression (e.g. Blazer et al., 1994). Numerous studies have shown that poverty is associated with increased risk for virtually all forms of psychological disorder. Often the correlation is bidirectional: people with disorders are too impaired to sustain work and income, and also poverty is a stress that may overwhelm healthy coping. In order to more closely characterise the causal direction of effect, Bruce, Takeuchi, and Leaf (1991) examined people who were below the poverty line in income, looking for the development of new onsets of disorders 6 months later in those who were previously well. They found, for example, that the poor were more than twice as likely to develop major depression as people who were not poor. Of course poverty itself is not the major mechanism causing disorder; it is likely the associated stress, strain, exposure to adversity and lack of resources to cope with difficulty that contribute to disorder. Such processes are reviewed more extensively in later chapters.

Also, unemployment or employment in lower status occupations are typically more likely associated with depression. Several studies have also found that being a homemaker (that is, not employed outside the home) is associated with higher levels of depressive disorder (e.g. Brown & Harris, 1978; Blazer et al., 1994). In addition, depression is usually found to be more common among those with lower levels of educational attainment (e.g. Regier et al., 1988; Wallace & O'Hara, 1992). Those with college education, for example, had lower rates, while those who failed to graduate from high school had the highest rates of depression (Blazer et al., 1994).

Finally, marital status is also related to depression. Those who are divorced have significantly higher levels of depression than either the continuously married or the never married (Blazer et al., 1994; Smith

& Weissman, 1992). However, it is also apparent that married individuals in unhappy relationships have a high risk for depression. For instance, Brown and Harris (1978) found that married women who lacked a close, confiding relationships with their partners were four times more likely to develop major depression when faced with a major stressor than stressed women who had such a relationship.

Overall, the demographic correlates of depression—such as gender, age, and social status—help point in the direction of causal factors. Clearly, any model of biological depression must acknowledge the tremendously important social factors that shape distributions of depressive disorders. On the other hand, any psychological models of depression must be able to account for the concentration of depressions among women, the young, and the disadvantaged. In the next chapters, we turn to an exploration of etiological models of depression.

Summary

- Depressive disorders are common, with 1 person in 6 having a diagnosable condition at some point in their lives.
- Women have twice as high rates as men worldwide, with explanations ranging from hormonal to sociopolitical suggesting that the lives of women are more stressful and that they have less effective resources for coping with depression.
- Depression is increasingly a problem for young adults and teenagers, probably due largely to changing social conditions.
- Among the elderly especially, depression may contribute to death through illness and suicide.
- There are cultural patterns in the way depression may be expressed.
- Any valid and comprehensive theory of depression must account for its prevalence in women, the young, and the disadvantaged.

Biological aspects of depression 4

There are several elements of depression that suggest that the role of biological features may be important. First, the symptoms themselves include physical changes: disruption of sleep schedules (insomnia or too much sleep), appetite changes leading to weight loss or gain, psychomotor changes, and the experience of fatigue, heaviness, and lack of energy. Second, it is well known that depression runs in families—although of course such patterns lend themselves to psychological as well as biological explanations. Third, the apparent success of antidepressant medications is consistent with a biological process in depression—although it would be fallacious to assume that an effective biological treatment implies a fundamental biological cause, since medications might have their effects by stabilising a process disrupted by psychological factors. Finally, it is also known that certain drugs used to treat medical illnesses may cause depression, and that particular kinds of head injuries and illnesses may also cause depression. These considerations all support the importance of viewing the possible biological origins of depression, and considerable research has been devoted to the study of depression from a biological perspective. This chapter reviews key developments.

Genetic research in depression

Traditionally, the methods of genetic research have included family studies, twin studies, and adoption designs. More recently, methods of molecular genetics and mathematical models have added to the array of genetic studies.

Family studies

Family studies identify a *proband* who has been diagnosed with the disorder and then interview or otherwise obtain information regarding the psychiatric status of each primary relative. The advantage of such studies is that they are reasonably easy to conduct, and therefore a considerable amount of information has been obtained regarding the patterns of familial transmission of unipolar depression. The disadvantage, however, is that results of such methods cannot be attributed entirely to genetic factors, since psychological variables such as being reared with ill relatives or exposed to common depressogenic processes cannot be ruled out as important determinants.

A number of studies of adult depressed probands have been conducted. Gershon (1990) reviewed 10 such studies of unipolar depressed patients, and found that the rates of depression in first degree relatives ranged between 7% and 30%—considerably higher than in the general population. In the Collaborative Depression Study of nearly 900 patients and controls, the rate of severe major depression involving hospitalisation, incapacitation, or psychosis was 10.4% in first-degree relatives of unipolar probands, compared with 4.9% of controls' relatives (Winokur et al., 1995).

Mild depression and dysthymic disorder.   Some of the genetic studies indicate that the increased rate of family members affected by depression applies only to severe depression (e.g. Torgerson, 1986). In the Winokur et al. (1995) study noted earlier, the unipolar and control groups did not differ in relatives' rates of depression when all levels of depression were included, but did differ when only severe depressions were counted. Thus, severe depression may be elevated in families, but milder forms of depression may be fairly common in both normal and patient families.

Less research has examined family patterns of dysthymic disorder, the milder, chronic form of depression. One recent study examined the family members of nearly 100 patients with early-onset dysthymia, patients with major depressive disorder, and nonpsychiatric comparisons (Klein et al., 1995). They found that dysthymia was significantly more common in the relatives of dysthymic patients than in either major depressed or normal comparisons, but that these families also displayed elevated rates of major depression. Both dysthymia and major depression in patients were also associated with elevated rates of personality disorders in relatives, although the association was especially strong for dysthymic patients. The authors conclude that there appears to be a familial link between dysthymia and major depression, but that dysthymia is somewhat distinct because it aggregates specifically in families of dysthymic patients.

Offspring of depressed parents.   Children of depressed parents appear to be at increased risk for developing depression as well as other disorders. From large-scale studies (e.g. Weissman et al., 1987) to relatively intensive small-scale studies (e.g. Gotlib & Lee, 1990; Hammen, 1991a; Klein, Taylor, Dickstein, & Harding, 1988), between 50% and 80% of children of depressed parents display a diagnosable disorder during childhood or adolescence. About 50% of the offspring display depressive disorders, but the full array of conduct, anxiety, and substance abuse disorders may also be present. While early onset of disorder may be an indicator of genetically transmitted dysfunctions, most of the offspring studies also indicate that the children in such families not only inherit whatever biological factors may contribute to psychiatric disorders, but they also "inherit" a variety of psychosocial disturbances such as dysfunctional child rearing and highly stressful family environments (e.g. Hammen, 1991a). Such characteristics of families of depressed parents are reviewed in later chapters.

Twin studies

In view of the difficulty in drawing conclusions about specifically genetic transmission from family patterns of disorder, many investigators have turned to *twin study* methods. Since identical (monozygotic) twins share 100% of their genes, they should be more similar to each other in the expression of a disorder (concordance) than would twins who are not identical (dizygotic) and who share an average of 50% of their genes. Indeed, earlier twin studies have generally indicated approximately 4 times higher concordance rates in monozygotic than dizygotic twins (65% to 14%) according to a review by Nurnberger and Gershon (1984). Two more recent studies are noteworthy for their improved methodologies and large sample sizes. McGuffin, Katz, Watkins, and Rutherford (1996) obtained a sample of 214 twin pairs through probands who had been inpatients in treatment for depression, located through the Maudsley Twin Registry. They determined that concordance for lifetime major depression was 46% for monozygotic twins, compared with 20% for dizygotic twins, and both rates were substantially higher than lifetime depression in the general population. McGuffin et al. (1996) concluded that genetic factors play a moderate role in family patterns of depression, and also suggested that genetics may be particularly important in recurrent depression with endogenous (melancholic) features.

Kendler et al. (1992) also tested the genetic versus shared environment hypothesis in their study of 1033 female twin pairs from the community-based Virginia Twin Registry. Using various diagnostic criteria to define depression, concordance between monozygotic (MZ) twins was higher than for dizygotic (DZ) twins (e.g. based on *DSM-III-R* depression 48% vs. 42%), and both groups had higher rates of depression than did the general population. Using advanced statistical models, the authors concluded that genetic factors play "a substantial, but not overwhelming, role in the cause of depression," and shared environmental factors did not play an important role. For shared environmental factors, the investigators used a measure of how often the twins, as children, shared a bedroom, had the same playmates, dressed alike, and were in the same classroom. In contrast, environmental experiences that were not shared as adults, such as life events, were hypothesised to play an important role in depression. Similar conclusions were reached in a follow-up study of the twin pairs (Kendler et al., 1993). The incidence of new depressions during a 1-year period was predicted "substantially but not overwhelmingly" by genetic factors (with 27% concordance for MZ twins and 17.6% concordance for DZ twins), according to the investigators, while "individual-specific environmental factors accounted for the remaining somewhat larger proportion of variance in the liability."

Issues in genetic research

Much of genetic research requires inferences from indirect evidence, whether using mathematical models to characterise heritability patterns or attributing familial depression to genetic transmission when it appears to run in families. Each method is subject to limitations. As noted, family studies cannot rule out the effects of environmental transmission. Twin studies, while less subject to similar limitations, cannot rule out the possibility that being an identical twin increases the risk of concordance for depression due to highly similar psychosocial experiences. Adoption studies in which biological offspring are raised by nonbiological relatives, could more convincingly separate nature from nurture, but represent very difficult samples to obtain.

Search for genetic defects in depression. One method that has the potential for resolving some of the limitations of genetic research is to locate a particular gene that is present in cases of depression. Methods of molecular genetics using recombinant DNA or presence of known genetic loci have explored genetic patterns in families affected by particular disorders such as bipolar illness. However, there are a number of factors that will be likely to prohibit such methods from being effective in unipolar depression (Blehar, Weissman, Gershon, & Hirschfeld, 1988). One problem is that unipolar depression is highly heterogeneous, probably encompassing a variety of subtypes. Another difficulty is that such methods are far more likely to be successful when there is a single gene with known modes of transmission, but most investigators have observed that the patterns of depression in families do not readily conform to known Mendelian patterns, suggesting more complex patterns that would be difficult to detect using molecular genetics methods. Moreover, it is obvious that many depressions arise directly from psychological and environmental factors, and therefore represent "phenocopies" that are indistinguishable from potentially genetically-based disorders. Such occurrences make it extremely difficult to select depressions for genetic study that are truly informative about genetic risk. For all of these reasons, methods of molecular genetics that have helped to identify particular genes for disorder are likely to be of little use in unipolar depressions.

What is transmitted?   Even if genetic factors play some role in risk for developing depression, the mechanism that is transmitted is unknown. As we explore in later sections, there may be various neuroendocrine or other processes that are good candidates but research has yet to indicate that they are markers of inherited traits.

Genetic factors are often regarded as *diatheses* in a diathesis-stress model; with respect to depression, such a model would hold that a genetic predisposition interacts with an environmental stressor to produce a depressive reaction. Traditionally, this form of gene–environment interaction suggests that an environmental factor affects people with the genetic predisposition to a disorder differently from how it affects people without the genetic predisposition. An example of this form of diathesis-stress interaction comes from the large Virginia twin study noted earlier. The study of female twin pairs yielded an intriguing view of the effects of having both genetic liability for depression and exposure to major stressful life events. Kendler and his colleagues (1995) examined the occurrence of significant negative life events and onset of major depression in the past year. They found that not only did the women who became depressed experience higher rates of stressful events, but also those with presumed genetic liability (e.g. were identical siblings of a depressed co-twin) were also more likely to be depressed than those with less liability. Most strikingly, there was an interaction of genetic liability and stress, such that the highest levels of depression were found in the group exposed to stress who were also most genetically at risk for depression. In contrast, women at lowest risk for depression (they were identical co-twins of non-depressed women) who experienced a severe life event were significantly less likely to become depressed. The authors suggest that genetic factors influence the risk of depression in part by lowering the sensitivity of individuals to the impact of stressful events.

An alternative to gene-environment interaction models of the diathesis-stress approach is noted by Rende and Plomin (1992), as genotype-environment correlation. In this alternative, the genetic predispositions may correlate with the environmental factors. An example of this effect is represented in a genetic family study by McGuffin, Katz, and Bebbington (1988a). These investigators determined not only that depression was more common in the relatives of probands than in the general population. They also demonstrated that social adversity and stressful life events were more likely to be present in the families of depressed probands (McGuffin et al., 1988b). It appeared that a common familial factor predisposed to both depression and occurrence of stressors. Thus, individuals created high risk environments by engaging in behaviours that caused life events that have been associated with depression onset. It is possible that the genetic influence on depression also contributed to the tendency to experience stressful life events—not an interaction of independent factors but a correlation between factors.

Neurotransmitters and depression

Historically, there has been considerable interest in the potential role of monoamine neurotransmitters (especially serotonin, norepinephrine (noradrenaline), and dopamine) in mood disorders. Neurotransmitters are, of course, the "chemical messengers" by which neurons communicate and link the regions and functions of various parts of the brain. The monoamine neurotransmitters were known to be especially important in the functioning of the limbic system of the brain (amygdala, hippocampus, hypothalamus, and related structures of the "old" brain), areas that play a major role in the regulation of drives (e.g. appetite) and emotion. Limbic system neurotransmitter pathways link this region with other parts of the brain, and also, through the hypothalamus, exert control over the endocrine and autonomic nervous systems (Shelton, Hollon, Purdon, & Loosen, 1991).

In the 1950s, several medications were observed either to cause or decrease depression, and it became known that they had their effects on the central monoamine neurotransmitters. For example, tricyclic antidepressants such as imipramine were found to block the synaptic reuptake of amines into the presynaptic neurons, thus increasing their availability (reviewed in McNeal & Cimbolic, 1986). Based on the apparent monoaminergic effects of drugs, Schildkraut (1965) articulated a catecholamine model of affective disorders that claimed depression results from insufficiencies of the monoamine neurotransmitters (primarily emphasising norepinephrine and serotonin), while mania resulted from too much. For about two decades, numerous studies of effects of various antidepressant medications focused on the immediate, acute, effects of antidepressant medications on various neurotransmitters.

However, difficulties with the simple catecholamine model became readily apparent. New generations of effective antidepressant medications appeared that did not have the same tricyclic neurotransmitter-increasing effects. Also it became clear that simple theories of excess or deficit were inadequate since antidepressant drugs have immediate effects increasing neurotransmitters but did not as immediately alter mood. It typically takes several weeks for the depression to diminish. This delayed effect appeared to be more in keeping with a longer-term mechanism, such as changes in the density or sensitivity of receptors in the neurons. As a result, interest turned away from the simple catecholamine theory to a greater focus on amine receptor systems (McNeal & Cimbolic, 1986). Moreover, monoaminergic activity was seen to be more irregular and complex than previously believed. Siever and Davis (1985) proposed a dys-regulation model of neurotransmitters in depression, hypothesising that instability, desynchronisation, and abnormal reactivity in the monoamine neurotransmitter system causes depression. However, it is unclear whether this is simply an accurate description of something that is the result of depression, or whether dysregulation is caused by yet another unknown abnormality—or whether this is the fundamental causal mechanism in depression. Most researchers believe that interactions between various neurotransmitter substances and systems will eventually prove crucial to a full understanding of depression, but the processes are so complex that we have so far achieved only partial understanding of how they work.

Neuroendocrine functioning in depression

The monoaminergic neurotransmitters play a crucial role in the various brain functions, including the limbic system. The hypothalamus exerts control over the endocrine and autonomic nervous systems. There has been considerable interest in the role of such processes in depression. For instance, in the search for differences between depressed and nondepressed persons, one of the most consistent findings concerns *cortisol* and related functioning of the *hypothalamic-pituitary-adrenal (HPA) axis*. The HPA axis is a neuroendocrine system involving complex interconnections between the brain, certain hormones, and various organs. It is centrally involved in the body's normal reactions to stress. When the person perceives stress, under the control of various neurotransmitters such as norepinephrine, serotonin, gamma-aminobutyric acid (GABA), and acetylcholine, the hypothalamus in the brain synthesises the hormone CRF (corticotropin-releasing factor), which then stimulates the anterior pituitary gland resulting in the synthesis and release of adrenocorticotropic hormone (ACTH). ACTH then circulates to the adrenal glands, located on the kidneys, which produce cortisol. Cortisol is a key hormone in the sympathetic nervous system, resulting in a variety of forms of physical arousal and activation. The presence of cortisol in the blood then inhibits further production of ACTH and corticotropin-releasing hormone (CRH). In normal people, therefore, this homeostatic mechanism prevents excessive or prolonged physiological arousal.

Cortisol hypersecretion.   Numerous studies have found elevated levels of cortisol in acutely depressed people compared to nondepressed (as well as increased levels of CRF). When the person is no longer depressed, cortisol levels return to normal. In addition to hypersecretion of cortisol, investigators have observed abnormalities in the regulation of cortisol. Specifically, when the HPA axis is "challenged" by administration of a synthetic cortisol called *dexamethasone*, in normal people the result should be temporary suppression of cortisol as described in the feedback loop noted earlier. However, many depressed individuals show an abnormal reaction consisting of "early escape" from the expected suppression of cortisol. That is, when tested a certain time after the administration of dexamethasone, they have higher cortisol levels than nondepressed persons.

Initially, clinicians welcomed the "dexamethasone suppression test" (DST) as a potential diagnostic aid, and believed that it might indicate a particular biological form of depression likely to respond to medication (e.g. Carroll et al., 1981; Holsboer, 1992). The apparent dysregulation of the underlying HPA axis was thought to play a causal role in depression. However, it has become apparent that abnormal DST reactions not only do not occur in all persons with major depression, but also they frequently occur in other patient groups, such as schizophrenics (e.g. APA Task Force, 1987). Moreover, among depressives the abnormal DST response is typically observed only in depressive states, and appears normal when the person is no longer depressed. The question of whether DST nonsuppression predicts response to treatment or future depressive status has been addressed in various studies. A recent review of more than 100 such studies drew several conclusions (Ribeiro, Tandon, Grunhaus, & Greden, 1993). First, pretreatment DST status was unrelated to treatment outcome and status following hospital discharge. Second, when depressed persons continued to show abnormal DST results (nonsuppression) even after treatment, they were more likely to relapse quickly and generally had a poorer prognosis than patients whose cortisol functions returned to normal after treatment. These patterns may suggest that depressed persons with abnormal cortisol mechanisms are "sicker" and therefore less responsive to treatment—or that there may be a subset of patients whose underlying disorder stems from dysregulation of the HPA. At the least, excess cortisol reactions appear to indicate an abnormal stress response. Tying the cortisol responses back to neurotransmitters, one suggestion is that decreased postsynaptic norepinephrine receptor density in the hypothalamus might block its ability to detect feedback signals from the circulating cortisol levels (McNeal & Cimbolic, 1986).

Elaborating the hypothesis of defective stress-feedback mechanisms, Gold, Goodwin, and Chrousos (1988) have postulated that some forms of depression may arise from acute, generalised stress that has failed to return to normal states when the precipitants are no longer present. These investigators have further speculated that the origin of the defective mechanisms may be genetic, or that the brain (and the complex neuroendocrine systems) may have been sensitised as a result of early, acute exposure to stress such that in adulthood the stress reaction may be readily activated even by mild or symbolic representations of stress precipitants. While there is no direct test of this integrative hypothesis, it represents a useful attempt to combine both biological and psychological factors in accounting for at least some forms of depression.

Circadian rhythm dysregulation

For some depressed persons, a pattern of recurrent episodes of depression, and the symptoms such as worse mood in the morning (diurnal variation) and early morning awakening have, along with other biological findings, led to the speculation that some depressions (and possibly bipolar affective disorders) may stem in part from some disruption of the circadian rhythms. Circadian rhythms are normal cycles of physical and behavioural processes that follow a 24-hour course linked with day–night changes. Sleep patterns, body temperature, and certain hormonal fluctuations are among the processes that follow a circadian rhythm pattern. For instance, as noted earlier, altered patterns of secretions of cortisol and pituitary-dependent hormones have also been observed in depressed patients (e.g. Pfohl, Sherman, Schlechte, & Stone, 1985). Patients may have elevated cortisol throughout the day, and show an increase during the night, rather than in the morning when it normally occurs (Thase, Frank, & Kupfer, 1985). And, as indicated above, DST nonsuppression reveals abnormal cortisol regulation.

Sleep disturbance patterns.   A number of studies have found disruption in sleep patterns, both behavioural and as measured by electroencephalogram (EEG) recordings. For example, over the past 25 years, three sleep pattern abnormalities have been well documented in depressed patients (Thase & Howland, 1995). One is sleep continuity problems, including difficulty falling asleep or staying asleep, and waking up early. These abnormalities are present in about 80% of people in a major depression, although they are not limited to depressive conditions (Ford & Kamerow, 1989; Kupfer & Thase, 1983). A second abnormality is decreased slow-wave (delta) sleep, as recorded by brain-wave activity during sleep (Reynolds & Kupfer, 1987). This pattern is most apparent in depressives with so-called endogenous (melancholic) features. The third abnormality is alterations in the nature and timing of Rapid Eye Movement (REM) sleep. As noted by Thase and Howland (1995), normal people experience the onset of the first REM period about 1 to 2 hours after falling asleep, with subsequent REM periods increasing in length and intensity occurring at about 90-minute intervals. About 50% of depressed patients, by contrast, have shortened REM latencies—that is, they begin REM sleep in less than 60 minutes, and increased REM activity with a shift of REM activity into the first few hours of sleep (REM density). Disturbed REM sleep may be a marker of a particularly pernicious form of depression, with an increased risk of relapse (Reynolds & Kupfer, 1987). However, there has been some question about the extent to which abnormal sleep EEG patterns normalise when the depressed person is no longer depressed. Several studies have suggested that sleep abnormalities are relatively stable, and remain unchanged when the depression remits (e.g. Giles et al., 1993). Thase et al. (1994) examined the sleep patterns of unmedicated male patients undergoing psychotherapy. They found that with clinical improvement, the sleep profiles showed a significant reduction in REM sleep density. However, there were no changes in reduced REM latency or slow-wave sleep. These results suggest either that the latter are stable traits—possibly serving as markers for future risk of relapse—or possibly they do return to normal levels with the passage of time.

Antidepressant medication treatment invariably suppresses REM sleep, and some have even argued that this effect may be a critical process in reducing depression. Interestingly, however, there is little evidence that depressed patients with REM disturbances mark a subtype of depression requiring biological treatment. Simons and Thase (1992) examined patients who had undergone cognitive-behavioural therapy. Dividing the patients into those with and without EEG sleep disturbances, they compared the groups on treatment outcome and follow-up status one year later. The two groups did not differ on depression levels at either point, and indeed, most of the patients improved significantly—regardless of EEG sleep disturbances. Thus, even if the groups might differ in their underlying biological pathology, they nonetheless were equally likely to benefit from psychotherapy.

Studies of depressed children and adolescents have not consistently found evidence of sleep disturbances similar to those of adults (e.g. Puig-Antich et al., 1982). As noted in a review by Rao et al. (1996), 9 controlled studies have been conducted, with 5 finding reduced REM latency, 2 reported higher REM density, and none reported changes in slow-wave sleep patterns. One explanation of inconsistent findings is maturational, that because of the brain's continuing development during adolescence, "adult" sleep patterns have not yet occurred, yielding variable and inconsistent results. Another source of inconsistencies may be methodological issues, in that early-onset (adolescent) depressives may contain a heterogeneous sample that includes undiagnosed bipolars while the control samples may include persons who are at risk for depression but have not yet shown it. Recently Rao et al. (1995) followed adolescent depressives for an average of 7 years, and were able to differentiate those who were truly recurrent unipolar depressives and those who truly did not ever develop depression, excluding all others from the originally studied sample. When the depressed and control groups were compared on their initial sleep data collected during adolescence, they differed in the predicted fashion on REM density and REM latency. Interestingly, these "depressive" patterns were also observed among the initially normal controls who went on to develop depression over the course of the follow-up.

It is of interest to note that abnormal sleep patterns may be familial, perhaps indicating a genetically transmitted marker or process of vulnerability. Giles, Roffwarg, Dahl, and Kupfer (1992) found correlated patterns of sleep abnormalities in youngsters and their parents in families with depression. Recently Lauer, Schreiber, Holsboer, and

Krieg (1995) studied sleep patterns of 54 healthy adults who were considered at risk for mood disorders because a close relative had an affective disorder. Compared to controls, the high risk individuals displayed reduced slow-wave sleep and increased REM densities; the authors suggest that such patterns may mark a vulnerability for future depression.

Taken together, the abnormal patterns of circadian rhythm functions such as cortisol secretion and sleep disturbances have suggested a dysfunction of some type. One hypothesis is that there is a disorganisation or desynchronisation of different cycles in relation to each other. Normally, REM patterns and cortisol fluctuate in synchrony with the sleep–wake cycle. Early morning awakening, diurnal variation, and the abnormalities noted have suggested a "phase advance" of the REM and cortisol secretion circadian rhythms in relation to the sleep–wake cycle. The desynchrony results in biological disturbances causing the symptoms of depression. Interestingly, sleep deprivation has been shown to reduce depression, at least temporarily, possibly by bringing the circadian rhythms back into alignment with each other (Wu & Bunney, 1990).

Circadian rhythms are related to day–night patterns, which of course are affected by season of the year. As noted in Chapter 1, a subgroup of depressed patients (including both unipolar and bipolar disorders) experience Seasonal Affective Disorder (SAD) marked by depression at certain times of the year (usually winter months in the Northern Hemisphere). We know that animal behaviours are highly affected by changes in light and temperature, with hibernation in winter months associated with decreased activity and increased sleep. Even normal humans report mild but significant seasonal changes in behaviour, such as sleeping and eating more, with less energy and activity in the winter months than in summer months (Kasper et al., 1989).

It has also been speculated that mood disorders might represent exaggerated seasonal variations. In general, it appears that more depressions occur in the Autumn and Winter (Goodwin & Jamison, 1990). Thus, one mechanism of depression (or at least SAD) might be abnormalities in light sensitivity or circadian rhythm functioning in response to detection of light. However, little direct evidence exists to clarify these processes or to demonstrate that they operate as etiological factors in mood disorders. Moreover, it should be noted that HPA functioning and circadian rhythms are not independent of neurotransmitter functioning. Indeed, complex relationships between these systems and acetylcholine, serotonin, norepinephrine, and dopamine have been noted (Thase & Howland, 1995). Thus, while investigators are gaining increased knowledge about various abnormalities associated with depression, their role as causal factors remains unclear, and their mechanisms of operation remain to be described.

Brain structure and functioning in depression

Individuals who sustain injuries or strokes in the frontal part of the brain have often been observed to display depression. One condition, *poststroke depression*, has been estimated to affect 30% to 50% of individuals after acute stroke. The quality of the depression is indistinguishable from major depressive episodes not caused by medical problems. Examination of the association between stroke location and presence of depression has suggested that the frontal regions and left side of the brain are especially critical, particularly the left frontal region, but the right posterior region of the frontal lobes may also be important in poststroke depression (Starkstein & Robinson, 1991). The frontal lobes control not only the higher intellectual functions such as planning and judgment, but they are also a major regulatory component of the limbic system which, as noted earlier, controls emotion and drive processes. Starkstein and Robinson (1991) speculate that stroke-induced damage to the biogenic amine pathways that connect the frontal regions to the limbic system may account for the symptomatology of depression.

Building on such observations and hypotheses, investigators have looked at the possibility of brain abnormalities in depressed patients. Neuroimaging studies, for example, have provided some evidence of structural abnormalities in the frontal regions of unipolar patients, particularly severely depressed patients (reviewed in Powell & Miklowitz, 1994). Recently, Coffey et al. (1993) used magnetic resonance imaging (MRI) analysis to demonstrate that depressed patients had lower frontal lobe volume than did controls, although there were no temporal lobe volume differences.

Another method for assessing frontal lobe functioning is electrophysiological (EEG) recording. Davidson and his colleague (e.g. Henriques & Davidson, 1990) reviewed evidence from various sources, concluding that depression is associated with a decrease in either left frontal or right posterior activation. They demonstrated left frontal hypoactivation in a sample of 15 unipolar depressed patients compared with normal controls (Henriques & Davidson, 1991). However, an important issue is whether such patterns are observed only in the depressive state, or whether they are stable, potential markers of vulnerability. To test this question, Henriques and Davidson (1990) evaluated individuals who previously had experienced a major depressive episode but who were now nondepressed, and compared them with never-depressed individuals. The former depressives were found to have the predicted reduced activation in the left frontal and right posterior cortical regions. Davidson speculates that deficits in left anterior activation reflect deficits in an "approach" system, and that individuals who display this type of frontal EEG asymmetry are more vulnerable to negative affective states—including depression, given sufficient environmental stress. As Henriques and Davidson (1990) note: "We view decreased left anterior activation as a diathesis that lowers the threshold for triggering emotions and psychopathology associated with deficits in approach (i.e., sadness and depression)."

Although intriguing, frontal lobe dysfunctions in depression are difficult to interpret. As noted by Powell and Miklowitz (1994), it is unclear if such patterns are an epiphenomenon of the vast neurochemical connections between this area of the brain and other structures that control mood and arousal—or whether frontal lobe dysfunctions reflect a primary etiological factor. This puzzle is revisited in a later section.

The role of female hormones in depression

In view of the gender differences in depression as noted in Chapter 3, it has been common to speculate that ovarian hormones likely play an important role in women's greater incidence of depressive disorders. The occurrence of premenstrual dysphoric disorder (or premenstrual syndrome, PMS), postpartum depressions, and the emergence of the gender gap in depression in early adolescence are all phenomena that are often used to attribute some depressions to hormonal shifts. However, the research on this topic is fraught with many methodological problems and inconsistent findings.

With respect to PMS, there has been considerable controversy about whether this condition actually exists. Interpretation of research on this topic has been coloured by political biases, poor methodologies, and overly simple theories (Gitlin & Pasnau, 1989). While the category of Premenstrual Dysphoric Disorder has now been placed in the *DSM-IV* as a condition requiring further study, it is unclear whether it reflects mostly a hormonal problem, a response to stressors, or pre-existing personality characteristics.

Postpartum depression actually refers to three distinct phenomena. *Postpartum blues* occur in a substantial percentage of women in the first few days after birth. Symptoms of crying, sadness, and upset are short-lived and rarely treated. They are thought to be consequences of the dramatic drops in estrogen and progesterone levels that occur at birth. Thus, this reaction is normal, and does not resemble the clinical condition of depression. *Postpartum major depression*, on the other hand, meets criteria for major depression and may occur in 10-15% of women after birth. Since only a minority of women experience such depressions, they are clearly not an inevitable response to hormonal changes. In general, women who do experience such depressions display psychosocial difficulties and prior histories of depression, as noted in Chapter 1 (e.g. Gotlib, Whiffen, Wallace, & Mount, 1991; O'Hara, Schlechte, Lewis, & Varner, 1991). The depressions may also be related to large changes in hormones and cortisol (Weissman & Olfson, 1995). Women who do develop postpartum depression appear to be at increased risk for developing future depressive episodes, as indicated in a $4\frac{1}{2}$ year follow-up (Philipps & O'Hara, 1991).

About one woman in 1000 has a *psychotic postpartum depression* with delusions. Women who have had one such postpartum psychosis have an elevated risk for subsequent such episodes. They are especially likely to occur among women with histories of bipolar disorder, but may also occur in unipolar depression. As Weissman and Olfson (1995) point out, some have speculated that postpartum psychotic depressions may be linked to low estrogen levels through a sensitisation of the central dopamine receptors.

The rise in depression rates in young women that appears to occur in puberty has been attributed to pubertal hormonal changes. The few studies that have actually examined depression and hormonal status in adolescents have failed to find a relationship (e.g. Angold & Rutter, 1992; Brooks-Gunn & Warren, 1989; see review by Nolen-Hoeksema & Girgus, 1994). The limited research on the topic suggests that a variety of psychosocial factors may better account for the emergence of sex differences in adolescence (Nolen-Hoeksema & Girgus, 1994).

In addition to the relatively transitory or peripheral role of hormones in these forms of depression, studies attempting to link adult depression to hormone levels has proven to be unconvincing (reviewed by Nolen-Hoeksema, 1990). Such studies have frequently been methodologically flawed, and many have found no relationship between moods and hormones.

The quest for the "biological" subtype of depression

In addition to the general search for biological factors in depression, another approach has been to search for a specifically biological subtype—presumably caused by some biological abnormality. As noted in Chapter 1, there have been various unsuccessful attempts to characterise such a subtype as distinct from a "psychological" type. Nevertheless, there is one descriptive subtype—based on its clinical presentation—that continues to be considered as a potential candidate: *melancholic depression*. "Melancholic" is preferred to the previous term, endogenous, because there is no evidence that such depressions arise spontaneously from some endogenous process in the absence of stressors (a topic reviewed in further detail in Chapter 6).

Melancholic depression is a type of major depressive episode characterised by psychomotor change (agitation or retardation), late insomnia (early morning awakening without being able to go back to sleep), weight and appetite loss, loss of pleasure, distinct quality of mood, diurnal variation of mood (commonly worse in the morning), excessive guilt, and delusions. Characterisation of the features of this subtype have been hampered by multiple overlapping definitions (Rush & Weissenberger, 1994).

The basis for pursuing melancholic depression as a possible biological subtype is that it has several features that distinguish it from nonmelancholic depression. It appears to be a good predictor of positive response to electroconvulsive therapy (ECT), and among the more severely depressed melancholic patients, to antidepressant medications. It is also associated with shorter REM latency and cortisol nonsuppression during the dexamethasone suppression test (Rush & Weissenberger, 1994). On the other hand, melancholic features do not appear to mark greater likelihood of family history (heritability) nor do they appear to predict a different course of illness than do nonmelancholic depressions (Rush & Weissenberger, 1994). Thus, further research is needed to determine the possible etiological significance of the melancholic subtype.

One study is an example of an effort to integrate biological and psychosocial approaches to depression by attempting to describe subtype differences. Monroe, Simons, and Thase (1992) asked the question of whether patients with endogenous depression (defined somewhat similarly to what is now called melancholic depression) could be further divided into potentially "psychosocial" and "biological" subtypes. Patients were categorised into subgroups who either had a severe stressor prior to the onset of their depression, or did not have a stressor. The groups were then compared on REM latency scores based on sleep EEG recordings. They found that the stressed depressives had essentially normal EEG patterns, whereas the patients who did not have prior stress had reduced REM latency values. They interpreted the results to suggest that acute, severe stress produced a type of depression marked by severe symptoms but normal biological sleep patterns, whereas patients without precipitating stressors may represent a different etiological subtype with indicators of sleep pattern disturbance. The effort to explore the possibility of different etiological processes in different subtypes of depression is an important direction to pursue.

Conceptual issues in the biology of depressive disorders

The task of identifying biological factors in depression is enormously complicated by the complexity of the interactions among various processes (e.g. circadian rhythms, neurotransmitters, brain regions, endocrine systems) as well as by the limited understanding of and tools for studying such processes. Compounding the difficulty of drawing useful conclusions, conceptual issues are often ignored. Two such difficulties are briefly discussed here.

Causality vs. correlation.   When depressed and nondepressed groups are compared and yield differences on a biological factor, what is the appropriate conclusion? Frequently, the conclusion or implication drawn is that the factor is of etiological significance—that is, it is the underlying cause of the depression. It is conceivable, even likely, that many biological "differences" simply reflect *consequences* of depression due to changes in sleep, appetite, or activity, or emotional distress. Or, they may be *correlates* of some other unknown process but in themselves have little etiological significance. The increasing use of longitudinal studies that examine depressed people during and after depressive episodes will help to determine which biological parameters are "state dependent" and simply reflect depression-related changes, and which are more stable. However, even if stable, it may still be difficult to conclude that the biological parameter has causal significance because it may reflect a residual of the depressive episode itself (a "scar"). Therefore, designs that are not only longitudinal but identify potential subjects at risk for depression but before they actually experience episodes may be needed to help clarify the status of the biological factor. It is further necessary to keep in mind that a putative "marker" or indicator of potential vulnerability may itself not have causal significance but may simply be a correlate or indicator of some other process that has etiological features.

This is not to say that "markers" or "correlates" may not be important to study. They may indeed help to clarify the pathophysiological process that occurs when depression is instigated for whatever reason. As such, they may play some important role in understanding the course or indicating a treatment mechanism. Unfortunately, however, they are often assigned causal significance not warranted by the design or data.

Static vs. transactional models.   Another conceptual challenge concerns the nature of the model of biological effects in depression. Some investigators appear to subscribe to simple "main effects" models, such as genetic defects or neuroendocrine dysregulation, implying that such factors are necessary and sufficient causes of depression. However, the genetic evidence does not support such a model (e.g. lack of complete concordance in monozygotic twins), nor is it clear that biochemical dysregulation is a causal rather than consequential feature. Most researchers appear to subscribe to diathesis-stress models, requiring a pathophysiological diathesis which must be triggered by some environmental or physical stressor. There are two difficulties with this approach, however. One is that there has simply been insufficient attention to an integration of biological and stress or psychosocial factors. Hopefully, this will change with increasing appreciation of the advantages of such models—and a few examples have been presented (or will be discussed in later chapters).

A second difficulty is that diathesis-stress models may tend to be static, focused on the interaction of the two factors but disregarding the potential dynamic mechanisms that might involve the influence of the diathesis and stress on each other. Several recent models, in contrast, suggest a highly transactional influence of the stress, episode, and diatheses on each other over time. For instance, Post (1992) has suggested that repeated episodes of both recurrent unipolar and bipolar disorder might alter the brain at the cellular level to change its sensitivity to stress—thus in time producing an organism reacting at such low levels of stress as to have virtually "autonomous" episodes. As noted earlier, Gold, Goodwin, and Chrousos (1988) proposed a model of depression which implicates defective stress regulation. Stemming from a possibly genetically-transmitted vulnerability in stress-homeostatic processes, a child exposed to chronic stress early in life would experience unusually intense and prolonged reactions that lead to the sensitisation of critical limbic sites in the brain. Such experiences and reactions may damage the homeostatic neuroendocrine processes especially in the developing brains of children. In turn, "sensitised" and improperly regulated stress reaction processes may mean that the individual is now predisposed to experience major depressive reactions when real—and possibly only when imagined or symbolic—stressors occur. To date, there is little research on humans that directly supports such transactional models, but studies that consider the effects of stressors and episodes on possible biological diatheses seem to be productive directions for future investigation.

Summary

- Overall, there is no definitive biological theory of the cause of depression, although there are several suggestive possibilities.
- Twin studies and family patterns suggest that some depressions have a genetic component, though its nature is unknown.
- Although antidepressant medications alter neurotransmitter functioning, there is no valid, simple theory that depression is due to excess or deficits of particular neurotransmitters.
- Abnormal levels and regulation of cortisol may suggest that depression is related to a defect in the stress response system.
- Sleep abnormalities, as well as cortisol abnormalities and seasonal patterns of depression, are consistent with a model of some depressions as a biological rhythm disturbance.
- Female hormones have been hypothesised as a crucial factor in the excess of female depression, but evidence of their importance in clinical depressions is weak.
- Integrations of biological and psychological models of depression are needed.

Cognitive and life stress approaches to depression 5

Sarah sips her coffee as she gazes out the window onto the busy street. She watches men and women walk briskly toward their destinations, and imagines that their lives are filled with purpose and meaning—but believes that hers will never be—no interesting job to go to, no eager completion of tasks, no important goal to pursue for the future. She watches couples pass the window, laughing and conversing, and feels a pang of loss. "I'll never have a relationship again," she thinks, "no one would want me, and I'll always be alone." As she often does these days, she leaves the coffee shop unrefreshed and feeling even worse than when she came in.

Sarah's reveries are typical of those of depressed people: a relentless focus on the negative aspects of herself, the world, and her future. Such thoughts are usually exaggerations or misperceptions of reality, but invariably they leave the person feeling overwhelmed and hopeless, accentuating or prolonging the symptoms of their depression. Many theorists argue that such negative thinking is not only part of the syndrome of depression, but may indeed reveal a pre-existing vulnerability to develop depression or to experience recurrences. That is, to the extent that such negativity of thinking is part of the person's *typical* way of perceiving the self and the world, they are prone to depression when something that they interpret as negative happens. In this chapter several of these models that emphasise primarily *cognitive* causes of depression are reviewed and evaluated.

Suppose that we also discover that Sarah's life changed dramatically a month ago, when her fiance broke off their relationship. She had dreamed of their life together, and was overwhelmed with hurt and anger when he told her he had found someone else. Her feelings rapidly turned into depression. As with Sarah, many people who experience major depressive episodes are reacting to undesirable negative life events. The role of stressful events and adverse life conditions has long been recognised as a contributor to depression, and in the second part of this chapter, we analyse this approach to understanding depression.

Cognitive and information-processing models of depression

Among psychological models of depression, no approach has stimulated more research in recent years than the cognitive model of Aaron Beck (1967; 1976) and several subsequent cognitive approaches. Although trained in the psychoanalytic perspective on depression that viewed the condition as introjected anger toward a lost relationship, more than anything Beck was struck by the negative thinking of his patients, the expressions of self-criticism and blame, the exaggeration of misfortune and the beliefs about personal helplessness and futility. He observed that such thoughts were dysfunctional—representing apparent distortions of reality and serving to prolong or exacerbate the symptoms of depression. Therefore, he formulated a cognitive model of depression with 3 key elements: *the "cognitive triad," faulty information processing,* and *negative self-schemas.*

The *cognitive triad* refers to characteristic thinking that emphasises negative cognitions (expectations, interpretations, perceptions, and memories) about the self, the world, and the future. Defeated, self-critical, and hopeless thoughts were believed to contribute to the mood, behavioural, physiological, and motivational deficits in depression. People who are depression prone are likely to think of themselves as defective; they view their circumstances and the world as defeating and depriving. They even think of the future as futile, with little possibility of positive change or desirable outcomes. These negative thoughts are *automatic,* according to Beck, in the sense that they occur spontaneously, without deliberate choice or conscious motivation. Obviously, carrying around the "cognitive triad" that leads individuals to automatically think negatively predisposes individuals to experience depression.

Moreover, as an additional component of his model, Beck argued that depressive thinking is typically distorted, that individuals selectively attend to the negative even when alternative positive events and interpretations are plausible, and greatly overgeneralise and magnify adversity while minimising or misinterpreting positive information. As in the example of Sarah earlier, there is no basis for her to conclude that she will never have a meaningful career or relationship—but her mood colours her thoughts in distorted ways, always emphasising the negative. Human *information processing* is characteristically biased in the sense that individuals are selective in what they attend to, and commit logical errors by leaping to conclusions that may not be warranted. Information-processing errors occur because people are guided by pre-existing beliefs and assumptions, and they "see" what they expect to "see" and believe that which supports their pre-existing beliefs.

More specifically, the third component of Beck's model is the idea of a *negative self-schema*. The schema concept has a long history in psychology, generally referring to organised representations of experiences in memory that serve as a kind of mental filter, guiding the selection, interpretation, and recall of information. Schemas are essential to all human information processing, serving the goals of speed and efficiency so that attention can be directed to "meaningful" information instead of laboriously processing all available information (e.g. Fiske & Linville, 1980). Thus, by selectively attending to or interpreting certain information, schemas help fill in "missing" information based on what is "expected." A schema about "JOHN" for example (tall, dark hair) helps us to rapidly spot him in a crowd, without seeing his face and without inspecting each and every person. Because they are like pre-existing filters or theories, however, errors are possible (e.g. we stop searching for John when we spot a tall, dark-haired man, but later discover that it wasn't John, who was actually sitting down so that we "ignored" him in our search for tall, dark-haired men). In exactly the same way as perceptual schemas, mental schemas of pre-existing beliefs lead to selective perception and interpretation of information that "fits."

A *self-schema* refers to organised beliefs and propositions about the self, and according to Beck, the depression-prone person holds a set of negative beliefs (or a mixture of negative and positive). These beliefs may be acquired in childhood, possibly as a result of repeated experiences with critical or rejecting parents. Because the schema is selective in "taking in" only confirmatory negative information, beliefs are retained despite accumulated evidence to the contrary. That is, a person who believes that it is terribly important to be perfect at all times and believes that he or she is basically incompetent is likely to pay attention to examples that support this belief while ignoring disconfirming information. He or she recalls mistakes but seems to ignore the preponderance of competent behaviour in his or her background.

Situations that are stressful and remind the individual of circumstances that were originally responsible for the acquisition of negative self-views are especially likely to activate the negative schema. Thus, a child often scolded for making mistakes might react to a poor exam performance with the "incompetence" self-schema. When activated, it directs his or her attention to any perceived flaws and exaggerates their significance, makes memories available that remind him or her of past shortcomings, and leads to thoughts about the future that include expectations of failure.

Beck has modified his views in various ways over time, an important change being the hypothesis that there are individual personality differences that define the types of negative events or instigators of depression, and that different symptom subtypes of depression might result from such personality differences (Beck, 1983). For example, a *sociotropic* personality style defines someone who bases self-worth on close connections with people and approval from other people. An *autonomous* personality style refers to someone whose sense of worth is based on achievement and independence. For an "autonomous" personality, losing at sports might activate depressive thoughts about the self but have little impact on someone with a sociotropic personality. On the other hand, the sociotropic personality might be upset over a perceived snub from someone—an event that the autonomous personality would be likely to ignore. Vulnerability, therefore, pertains to the dysfunctional beliefs and thoughts that are activated when events in the relevant domain occur that are interpreted as depletions of self-worth.

Helplessness and hopelessness models of depression. Martin Seligman (1975) and his colleagues originally observed that animals who had been exposed to uncontrollable aversive conditions failed to take action to escape such situations when outcomes were no longer uncontrollable, as if they had learned to be helpless. Seligman applied this hypothesis to human depression, suggesting that when one has erroneous expectations that no control is possible (in obtaining desirable outcomes or preventing undesirable ones), one fails to take action and experiences depressive symptoms. Later, the model was refined to include the individual's perceptions of the *causes* of uncontrollable outcomes. Abramson, Seligman, and Teasdale (1978) developed the *attributional model* that linked depression to the tendency to ascribe the causes of negative events to qualities of the self perceived to be unchanging and pervasive. Negative outcomes attributed to unstable or specific causes, for example, might provoke different reactions rather than depression. For example, a person who experienced the loss of a desirable job might become depressed if he or she interpreted the cause of the job loss to be a quality of the self that is global and

unchangeable, such as lacking "intelligence." Seligman later argued /
that some people characteristically show a "negative explanatory
style" of stable, global, and internal causal attributions for negative
events. That is, he moved the focus away from causal attributions
about specific undesirable situations toward a more general tendency
to see all negative events in certain ways. Thus, when something bad
or undesirable happens, those vulnerable to depression are more
likely to believe that it was caused by global and persisting qualities
of themselves that presumably are undesirable and unchangeable.

More recently, a revised *hopelessness model* of depression has been
articulated by Abramson, Metalsky, and Alloy (1989), intended to
characterise a subset of depressed people rather than serving as the
explanation for all depression. In this model, hopelessness (consisting
both of negative expectations about the occurrence of a highly valued
outcome and perceptions of helplessness to change the likelihood of
the outcomes) is the cognition that immediately causes depressive
reactions. In turn, hopelessness is the outcome of negative life events
that are interpreted negatively, in terms of stable and global causal
attributions for the event, or inferred negative consequences of the
event and/or inferred negative characteristics of the self given the
event's occurrence.

Recently, Rose et al. (1994) searched for the subtypes or characteristics of depressed people who display the hopelessness cognitions.
They examined the hopelessness cognitions of various nosological
groups (such as endogenous vs. nonendogenous, chronic vs. episodic
depression) as well as groups formed by different demographic and
background variables. They found that patients with the most negative hopeless cognitive styles were those who had personality
disorders (especially borderline personality disorder), adverse childhood histories in the form of sexual abuse or negative, controlling
family environment, and severe depression. Further research will be
needed to confirm whether this subgroup marks a cognitively vulnerable group that is at risk for future depression.

Other cognitive models of depression.   There have been additional approaches to depression that emphasise dysfunctional cognitions. There is not sufficient space to present them in detail, but they
have been influential with many of their elements incorporated into
the information-processing or other broad models. Rehm (1977) articulated and verified elements of a *self-control* theory of depression,
postulating that depressed people have deficits in the elements of
self-regulation: self-observation, self-evaluation, and self-reinforcement.

For example, depressed people selectively observe negative events to the relative exclusion of positive, and they set unrealistically high, global standards for themselves—making attainment unlikely. Moreover, they evaluate themselves negatively, and even if successful, devalue positive outcomes or attribute them to luck or factors for which they cannot take credit. Also, depressed people are skimpy in their rewards for desirable behaviour, while being excessively self-punishing for perceived inadequacies.

Nezu and colleagues (Nezu, 1987; Nezu, Nezu, & Perri, 1989) proposed a *problem-solving deficit* model of depression in which depression results from and is perpetuated by ineffective skills in problem solving when stressful events occur. Although not exclusively cognitive in its focus on actual problem-solving skills, the model emphasises several cognitive elements of the problem-solving process: problem orientation and definition in which a potential problem is defined or interpreted in a dysfunctional way (e.g. perceived as a threat, or attributed to the self), plus difficulties in generating and selecting alternative solutions. That is, a person may not be able to imagine effective solutions or select appropriate choices among the various possibilities. Such deficiencies could stem both from lacking skills and from negative cognitions about the self and situations.

Several investigators have noted that depressed people exhibit a heightened state of self-awareness, or *self-focused attention*. During such inward focus, individuals invariably magnify their negative appraisals of themselves and the significance and meaning of their negative experiences. Pyszczynski and Greenberg (1987) and Ingram (1990), for example, propose that self-focus increases negative affect and self-criticism, magnifies the perceived negative consequences of undesirable events, and potentially interferes with appropriate social and adaptive functioning, thereby contributing to a vicious cycle. A somewhat related version of this approach has been proposed by Nolen-Hoeksema (1991), as noted in Chapter 3 as an explanation for sex differences in depression, and as a theory about duration rather than onset of depression. She proposed that a *ruminative* response to depression (turning inward, reflecting on feelings, analysing the self, etc.) is a typically passive, female style of responding to dysphoric feelings. Unfortunately, it leads to the exacerbation of symptoms because individuals are less likely to effectively solve the problems that triggered their reactions and may selectively focus on negative interpretations. A number of naturalistic and experimental studies have supported the idea that rumination, compared with *distraction*, is associated with more dysphoria, less effective problem solving, and more negative thinking about the self and future (Lyubomirsky & Nolen-Hoeksema, 1995; Nolen-Hoeksema, 1991; Nolen-Hoeksema, Parker, & Larson, 1994).

Self-concept in depression. A frequent theme in many of the cognitive models of depression is that of negative views of the self, a deep-seated belief that one is defective, unworthy, unwanted, or incapable of obtaining or keeping important sources of meaning and gratification. Roberts and Monroe (1994) note, however, that overall self-esteem in terms of conscious feelings of self-worth, is not a reliable predictor of depression. Instead, they propose a multi-faceted approach to dysfunctional self-processes. They propose that dysfunctions of the self that contribute to vulnerability include 1) possessing relatively few, rigid, or externally based sources of self-worth, or 2) abnormally low self-esteem that is triggered by relevant events or negative mood, or 3) possessing unstable, highly fluctuating self-worth. In a later section, self-esteem as a consequence of adverse social conditions—and as a contributor to risk for depression in the face of severe stress—is discussed.

Evaluating cognitive vulnerability models

There are a number of issues that have been pursued in the empirical evaluation of the cognitive models of depression. The following sections are organised around some of the major questions.

Depression and negative cognitions

Probably hundreds of studies have tested the question of whether depressed people think more negatively than do nondepressed comparisons. The great majority of cross-sectional studies have supported this idea (reviewed in Gotlib & Hammen, 1992; Haaga, Ernst, & Dyck 1991; Segal & Ingram, 1994). For example, currently depressed individuals interpret hypothetical situations more negatively and make more negative predictions about the future (e.g. Hammen & Krantz, 1985) and display more global and stable negative attribution style (Gotlib et al., 1993; Sweeney, Anderson, & Bailey, 1986). Depressed people retrieve more negative memories than nondepressed people (e.g. Clark & Teasdale, 1982), and are more negative about themselves and hopeless about their futures (e.g. Blackburn, Jones, & Lewin, 1986; Bradley & Mathews, 1983). Thus, on nearly every measure of negative thinking about the self, the past, current and future circumstances, depressed people do appear to emphasise the negative—a process that is likely to contribute to the perpetuation or deepening of their depressed mood. Whether such negative thinking plays a *causal*, rather than merely descriptive, concomitant, role in depression, however, is a different question, addressed in a later section.

Distortion, bias, or depressive "realism."   Although Beck noted that the thinking of depressed people is often illogical and unrealistic (which he termed depressive distortion, implying deviant perception of objective reality), others characterised the thinking as negatively "biased" (consistent negativism across times and situations) rather than distorted. Still others have claimed that depressive thinking is actually more realistic ("sadder but wiser") than that of nondepressed individuals who often have positive illusions and esteem-enhancing positive biases (e.g. Alloy & Abramson, 1979). After a review of studies bearing on this topic, Haaga et al. (1991) conclude that the best interpretation is that the thinking of depressed people is biased in a negative direction more than it can be said to be distorted compared to absolute standards of objective reality. What appears to be "realism" may be a function of the match between the feedback to be perceived and subjects' prior beliefs, rather than a general flexible assessment of reality (Dykman, Abramson, Alloy, & Hartlage, 1989).

Negative thinking as a cause of depression

Testing the causal status of cognitive vulnerability has proven to be more problematic than demonstrating that people think more negatively when they are depressed. Relatively few longitudinal designs have been conducted to evaluate the question of whether cognitive vulnerability in never-before-depressed individuals predicts onset of depression. Lewinsohn, Steinmetz, Larson, and Franklin (1981) evaluated a large community sample on a composite measure of dysfunctional cognitions, but found no differences between those who eventually became depressed and those who did not (although they did not test the interaction of stressors with the cognitive diathesis). Most other longitudinal studies have involved predictions not of initial onset of depression, but of recurrence or exacerbation in people who were previously depressed or showed symptom elevations. Haaga et al. (1991) reviewed 5 such studies, and none of them indicated that negative cognitions added significantly to the prediction of later symptoms once initial depression level was controlled (and only a few tested the interaction of cognitions and stress). A set of short-term longitudinal studies reviewed by Barnett and Gotlib (1988) that used attribution style as the cognitive diathesis yielded mixed results, with most studies failing to support the predictive effect of negative attributions on later depression following stressors. Barnett and Gotlib (1988) concluded that depressive attributional style was generally not an antecedent of depression nor a predictor of increased depression over time. Several more recent experimental investigations (e.g. evaluating students' depressed mood following exam failure as a function of prior attribution style) have found results consistent with the attributional style vulnerability prediction (e.g. reviewed in Abramson & Alloy, 1992). Additional longitudinal research by Abramson and Alloy is currently underway to test the hopelessness model of depression as a theory of depression onset in never-before depressed students.

State-dependent cognitions. One of the implications of the cognitive vulnerability models is that the presence of dysfunctional cognitions or schemas distinguishes between those who are depressed and those who are not—even when the person is not presently depressed. That is, the vulnerability remains, even when the person is not depressed, and presumably increases the risk for future depression. Numerous studies have tested this hypothesis by comparing non-depressed and formerly depressed (recovered) groups on various measures of presumed cognitive vulnerability (reviewed in Segal & Ingram, 1994). The great majority of the studies found that recovered depressed patients did not differ from nondepressed comparisons, or displayed significantly lower scores when recovered. The results were consistent across various instruments, such as the Attribution Style Questionnaire (e.g. Dohr, Rush, & Bernstein, 1989; Hamilton & Abramson, 1983; Seligman et al., 1988), or the Dysfunctional Attitudes Scale (e.g. Blackburn, Jones, & Lewin, 1986; Hamilton & Abramson, 1983; Hollon, Kendall, & Lumry, 1986; Silverman, Silverman, & Eardley, 1984; see also Gotlib et al., 1993; Lewinsohn, Steinmetz, Larson, & Franklin, 1981; Rohde, Lewinsohn, & Seeley, 1990). Numerous studies indicated that treated depressed patients showed significant declines in levels of dysfunctional or depressogenic cognitions (e.g. reviewed in Segal & Ingram, 1994).

A few studies found that remitted depressed patients continued to have elevated cognitive dysfunctions compared to controls, but many of the patients also continued to show residual depressive symptoms (e.g. Dobson & Shaw, 1986; Eaves & Rush, 1984). Several studies also suggested that patients who initially had higher levels of dysfunctional cognitions were at greater risk for relapse following recovery (e.g. Hollon, Evans, & DeRubeis, 1990; Thase et al., 1992). Thus, while the level of depressogenic cognitions during the depressed state may have some predictive value concerning future depression, the bulk of the evidence fails to support the assumption that such cognitions are stable traits that might cause vulnerability to depression. Some have interpreted such findings as casting doubt on the cognitive formulations of depression (e.g. Coyne, 1992). However, Segal and Ingram (1994) caution against such an interpretation, noting that many of the studies did not control for the presence of symptoms during remission, used varying definitions of recovery, and generally failed to take into account the potential role of the type of treatment on changing cognitions. More importantly, they argue that failure to find evidence of dysfunctional cognitions when the person is not depressed does not mean that they do not exist. Rather, such cognitions may be "latent" or inaccessible unless they are activated by a relevant "challenge" much the same way that biological dysregulation may not be apparent unless activated by a stressor or by a biochemical challenge such as synthetic cortisol (as in the dexamethasone suppression test described in Chapter 4).

Priming and activation of cognitive vulnerability

In the light of research that demonstrated that when no longer depressed, individuals' cognitions resembled those of nondepressed persons, investigators proposed that cognitive vulnerability takes the form of "latent" schemas or processes that can be observed and measured only when they are activated. Based on the schema model described earlier, access to cognitions and experiences is highly influenced by mood and current context. When the person is not depressed, or is given tasks requiring reports of current attitudes and beliefs, their depressogenic schemas remain hidden. According to this approach, vulnerable individuals may be distinguished by the availability of negative thinking only once such thinking has been "primed," or activated, by negative mood, stressful events, or negative cognitions.

There are several types of "priming" paradigms that have been used in experimental tests of the hypothesis of underlying depressogenic schemas. One method induces depressed mood by having subjects read depressive words or phrases or listen to sad music. For example, Miranda and Persons (1988) used a mood induction procedure for women who had a prior history of depression or no prior history; both groups were currently nondepressed. Following the mood induction procedure, a measure of dysfunctional cognitions indicated more negative cognitions as depressed mood increased but only for the women with former depression. Thus, the women vulnerable to depression (indicated by previous episodes) appeared to possess underlying negative cognitions that became accessible during mildly depressed mood (see also Miranda, Persons, & Byers, 1990; Teasdale & Dent, 1987). Similarly, the degree of negativity of cognitions during a depressive episode was found to predict who remained depressed and who recovered 5 months later in a sample of 53 depressed women (Dent & Teasdale, 1988). The accessibility of the negative thinking during depression was hypothesised to indicate an underlying cognitive structure that created a risk for persisting depression.

A different type of priming used to test whether an underlying vulnerability cognitive structure exists employs words or phrases that are associatively (semantically) related to a target word or phrase. If the prime and the target are indeed related in the person's underlying schema, the prime makes the target word more accessible. In the primed Stroop colour-naming procedure a person sees or hears a word, followed by a presentation of a related or unrelated word; the latter is presented visually printed in colour and the person's task is to state the name of the colour as quickly as possible. For example, if the first or prime word is "tree" and the target or colour word is "oak," to the extent that these concepts are related to each other in the person's cognitive structure, the more the associative connection *interferes* with simply stating the colour in which the word is printed (e.g. red). Thus, it takes longer to state the colour when the prime and the target are related.

Studies of depression using this paradigm have generally found that depressed people show slower colour naming for negative words than for neutral words (e.g. Gotlib & McCann, 1984) or slower colour naming for self-descriptive negative words compared to nonself-descriptive words (e.g. Segal, Hood, Shaw, & Higgins, 1988). Recently, Segal et al. (1995) selected target words that were highly meaningful to each individual, and also employed as primes certain phrases with interpersonal content (such as "hard to trust others"). Different combinations of self-descriptive or nonself-descriptive primes and targets were presented in the Stroop colour-naming procedure to currently depressed patients or nondepressed persons. As hypothesised, more interference (slower colour naming) occurred for depressed people when presented with negative self-descriptive primes and target words. The pattern supported the idea of underlying negative cognitive structures of interrelated beliefs and self-concepts. Recently, using a variety of information-processing tasks with a "self-focus" instructional priming procedure, Hedlund and Rude (1995) similarly found that formerly depressed persons exhibited a negative bias in their performances compared to never-depressed persons. Moreover, questionnaire measures such as the Dysfunctional Attitude Scale failed to show such differences, reinforcing the idea that vulnerability may be better revealed in subtle information-processing tasks that do not rely on consciously available representations of cognitions.

Overall, therefore, Segal and Ingram (1994) conclude that priming methods are a good way of testing the idea of "latent" cognitive structures. These structures are activated under certain conditions, and when activated produce the nature and extent of negative thinking that intensifies and prolongs depressive experiences. The relatively recent priming studies are generally supportive of the cognitive model of depression, and provide evidence of a mechanism to account for vulnerability to recurrence of depression. However, considerably more research is needed to test whether such vulnerabilities predict onset of first depression, or recurrence, and how such vulnerabilities might affect the severity and course of depression.

Models of depressive information processing. Although these studies are consistent with the idea of organised content stored in memory that is activated under certain conditions, there remains considerable uncertainty and debate about the nature of the representation in memory (Segal et al., 1995; Teasdale & Barnard, 1993). While some cognitive models initially emphasised stable dysfunctional cognitions that are present before—and after—depressive experiences, the findings of apparently unstable, mood-related cognitions led to clarifications of the underlying information-processing mechanisms. Teasdale (1983; 1988) proposed a Differential Activation Hypothesis that suggested that individuals differ in the extent of patterns of negative thinking that are associated with depressed mood and stressors. Individuals are vulnerable to develop severe and potentially recurring depression only to the extent that negative moods and events are associated with strongly negative cognitions, presumably acquired through learning experiences. Borrowing from Bower's (1981) associative network model of moods and memory, Teasdale hypothesised that emotions and associated cognitions are linked in memory, so that when a mood is activated, representations of events and cognitions that are associated with it in memory may also be made accessible. Thus, according to Teasdale, an event such as an interpersonal rejection might make someone feel upset, but if the mood experiences that are activated are also associated with various other events in memory, such as recollections of past rejection by others and harsh self-critical thoughts and beliefs about the futility of future interpersonal success, then that individual might experience a depressive reaction.

More recently, Teasdale (e.g. Teasdale & Barnard, 1993) have offered a different model, hypothesising that what gets activated in depressed mood is not a set of individual cognitions, but rather an entire "mental model" is activated that involves globally negative views of the self and beliefs about the need for social approval or personal success. Different moods involve different mental models, and a person vulnerable to depression is believed to have acquired a schematic model that contains global dysfunctional views of the self. Recently Teasdale et al. (1995) reported results from an experiment supporting their view that cognitive vulnerability occurs in global mental models rather than in simply more negative beliefs accessible during depressed mood. Considerable further work is needed, however, to clarify the mechanisms and processes underlying dysfunctional information processing and its role in vulnerability to depression.

Specificity of depressive cognitions

Are certain kinds of negative cognitions specific to depression rather than other forms of psychopathology? As indicated earlier, there is considerable evidence that during depressed states individuals are characteristically negative about themselves and circumstances, but maybe negativism is present in many forms of disorder, such as alcohol dependence, eating disorders, or anxiety disorders. Studies comparing depressed individuals to others with nondepressive disorders have been relatively infrequent, and the results have been somewhat mixed. Some have found specificity on the Dysfunctional Attitude Scale with depressed patients scoring higher than non-depressed patients (e.g. Silverman, Silverman, & Eardley, 1984; Hamilton & Abramson, 1983), while others have not found such differences (e.g. Hollon, Kendall, & Lumry, 1986)—although the latter did find specificity on a measure of negative automatic thoughts. Similarly, mixed results have been obtained for the Attribution Style Questionnaire (e.g. Asarnow & Bates, 1988; Curry & Craighead, 1990). In a sample of adolescents receiving diagnoses of depression or of nondepressive disorders, Gotlib et al. (1993) found that depressed youth had significantly higher scores on a composite "negative cognitions" scale, but did not differ from nondepressed subjects on scores of dysfunctional attributions. Both depressed and nondepressed-diagnosed groups scored higher on dysfunctional attributions than did never-depressed controls. A more extended review of specificity results is reported in Haaga, Dyck, and Ernst (1991), who conclude that on the whole, the results demonstrate fairly good specificity, in that depressed persons are more likely to view themselves and the future negatively; group differences are less apparent when psychiatric comparison groups contain individuals who are also depressed in addition to having nondepressive disorders.

A particularly stringent test of specificity would compare depressed people with anxious subjects, because both represent an internalised, emotional disorder with exaggerated negative beliefs. Most studies comparing depressed and anxious patients have found that depressed individuals do differ from anxious patients (e.g. Beck et al., 1987; Beck, Steer, Epstein, & Brown, 1990; Blackburn, Jones, & Lewin, 1986; Clark, Beck, & Brown, 1989). Depressed individuals are particularly distinct from anxious persons in the emphasis on personal inadequacy and worthlessness, while anxious people focus on perceived future danger.

Overall evaluation of cognitive models of depression

Much of the increased knowledge about depressive disorders that has been acquired in the past 20 years may be attributed to the extremely active research programmes stimulated by cognitive models of depression. Nevertheless, that volume of research has also revealed many shortcomings of the cognitive models. One the one hand, it can be said that cognition is vital in understanding depressive reactions to stressful events, since the meaning, interpretation, and responses to the events are all products of thought. Once instigated, negative thoughts and dysphoric moods profoundly affect each other.

On the other hand, the cognitive approach has been open to various criticisms intended to question its presumed primary, causal role. As noted, there are gaps in the empirical basis of the etiological portion of the model, with need for more longitudinal studies of depression onset and recurrence. Methodological and conceptual issues are still active topics of research. For instance, how can cognitive vulnerability best be measured, since current mood appears to affect self-reported cognitions that are accessible to consciousness thereby making it difficult to rule out the possibility that cognitions are the concomitants or *consequences* of dysphoric mood, rather than the reverse? Some are calling for increased use of information-processing tasks to uncover possible structural aspects of cognition not open to conscious reflection. Thus, many are emphasising the need for primary or activating procedures as a necessary step in making "latent" cognitive content and structure more accessible (e.g. Segal & Dobson, 1992; Segal & Ingram, 1994). There also remain considerable gaps in our knowledge of the mechanisms of dysfunctional information processing, if it exists, and how it is acquired.

Another set of criticisms emphasises the oversimplicity of the focus on cognition as the major diathesis in depression. Many have drawn attention to the nearly exclusive focus on internal cognitive events to the relative neglect of the environmental and social context in which the person lives. For example, the lives of depressed people are often extremely stressful and deficient in resources (e.g. Coyne, 1992; Hammen, 1992). As part of the external context, the role of interpersonal relationships including intimate, social, and family relationships has not been fully integrated (e.g. Gotlib & Hammen, 1992). Relatedly, many have called for much more integrative models that account for biological as well as personality, social, environmental, and developmental aspects of depression. In subsequent sections and chapters, several of these alternative and integrative approaches are discussed.

Stressful events and circumstances and their role in depression

It is a commonsense observation that "depressing" events lead to depression. But this simple observation is deceptive, because of difficulties in conceptualising and measuring negative events, and in determining the mechanisms that account for the association between life events and depression. Nevertheless, it appears that stress plays at least a triggering role in many depressive episodes.

Empirical associations between life events and depression

Early studies, using life-event checklists, commonly found modest but significant associations between stressful events and depression, both in community residents and clinical patients (e.g. Billings & Moos, 1982; Lloyd, 1980; Thoits, 1983). Questionnaire methods may be limited, however, by differences in individuals' interpretations of the same item ("family member has significant health problem"), inclusion of some items that might actually be symptoms (e.g. "difficulty sleeping"), as well the issue of measuring the level of stressfulness of events. For instance, if individuals rate their own items for stressfulness, their interpretations may be biased by their depression and by their tendencies to blame events for their depression. Subsequent research attempted to address many of these issues by improving the methods of determining stress occurrence and evaluating its impact, as well as developing procedures for measuring different levels of stress such as episodic vs. chronic stressors, and major vs. minor events (sometimes called "daily hassles").

Using a variety of procedures, investigators have clearly demonstrated that depressed patients experience higher levels of life events in the year before a depressive episode (e.g. Dohrenwend et al., 1986). Dohrenwend and colleagues (Shrout et al., 1989) provided a particularly stringent test of the causal role of stressors by limiting the association to "fateful" loss events outside the person's control such as the death or illness of another person (and thereby uninfluenced by depressive symptomatology), finding a significant association between such events and subsequent depression. Several large-scale samples of community residents have also demonstrated a significant association between stressful events and depression, in models emphasising not only negative events but also chronic stressful conditions and social supports such as family or marital functioning (e.g. Billings, Cronkite, & Moos, 1983; Holahan & Moos, 1991; Lewinsohn, Hoberman, & Rosenbaum, 1988).

Perhaps the most highly regarded method of assessing stress was developed by George Brown and colleagues (Brown & Harris, 1978), now called the Life Events and Difficulties Schedule (LEDS). An intensive interview procedure, it elicits respondents' descriptions not only of recent events but also the context in which they occurred. For instance, the end of a marital relationship—or even the loss of a pet—has enormously different significance depending on the surrounding circumstances. Interviewers prepare narrative accounts of the event in its surrounding circumstances, which are then reviewed by a rating panel for objective "threat" of the event: how would the typical person experience the same event under the same circumstances? The raters make their judgment on a scale without knowledge of the person's actual emotional reaction. Brown has conducted several community studies of English women, and others have also used the LEDS methods. Figures 5.1 and 5.2 present summaries of the findings of these studies.

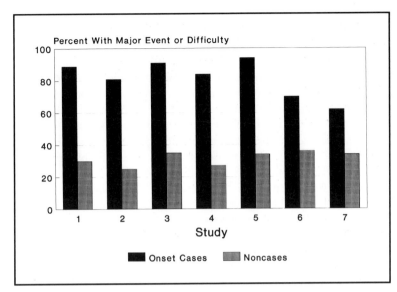

FIG. 5.1.
Life events and
onset of
depression: LEDS
method/community
samples (adapted
from Brown &
Harris, 1989).

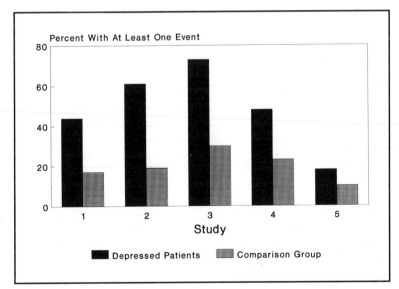

FIG. 5.2. Life
events and onset
of depression:
Patient samples
(adapted from
Brown & Harris,
1989).

These figures illustrate that, for both community and patient samples, major stressors were more likely to occur to those who had a depressive episode than to those who did not.

Theoretical accounts of the link between stressors and depression

In the sections to follow, several theories about the relationship between stress and depression are discussed. At the extreme, certain perspectives view stressors as irrelevant to the etiology of depression (e.g. endogenous depression) and focus instead on biological models of causality. Another approach is a classic diathesis-stress model, in which stress is a necessary component, activating the underlying diathesis for depression; there are different versions of this approach.

The search for "endogenous" depression.   The history of depression research is punctuated with the search for a "biological" subtype of depression in contrast to a psychological subtype. The terms melancholic, endogenous, and autonomous have been contrasted with reactive, situational, and neurotic, to name a few proposed distinctions. For many years the term "endogenous" was used to define a depression that was presumably due to the unfolding of a biological process, and characterised both by an *absence* of stress as a precipitant and by unique symptom features. Thus, the theory holds that some forms of depression arise in the absence of stress.

Some years ago empirical support for the distinction between an endogenous and nonendogenous (stress-reactive) depression was initially based on statistical procedures in which characteristics are analysed for the extent to which they naturally cluster together. Such studies of clinically depressed patients found support for distinct symptoms (such as waking up early, being physically slowed down, weight loss, and others) clustered along with *absence of stress as a trigger* of the depression (e.g. Garside et al., 1971; Kay, Garside, Beamish, & Roy, 1969; Kiloh, Andrews, Neilson, & Bianchi, 1972; Mendels & Cochrane, 1968). However, as Paykel, Rao, and Taylor (1984) pointed out, these studies were often flawed by inclusion of items in the factor analysis that might have spuriously accounted for the apparent association between endogenous symptoms and absence of stress (for example, older age and certain personality traits are less associated with event occurrence).

More recently, two approaches have been used to examine whether a particular type of depression is associated with stress (or not associated with stress). One method compared depressed groups with low or high levels of prior stress, to determine whether the groups showed distinct symptom characteristics. These studies found either few or no symptom differences (e.g. Brown, Ni Bhrolchain, & Harris, 1979;

Copeland, 1984) or found the *opposite* pattern of patients with major stressors having more of the endogenous symptoms (Bebbington, Hurry, & Tennant, 1988; Dolan et al., 1985). An alternative research strategy was to compare patients with and without the endogenous symptom profile on presence of stressful events prior to their episodes. In general these studies found that both groups had elevated rates of stressors (e.g. Bebbington, Hurry, & Tennant, 1988; Cornell, Milden, & Shimp, 1985; Monroe et al., 1985; Zimmerman, Coryell, Pfohl, & Stangl, 1986).

These two lines of study would seem to indicate that there is little evidence of a distinct stress-absent type of depression. However, two recent studies using the LEDS contextual threat methods have found some support for the hypothesised "endogenous" type of depression. Patients with endogenous symptoms were less likely to report stressors prior to their episodes—but the findings appeared to hold only for those with recurrent depression (Brown, Harris, & Hepworth, 1994; Frank et al., 1994). However, because of the lack of consistent empirical support, the term "endogenous" is no longer used to describe patients with the characteristic symptoms of early awakening, psychomotor slowing, weight loss and the like—because the term erroneously implies that the symptoms are biological and unrelated to stress. Instead, the descriptive term "melancholic" is used to characterise those depressions that have the particular features noted, but it does not imply causality due only to biological factors in the absence of stress.

A different approach to the diathesis-stress approach to depression has been to establish whether certain biological predispositions render a person especially susceptible to develop depression in the face of stress. Somewhat surprisingly, there have been relatively few such investigations. As noted in Chapter 4, the Kendler group (Kendler et al., 1995), found that the risk of onset of major depression was highest in subjects who had both a genetic liability for depression (they were the monozygotic co-twins of women who had a history of major depression) and a recent severe stressor (assault, serious marital problems, divorce or breakup, or death of a close relative). Although stressful events were significantly predictive of depression in all subjects, it seemed that those at genetic risk were most susceptible. The mechanism that might account for reactivity to stress remains to be clarified, but as noted in the previous chapter, several models suggest defects in the biological systems responsible for reacting to—as well as recovering from—perceived stress. These models also suggest that stressors might actually alter the biological mechanisms over time, possibly creating increased sensitivity to stress (e.g. Gold, Goodwin, & Chrousos, 1988; Post, 1992).

Cognitive diathesis-stress models. Most life stress researchers adhere to diathesis-stress models, in which stressors precipitate a depressive reaction as a function of the individual's interpretation of the negative event. That is, the event's occurrence as such is not crucial, but rather the person's *appraisal* of the event—and its consequences—determine whether or not depression ensues (e.g. Lazarus & Folkman, 1984). For some investigators, like Beck and the attributional/hopelessness theorists described earlier, cognitive schemas or dysfunctional explanatory style represent the underlying vulnerability, because they predispose the person to interpret the event and its aftermath in hopeless, self-deprecating ways that elicit depression. The nature of the stressor itself is relatively unimportant to these theorists—except that it must be "meaningful" to the individual in the sense that it elicits the interpretation of hopelessness or worthlessness. In these models the objective magnitude of the event may be exaggerated, so that even fairly minor events may trigger depressive reactions if they are subjected to biased interpretation arising from the cognitive vulnerability.

By contrast, George Brown, who is a sociologist, and his colleagues have articulated a model based on characteristics of the stressful life events themselves, and their occurrence in a particular psychosocial context that elicits or reinforces cognitions of hopelessness and low self-esteem. In this model the vulnerability factors are features of the person's current and historical context that promote the experiences of hopelessness. According to Brown, it is the occurrence of major life events or ongoing difficulties (chronic strains) that precipitate depression under vulnerable conditions. Thus, rather than minor stressors or even an accumulation of moderately stressful events, a severe event or major ongoing strain is considered crucial. Given the occurrence of such an event or difficulty, the presence of what Brown terms *vulnerability* factors greatly increases the likelihood of depression (Brown & Harris, 1978). These factors were empirically identified, based on a large community study of working-class women, and included lack of an intimate or confiding relationship (e.g. a poor marital relationship), loss of the mother before age 11, having 3 or more children at home under the age of 14, and lack of full- or part-time employment outside the home (Brown & Harris, 1978). In a subsequent longitudinal study of working-class women, Brown, Bifulco, and Harris (1987) refined the prediction of depression in response to a severe event or major difficulty by specifying that the event represented a loss (such as an important person, belief, role, object, health) and that it "matched" a particular role to which she was committed or represented a conflict between roles. For example, if Mrs Jones and Mrs Smith both had teenage sons who were arrested for shoplifting (a severe event), Mrs Jones might become depressed because the event represented a "loss" of her views of her son as honest and reliable, and a "match" with her major role commitment to being a mother. Mrs Smith, on the other hand, might not become depressed because she already knew her son had a propensity for getting into trouble and she herself was more invested in her career than homemaking now that the children were older.

According to Brown's model (e.g. Brown & Harris, 1989), the important mediator of the link between stressors and depression is the meaning of the event. Specifically, severe events that give rise to a lack of hope for better things induce depression; low self-esteem prior to the event is likely to give rise to hopelessness. Several studies have shown, for example, that low self-esteem is a risk factor for depression (Brown et al., 1986). Low self-esteem is hypothesised to be the outcome of the vulnerability factors, particularly social support factors such as the lack of a confiding relationship or poor quality of the woman's close relationships (Andrews & Brown, 1988). Indeed, as shown in a 7-year follow-up, women whose negative self-esteem improved, compared to those who didn't, were likely to have experienced positive changes in their close relationships as well as other positive events (Andrews & Brown, 1995).

Although Brown's model is different from Beck's in its focus on the nature and context of life events, they are somewhat similar in the emphasis on cognitive mediation of the effects of stress. Brown and Harris (1989), like Beck, emphasise the interpretation of the event as a depletion of the sense of self-worth and identity. In Brown's research such cognitions are inferred and rated by the investigator through discussions with the subject about her life circumstances, whereas more traditional cognitive researchers have generally elicited direct reports of cognitive appraisals from the subject. However, a major point of disagreement is the extent to which the individual is viewed as having distorted interpretations of events, with Brown and others arguing that it is severe negative events and adversity—not minor, exaggerated misfortunes, that cause depression.

Personality and depressive reactions to specific life event types.
Beck (1983) and others including psychodynamically-oriented theorists (e.g. Arieti & Bemporad, 1980; Blatt et al., 1982) proposed that individuals may be particularly vulnerable to some stressors more than others. Specifically, individuals differ in the sources of their self-esteem and sense of mastery, with some individuals experiencing personal worth as deriving from the achievement of highly valued goals and control, while others are more likely to invest themselves and their self-definitions in personal relationships with others. The former type is variously termed autonomous, dominant goal-oriented, or self-critical, while the latter may be termed sociotropic, dominant-other oriented, or dependent (reviewed in Nietzel & Harris, 1990). Vulnerability, therefore, might consist of attitudes, beliefs, and values about the self and its sources of worth. Thus, a major stressor that was interpreted as representing a depletion in the sense of worth or competence would provoke a depressive reaction.

Several studies have tested this model, refining the depression-life stress link to include those events whose content matches the presumed underlying vulnerability. Hammen, Marks, Mayol, & deMayo (1985), for example, found that college students were indeed significantly more likely to show depression following events matching their personal beliefs and values than when negative events occurred that did not match that domain; the effect was especially marked for the combination of interpersonal or sociotropic views and negative interpersonal events. Two other cross-sectional rather than prospective studies using college students found similar results (Robins & Block, 1988; Zuroff & Mongrain, 1987). Studies based on clinical samples have also supported the importance of specifying the match between event content and personal vulnerability (Hammen, Elliott, Gitlin, & Jamison, 1989; Robins, 1990; Segal, Shaw, Vella, & Katz, 1992). With the exception of the Segal et al. (1992) study, the other investigations found particular support for the link between sociotropy or dependency and interpersonal negative events; Segal et al. (1992) found support for the link between self-criticism and negative achievement events.

These studies indicate that the general link between depression and stressors can be refined and made stronger by clarifying the areas of personal vulnerability, such that depression is predicted to occur only when negative events in that domain occur. Except for specifying two general domains of vulnerability, achievement and interpersonal, this approach is somewhat similar to that of Brown, as noted earlier, who assessed women's "commitments" and values based on interviews.

The generation of stress by depressed people. Although various stress researchers have noted that the depression-stress association is bidirectional (e.g. Monroe & Simons, 1991), most have viewed the possibility that depression causes stress as a methodological nuisance factor prompting careful methodological controls before drawing conclusions about the causal connection between the variables. However, given that the impact of stress on precipitating depressive reactions is now well established empirically, it is important to evaluate whether depressed individuals actually contribute to the occurrence of stress. Hammen (1991b) compared the stressful events in the lives of demographically similar unipolar depressed women patients with bipolar, medically ill, and nonpsychiatric women over a 1-year period. The unipolar depressed women had significantly more events to which they had contributed, accounted for largely by interpersonal and conflict-related events. Obviously, characteristics of the women that contribute to difficulties in resolving interpersonal disputes may be one factor contributing to stressors. Recently, Davila et al. (1995) demonstrated that indeed, relatively dysfunctional interpersonal problem-solving strategies contributed to the occurrence of stressors in young women, and the stressors in turn predicted depression. Thus, the stress-depression association may be a reciprocal, self-perpetuating cycle possibly helping to account for the typical pattern of recurrent depression.

Summary

- Cognitive models of depression, orginating with Beck, emphasise negative thinking as a factor causing or maintaining depressed symptoms.
- Different versions of cognitive models variously emphasise self-schemas, self-esteem, attributional style, hopelessness, self-regulation—and other aspects of depressive thinking.
- Ample evidence supports the hypothesis that depressed people are biased in negative directions while depressed, but less research supports a causal role of negative thinking in causing depression.
- Stressors play an important role in triggering depressive reactions.
- Current stress and cognition models emphasise that the "meaning" of the event to the individual determines whether it will trigger depression.
- There is little evidence of a biological subtype of depression that occurs in the absence of precipitating stressors, but truly integrative models are not yet well developed.

Social aspects of depression 6

Most forms of psychological disorder affect individuals' interpersonal lives, impairing their social functioning by altering interpersonal behaviours and the quality of relating to others. Depression is no exception, because the symptoms of depression interfere with normal relationships. But even more importantly, several perspectives about the causes of depression emphasise the role of relatedness to others as a fundamental contributing factor. In this chapter, therefore, various topics are explored. There is no single interpersonal perspective on depression; instead there are diverse topics of study, such as family functioning, attachment, marital adjustment, loss and bereavement, and the effects of stressful interpersonal events, and social skills. Difficulties in social relatedness have been variously viewed as concomitants of being in a depressed state, consequences of depression that have negative "side effects", and as fundamental causal factors in depression.

In this chapter, the first section is on depression in the family context, further divided into sections discussing family-based causes of depression and those discussing interpersonal *consequences* to family members. A second major section discusses other social relations besides those focused on the family, reviewing research on indications that depressed people are "rejected" by others because their depression is aversive, and on interpersonal events as stressors causing depression. Throughout, however, the distinction between depression as a cause of interpersonal difficulties and depression as a result of interpersonal problems is somewhat arbitrary. Or perhaps more precisely, the associations are bidirectional—eventually, even if some social difficulties are the result of depression, they may perpetuate or create depression because they are stressful for the depressed or depression-vulnerable person. That is, vulnerability to depression may arise in the early family environment; the interpersonal consequences of depression might also contribute to further symptomatology; and deficits in social behaviours set the stage for stressful events and circumstances that may lead to depression.

Depression in the family context

Both psychodynamic and social learning theory models of human development emphasise the importance of experiences in early childhood in the family environment. When those experiences are dysfunctional or when the child lacks critical experiences such as a close bond with a stable caretaker, he or she may develop in maladaptive ways. Both of these models hypothesise that depression might be a form of psychopathology resulting from certain unique family experiences.

The original *psychodynamic* approach, which has evolved into a contemporary version called object relations theory, emphasised that depression is similar to bereavement, and results from the loss of an important "object". Loss of an important other person, especially in childhood, produces sadness and other experiences of mourning, but unlike bereavement, according to the traditional psychodynamic model, loss can cause self-deprecation, guilt, and related symptoms of the depression syndrome due to introjected anger toward an ambivalently loved lost object (the theory of anger turned inward).

More recently, John Bowlby (1978; 1981) has articulated a model of the importance of early attachment bonds between the infant and caretaker which has implications not only for depression, but for key elements of individual personality and adaptive functioning. Specifically, Bowlby argued that infants have an innate and fundamental tendency to form attachment bonds to a primary caretaker, in the service of protection and survival. Further, the development of a stable and secure attachment bond is essential for healthy development. An infant with a mother who is consistently responsive, accessible, and supportive will acquire a "working model" (that is, cognitive representations) of the self that is positive. The child will be able to use the relationship as a "secure base" from which to explore the environment and acquire essential skills, and will form representations (beliefs and expectations) of other people as trustworthy and dependable. If, however, the attachment bond is insecure due to actual disruption or loss, or to maternal rejection, unresponsiveness, or inconsistency, the person becomes vulnerable to depression. The individual acquires negative cognitions about the self and others. Insecurely attached children, for instance, may be highly anxious and needy, or alternatively, may deal with the lack of attachment by being avoidant or rejecting of closeness. In later life, actual or threatened loss of close relationships may trigger not only mourning, but also self-criticism, feelings of abandonment, hopelessness and helplessness, and related depressive symptoms. There is a considerable body of empirical work validating Bowlby's ideas about attachment security in infants and its consequences for healthy or maladaptive development (e.g. reviewed in Blatt & Homann, 1992; see also Cicchetti & Schneider-Rosen, 1986). Studies specifically linking attachment quality and loss to depression are reviewed in a later section.

The *cognitive social learning* perspective on the role of early family experiences on depression is more general than the attachment model, and has been less well elaborated as a model of depression than has the developmental psychopathology model based on attachment theory. Its essential tenets are that adaptive skills and cognitions are acquired through learning during childhood. Parent–child interactions that lead to the child's acquisition of dysfunctional self-schemas or nega- tive explanatory style (as discussed in Chapter 5) set the stage for vulnerability to depression in the face of stress. For example, Brewin, Firth-Cozens, Furnham, and McManus (1992) found that recollections of inadequate parenting were associated with self-critical tendencies, and such cognitions might predispose someone to depressive reac- tions. Moreover, learning by observation of the parents—as well as through direct reinforcement contingencies—influences acquisition of cognitions and behaviours. Thus, modelling depressed parents' views of the self or world, or being treated harshly, may contribute to the cognitive vulnerability to experience depression under provoking circumstances such as loss or failure. Since coping with stressors throughout life requires learning appropriate problem-solving and coping skills, deficiencies in these areas might also create vulnerability for depression. In general, research directly bearing on the childhood acquisition of maladaptive cognitions and skills relevant to depression has been relatively sparse. As reviewed in subsequent sections, how- ever, numerous studies are consistent with the basic perspective of cognitive social learning theory.

The family context is also important in depression from the oppo- site perspective: the enormous impact of a parent's depression on others in the family. Depressed parents commonly have difficulties in their parenting roles, and such dysfunctions may contribute to the high rates of depression and other disorders in the children. Marital relationships may also suffer as a result of the depression of one of the partners. In other cases, the depressed individual may experience relating to family members as highly stressful, and this stress may contribute to further depression. Research on the relationship between depression and parental and marital functioning is reviewed later.

Family relationships as potential causes of depression

We turn first to various lines of research investigating the importance of early family experiences on development of depression.

Early loss and depression.   Numerous studies have tested the theory that depression is often caused by loss of a parent in early childhood, presumably creating a vulnerability to become depressed later in life if a real or threatened loss of a loved one reactivates the despair of the early loss. When the histories of depressed adults have been examined for evidence of loss, the results have been mixed. Based on the earlier research, two reviews concluded that there was a significant association between depression and early childhood loss (Lloyd, 1980a; Nelson, 1982), while two studies concluded that there was no such relationship (Crook & Eliot, 1980; Tennant, Bebbington, & Hurry, 1980). Several more recent studies have clarified the contradictory findings, by suggesting that it is not parental loss as such that creates risk for depression, but rather the quality of parental care following the loss. That is, parental loss followed by lack of quality and inconsistent care for the child does seem to be predictive of later depression (e.g. Bifulco, Brown, & Harris, 1987; Harris, Brown, & Bifulco, 1986). Harris and colleagues hypothesise that the adult women in their studies who lost a parent in childhood and were then subjected to poor care were likely to experience lowered self-esteem. Later on, exposure to highly stressful life events, therefore, might cause a generalised sense of hopelessness, hence depression, in those with low self-esteem.

Attachment and depression.   Few studies are available to directly assess Bowlby's hypothesis of a link between insecure mother–child attachment and vulnerability to depression later in life. However, several studies, using various methods of assessing "attachment" including self-reported attitudes toward parents, have shown that depressed children and adolescents report less secure attachment to parents, compared with nondepressed comparison groups (e.g. Armsden et al., 1990; Kobak, Sudler, & Gamble, 1991). Kobak et al. (1991) and Hammen et al. (1995) also showed that adolescents were more likely to become depressed following stressful life events if they had more insecure attachment representations of their parents. A study of clinically depressed women patients found that they reported significantly less attachment to their mothers than did nonpsychiatric controls (Rosenfarb, Becker, & Khan, 1994).

Studies of nonhuman primates permitting experimental control over mother–infant separation and quality of care have provided clear evidence of the importance of mother–infant attachment to healthy development (e.g. Harlow & Suomi, 1974). Recently, research has shown that separation from the mother or attachment figure produces emotional and behavioural disruptions in infant monkeys that resemble depression. Separations also result in increased cortisol and lower norepinephrine just as with some depressed human adults (Suomi, 1991a). Infant monkeys raised by peer monkeys instead of by their own mothers (an experimental model of "insecure attachment"), when compared to mother-reared infants, appeared to be more vulnerable to "depressive" reactions later in life when briefly separated from other monkeys (Suomi, 1991b).

Early family relationships reported by depressed adults. Taken together, the few attachment studies support a link between quality of early childhood attachment and vulnerability to depressive reactions. More extensive evidence of depression vulnerability may be found when the general concept of quality of parent–child relationships—rather than attachment as such—is considered. Numerous studies of depressed adults have asked them about their recollections of their relationships with parents.

In general, the retrospective studies are fairly consistent: depressed adults report more adverse relationships with their parents during childhood. For example, a large study of depressed inpatients compared their perceptions of parents with those of nondepressed nonpatient controls (Crook, Raskin, & Eliot, 1981). The depressed patients described both mothers and fathers as more rejecting, controlling, and as demonstrating hostile detachment, compared with the reports of the nondepressed controls. Similar findings have been reported in nonpatient community samples, in which relatively more depressed individuals reported more negative views of the parents (e.g. Blatt, Wein, Chevron, & Quinlan, 1979; Holmes & Robins, 1987, 1988). Andrews and Brown (1988), for example, found that women who became clinically depressed following occurrence of major life events were more likely to report lack of adequate parental care or hostility from their mothers, compared to those who did not become depressed (see also Brown & Harris, 1993). In reviewing the extensive literature on depressed individuals' recollections of parents, Gerlsma, Emmelkamp, and Arrindell (1990) concluded that parental childrearing styles that included low affection and more control (overprotection), were especially consistently related to depression.

Recently, research shows that such parental styles were not only associated with the occurrence of depression, but also with its course features. For instance, Lizardi et al. (1995) examined the childhood experiences of patients who had diagnoses of *early onset dysthymic disorder*, and found that they were significantly more likely to have experienced negative relations with their parents than were comparison groups of normal controls or those with major depressive episodes. In another study, severity of symptoms, as well as highly negative cognitions, were particularly associated with adverse family experiences including harsh, rigid control, overprotection, or sexual assault (Rose et al., 1994). Gotlib, Mount, Cordy, and Whiffen (1988) examined the reports of women with or without postpartum depression concerning their own parents' childrearing styles. They found that the depressed women reported less maternal and paternal care and more maternal overprotection. Also, a further study of postpartum depressed women found that negative perceptions of parents predicted the onset of depression during the postpartum period, and more negative perceptions predicted slower recovery (Gotlib, Whiffen, Wallace, & Mount, 1991).

Although the research links depression with somewhat general parental styles reflecting negativity (criticism, low affection or care, overcontrolling), some investigators suggest that different types of depression might be associated with more specific patterns. Blatt and Homann (1992), adopting a psychodynamic object-relations model of depression, argued that insecure attachment characterised by anxiety and neediness would lead to a depression focused on dependency and concerns about abandonment ("anaclitic" depression characterised by helplessness and weakness). Insecure attachment characterised by an avoidant or dismissive reaction toward others, on the other hand, would lead to a depression focused on issues of self-worth, self-criticism, and achievement (an "introjective" depression, characterised by feelings of inferiority, failure, and guilt). Note that these concepts are somewhat similar to the ideas of "sociotropic" and "autonomous" depression discussed in Chapter 5, predicting individual vulnerability to specific types of stressors (interpersonal, achievement) that define the person's central area of self-definition. According to Blatt and Homann (1992), introjectively depressed persons are likely to have had parents who set high standards, and are harshly critical, intrusive, and controlling in an attempt to get their children to meet their high expectations. As a result, the child constantly berates herself or himself, and attacks the self as worthless. Research is needed to verify these hypotheses, but they provide an initial step in making more specific predictions about early experiences and later depression.

Since there have been virtually no longitudinal studies following children raised in families with negative parenting into adulthood to see if they become (or remain) depressed, conclusions are based on retrospective reports by depressed adults about their childhood experiences. Some have been sceptical about the validity of these reports, arguing that depressed peoples' negative cognitive biases might extend to perceptions of their parents. However, Brewin, Andrews, and Gotlib (1993) have argued that there is little evidence that such bias invalidates the reports of depressed patients. They cite studies suggesting that alternative sources of information (such as parents' or siblings' reports) attest to the accuracy of retrospective accounts.

In addition to retrospective reports by depressed adults, there is evidence that current quality of family life affects depression. When the quality of the marital and family relationships is evaluated, studies have consistently found that family members who are critical, unsupportive, or generally display negative family interaction patterns predict less likelihood of recovery or greater likelihood of a relapse of depression for the depressed family member(Billings & Moos, 1985b; Hooley & Teasdale, 1989; Keitner et al., 1995; Swindle, Cronkite, & Moos, 1989).

Specific childhood stressors and vulnerability to depression.   In addition to loss and inadequate parenting, several studies point to the impact of particular childhood stressors. A large-scale epidemiological study of community residents who met criteria for major depression found that several childhood adversities (parental drinking, parental mental illness, family violence, parental marital problems, deaths of mother or father, and lack of a close relationship with an adult) were predictive of onset of depression. Three early adversities, parental mental illness, violence, and parental divorce, were significantly predictive of recurrence of depression (Kessler & Magee, 1993). The importance of parental mental illness—particularly depressive disorders—contributing to depression is discussed more fully in a separate section.

Several studies have indicated that the experience of childhood physical and sexual abuse may be associated with later depression (and other disorders) (e.g. Andrews, Brown, & Creasey, 1990; Bifulco, Brown, & Adler, 1991; Brown & Anderson, 1991; Brown & Harris, 1993). Andrews, Valentine, and Valentine (1994) found that childhood abuse was especially associated with chronic or recurrent depression. Similar findings were reported for those with early-onset dysthymia which by definition is a chronic disorder (Lizardi et al., 1995). Sexual assault, defined as use of pressure or force to have sexual contact, was found to be related to later depression and other disorders for both men and women; *childhood* sexual assault was particularly related to likelihood of adult disorders including depression (Burnam et al., 1988).

The mechanisms by which specific childhood stressors such as physical or sexual abuse have their effects on later depression is not known directly. However, such experiences are highly likely to occur in the context of parental lack of care. Thus, it is unclear whether abuse itself, or the underlying parental rejection or inadequate care, accounts for the effects on children's self-concept and interpersonal competencies.

Family relationships of depressed children. An alternative strategy for investigating the role of early family experiences in depression is to examine depressed children: what are the features of their family life? Numerous studies now confirm the hypothesis of disrupted family environments and relatively dysfunctional relationships between parents and children (reviewed in Hammen & Rudolph, 1996; Kaslow, Deering, & Racusin, 1994). For instance, high levels of chronic stress including divorce, parental death, child maltreatment, and parental occupational and social difficulties have been reported (e.g. Burbach & Borduin, 1986; Toth, Manly, & Cicchetti, 1992; Warner et al., 1992; Weller, Weller, Fristad, & Bowes, 1991). Moreover, depressed children report less social support, potentially exacerbating the ill effects of stressful family life (e.g. Armsden et al., 1990; Compas, Slavin, Wagner, & Vannatta, 1986; Daniels & Moos, 1990).

The quality of parent–child relationships is frequently impaired for depressed children. Both clinical and community samples of depressed youngsters report relatively negative interactions with their parents (e.g. Cole & McPherson, 1993; Garrison et al., 1990; Larson et al., 1990; Hops, Lewinsohn, Andrews, & Roberts, 1990; Puig-Antich et al., 1993; Stark, Humphrey, Crook, & Lewis, 1990). Both parent–child conflict and marital discord appear to be associated with depression in youngsters (e.g. Burbach & Borduin, 1986). Moreover, critical and overinvolved parental attitudes toward, or interactions with, the depressed child have been found to characterise occurrences of depression and predict a worse course of depression (Asarnow, Goldstein, Thompson, & Guthrie, 1993; Hamilton, Hammen, Minasian, & Jones, 1993)—just as they do in families of depressed adults.

While quality of family relationships appears to be relatively negative in depressed children and adolescents, they may be especially detrimental to children who are particularly reliant on families for support and protection. As children become adolescents, they may turn more to peer relationships for such support, so that the quality of family life is less directly predictive of depressive experiences (e.g. see Hammen & Rudolph, 1996).

Commentary on early life experiences.   This brief review of research indicates that the quality of early life experiences in the family may contribute to depression. The quality of the attachment bond, the experience of critical, rejecting, or overcontrolling parenting and disrupted family life appear to set the stage for depression. Children exposed to such experiences may become depressed, while adults who experienced such events in childhood may be vulnerable to depressive reactions when faced with triggering experiences. Most of the research to date is correlational, however, with little direct evidence of a causal relationship between early negative events and depression. Nevertheless, the associations are robust and well-replicated, suggesting that disruption of close family relationships may be a critical vulnerability factor for depression. Although research has yet to fully clarify the mechanisms accounting for the associations with depression, two are likely to be important. One is that maladaptive family relationships create negative cognitions about the worth and competence of the self. The other is that poor early relationships impair important adaptive skills that would help to avoid or resolve stressful situations, thus contributing to vulnerability to react with depression when a negative event is encountered that is interpreted as a depletion of the self and beyond one's ability to repair.

Impact of depression on family relationships

Not only do some forms of depression appear to result from inadequate emotional connectedness with parents, but also depression appears to create interpersonal disruptions in families. In the following sections, ways in which depression is associated with dysfunctional family interactions are discussed. In these ways, depression may induce negative reactions in others and promote disturbed interactions; in turn such stressful relationships may contribute to further depression.

Depression and family burden.   Coyne (1976) was one of the first to hypothesise that depressive symptomatology may be maintained or worsened by the responses of others with whom the depressed person interacts. While others may initially respond to depression with concern and compassion, their reactions eventually turn to rejection and hostility because of the aversiveness of depression. This prediction has been verified in many studies, which are reviewed in a later section. In the marital or family context, in particular, the consequences may be especially detrimental to all parties, because depression is a burden on others while at the same time others' resulting rejection or withdrawal may make the depressed person feel worse. In one study of the perceived effects of living with a depressed person, the spouses or other relatives reported negative reactions to numerous depressive symptoms, and approximately 40% of the relatives experienced distress severe enough to warrant the need for treatment (Coyne, Kahn, & Gotlib, 1987). A further study of spouses of depressed patients indicated marked difficulties, including restricted social activities, reduced income, and increased marital difficulties associated with a depressed mate (Fadden, Bebbington, & Kuipers, 1987). As noted earlier, other studies have indicated that the negative attitudes of relatives may predict a more protracted course of depression or relapse (Hooley, Orley, & Teasdale, 1986; Hooley & Teasdale, 1989; Keitner et al., 1995).

In addition to a generally difficult burden for families, having a depressed adult in the family is also associated with two specific negative outcomes: quality of the marital relationship and the impact of parental depression on children.

Marital problems and depression.   There is a large body of research showing an association between marital status or quality and depression. Studies of marital couples in which one is clinically depressed have shown relatively negative interaction patterns marked by hostility, tension, difficulty resolving conflict, and reports of marital difficulties associated with depression (e.g. Fadden et al., 1987; Gotlib & Whiffen, 1989; Hinchliffe, Hooper, & Roberts, 1978; Kahn, Coyne, & Margolin, 1985; see review in Gotlib & Hammen, 1992). However, it is not clear whether marital distress is simply a temporary reaction to depression. Studies that have followed depressed patients and their spouses after symptomatic remission have generally found evidence of *enduring* marital dissatisfaction and difficulties (e.g. Coryell et al., 1993; reviewed in Barnett & Gotlib, 1988). A recent 5-year study of patients with unipolar depression indicated that these patients were less likely to be married, and if married more likely to divorce than nondepressed controls. Moreover, of those who stayed married, unipolar patients reported that the quality of their marriage was poorer than did controls (Coryell et al., 1993).

Other lines of research suggest that being married—and especially being in a marriage with a confiding, intimate relationship with the spouse—is protective against depression, even in the face of major stressors (e.g. Bebbington, 1987; Brown & Harris, 1978; Gotlib & Hammen, 1992). On the other hand, marital distress can lead to depressive episodes—or marital conflict and criticism can prolong depression or precipitate relapses (e.g. Hooley & Teasdale, 1989; Gotlib & Hammen, 1992; O'Hara, 1986). Thus, there is good evidence of an association between depression and marital difficulties, but the direction of causality is mixed, and indeed, in many couples, it is likely to be a circular process in which depression and marital difficulties exacerbate each other.

The interpretation of causal directions of effect in marital relationships and depression is further complicated by "assortative mating," the observation that depressed people often marry others who also have psychiatric disorders (e.g. Hammen, 1991a; Merikangas, Weissman, Prusoff, & John, 1988; Rutter & Quinton, 1984). Marriages in which both partners suffer from emotional, personality, or substance abuse problems are highly likely to be marked by distress and poor conflict resolution, as well as punctuated with the stressors associated with such lifestyles.

Taken together, the studies of marital functioning suggest several issues of relevance for the functioning of depressed people: they are difficult for others to interact with and may place burdens on the relationship; they may be highly prone to depressive reactions to disturbances in their close relationships; marital problems, whatever their causes, may be intensified among depressed people because of their interpersonal vulnerabilities and difficulties in resolving social problems—and possibly because of marrying dysfunctional mates.

Children of depressed parents. Numerous studies of children—including infants and toddlers, school age, and adolescent offspring—of depressed parents have been conducted, the majority with the mother as the depressed parent. Depression measured either as an elevated score on a self-report inventory or as a clinical diagnosis, has been shown to be associated with dysfunctional adjustment and diagnosable conditions in the offspring.

A number of observational studies of nondepressed compared with depressed women interacting with their babies or young children have indicated that depressed mothers are unresponsive or non-contingently responsive, or negative and rejecting, while the babies themselves are wary or distressed. Even mildly or transiently depressed mothers may elicit negative reactions in their infants. Some of these studies are noted below in a discussion of quality of parent–child relations. One of the most extensive studies of young children of clinically depressed (both unipolar and bipolar) mothers has been conducted at the National Institute of Mental Health (NIMH) Laboratory of Developmental Psychology. Infants and toddlers of such mothers have problems regulating emotional reactions including aggression, and engaging in cooperative interactions with others (Zahn-Waxler, Cummings, Iannoti, & Radke-Yarrow, 1984; Zahn-Waxler, Cummings, McKnew, & Radke-Yarrow, 1984; Zahn-Waxler, McKnew, Cummings, Davenport, & Radke-Yarrow, 1984). Other studies have shown that babies of depressed women display emotional and behavioural disturbances, delayed expressive language development, and lower cognitive development (Cox, Puckering, Pound, and Mills, 1987; Pound, Cox, Puckering, & Mills, 1985; Whiffen & Gotlib, 1989).

One of the strongest and most widely replicated findings concerning the infants and toddlers of depressed women is insecure attachment—presumably due to depressed mothers' insensitivity and negativity. Young children of depressed women displayed higher rates of insecure attachment (e.g. Cohn et al., 1986; DeMulder & Radke-Yarrow, 1991; Lyons-Ruth, Zoll, Connell, & Grunebaum, 1986; Murray, 1992; Radke-Yarrow, Cummings, Kuczynski, and Chapman, 1985).

Several well-controlled studies of *school-age* offspring of depressed parents that used clinical diagnostic criteria are summarised in Table 6.1. They yield three consistent results: children of depressed parents have elevated rates of diagnoses compared with normal comparison families; children of depressed parents have higher rates of affective disorders, particularly major depression, than any other disorders; such offspring also have elevated rates of other disorders and commonly experience multiple disorders, including anxiety, substance use, and disruptive behaviour disorders.

A number of other offspring studies have employed additional indicators of children's functioning besides diagnosis, including self- or parent-reported depression and other symptoms. These studies have reported higher levels of symptoms in the children of depressed

TABLE 6.1
Diagnostic outcomes of children of clinically depressed women

Study	Percentage receiving diagnosis by category				
	Any	Major depression	Disruptive behaviour	Substance use	Anxiety
Hammen, 1991a (ages 8–16)					
Unipolar	82	45	32	23	27
Bipolar	72	22	22	11	11
Medically ill	43	29	14	7	7
Normal	32	11	8	3	8
Keller et al., 1986; Beardslee et al., 1988 (ages 6–19)					
Unipolar	65	24	30	13	19
Normal	nr	nr	nr	nr	nr
Klein et al., 1988 (ages 14–22)					
Unipolar	51	9	13	11	15
Medically ill	21	0	6	6	3
Normal	24	0	0	8	5
Orvaschel et al., 1988 (ages 6–17)					
Unipolar	41	15	nr	nr	20
Normal	15	4	nr	nr	9
Weissman et al., 1987 (ages 6–23)					
Unipolar	73	38	22	17	37
Normal	65	24	17	7	27

nr = not reported; children may have more than one disorder

parents (Breslau, Davis, & Prabucki, 1988; Hirsch, Moos, & Reischl, 1985; Lee & Gotlib, 1989a,b). Finally, it should be noted that studies of psychosocial functioning of the school-age offspring of depressed women have also reported academic and social problems (e.g. Anderson & Hammen, 1993; Weissman, 1988), intellectual impairment (Kaplan, Beardslee, & Keller, 1987; but see Weissman, 1988, for discrepant results), and negative cognitions about the self (e.g. Jaenicke et al., 1987).

Relatively few studies have followed up children of depressed parents to determine the stability of their diagnoses or dysfunctions over time, but those that have been conducted indicate continuing impairment (Billings & Moos, 1983; Hammen, Burge, Burney, & Adrian, 1990; Lee & Gotlib, 1989b; Warner et al., 1992).

Taken together, the studies focusing on children of unipolar depressed women uniformly indicate impairments in the functioning of the children—at all ages, and across samples of women with depression ranging from mild self-reported symptoms to clinically diagnosed, treatment samples. The problems include both high rates of significant disorders including both depressive and nondepressive diagnoses, as well as academic, cognitive, and social difficulties. The limited longitudinal data suggest that the children's dysfunctions persist even when maternal symptoms have remitted—although little research has specifically examined the influence of depression severity, frequency or chronicity, and timing of maternal symptoms in relation to children's adjustment. Although severe and repeated depression would be likely to cause the most negative consequences for children, it is likely that even relatively mild but persisting or recurring symptoms may exert long-lasting effects. Even mild depression may result in disruptions of children's development of normal skills, putting the child at a disadvantage in dealing with challenges and mastery of new tasks.

Social behaviours of depressed persons

The research on family functioning indicates that depressed people experience difficulties in their relationships with their parents as children, and with their spouses and children when adults—and that depressed children also experience problems in their interactions with family members. What about more general social relationships with others, including strangers? What is the nature of interpersonal difficulties that depressed people have, and how might social difficulties or vulnerabilities lead to depression? In the following section the extensive research is organised into two major topics: interpersonal characteristics of depressed persons, and the impact of stressors under conditions of interpersonal vulnerabilities.

Interpersonal characteristics of depressed persons

This section explores the extent to which there may be characteristics of depressed people that reflect cognitions or behaviours that have negative consequences on their relationships with other people.

Responses of others to depression. Beginning with the hypothesis of Coyne (1976) noted earlier, numerous studies have examined the proposition that depression elicits negative responses from others. A variety of controlled, simulated laboratory experiments have documented that, indeed, interacting with a depressed person often (although not invariably) results in negative emotional reactions in the other person, relatively more negative verbal and nonverbal interactions, and indicators of rejection (e.g. Gotlib & Beatty, 1985; Gotlib & Meltzer, 1987; Hammen & Peters, 1977; Stephens, Hokanson, & Welker, 1987; Strack & Coyne, 1983).

A key question raised by this literature is whether responses by strangers to a depressed person might reflect "real" relationship patterns. To examine the interpersonal rejection hypothesis in a more natural fashion, Hokanson and his colleagues explored the reactions of college roommates to their relatively depressed partners over an academic year. Howes, Hokanson, and Loewenstein (1985) selected initially unacquainted pairs, and analysed their mood and social interaction results according to the Beck Depression Inventory scores of the depressed partner over time. They found that roommates of persons who remained relatively depressed over the study had roommates who themselves became progressively more dysphoric over several months; both members of the pairs perceived that the more depressed roommate became increasingly dependent. In other analyses, roommates diagnosed as depressed reported less social contact with their roommates and low enjoyment of the contact, while the roommates also reported low enjoyment of contact and aggressive-competitive reactions toward the roommate (Hokanson et al., 1989). In fact, Hokanson, Hummer, and Butler (1991) found that the stably depressed subjects perceived high levels of hostility and unfriendliness in their roommates. Taken together, these patterns are consistent with those from many of the simulated interaction studies with strangers: depressed persons elicited more negative emotions and relatively greater social rejection from nondepressed others.

Mechanisms of interpersonal difficulties in depressed persons.
Several mechanisms have been hypothesised to account for depressed persons' elicitation of negative reactions from others. Coyne and colleagues (e.g. Coyne, Burchill, & Stiles, 1991) speculate that depression induces negative mood which is aversive to others, leading to rejection—but also that neediness or reassurance-seeking may actually provoke negative reactions, especially when the depressed person appears unable or unwilling to accept the reassurance or take the steps the nondepressed partners thinks are needed to overcome depression. As explored in Chapter 4 on cognitive models, depressed people may appear to be unreasonable and irrational in their worries, insecurities, and lack of apparent motivation and energy—so that their "inconsolability" is irritating and burdensome to those trying to help.

Various deficits in social skills have also been hypothesised to account for negative reactions to depressed people. Studies have indeed shown that both depressed persons themselves, as well as observers, rate them as less socially skilled than nondepressed persons (e.g. Dykman, Horowitz, Abramson, & Usher, 1991; Youngren & Lewinsohn, 1980). Actual deficits noted when individuals are depressed include less fluent and more monotonous speech, and poor eye contact (reviewed in Segrin & Abramson, 1994). Segrin and Abramson (1994) argue that such "depressive" behaviours elicit negative reactions from others because they violate certain norms of commun- ication such as responsiveness, politeness, and expectations of involve- ment. That is, they fail to engage others and respond with interest and attention, so that interacting with them is aversive and unrewarding.

Certainly, in the depressive state, the symptoms of apathy and anhedonia, social withdrawal, low energy, and others create obstacles to pleasant and constructive communication. A key question, however, is whether depressed individuals may have relatively stable social characteristics that might contribute to vulnerability to develop depression, or whether their social deficiencies are temporary symptoms of the depressive state. This question requires discussion of enduring traits such as dependency, negative interpersonal cognitions, and deficiencies in social problem-solving skills.

Personality traits: dependency and introversion. Self-reported dependency feelings and beliefs are more commonly reported by women than men (e.g. reviewed in Bornstein, 1992). Clinical lore and empirical observations have noted that an important predictor of depression is dependency—emotional reliance on others, the belief that the affection, acceptance, and support of other people is essential to personal worth. There are two versions of this approach—one emphasising trait dependency as a vulnerability factor, and the other emphasising a diathesis-stress model that depression occurs when a match between interpersonal stressors and underlying dependency motives and cognitions occurs.

The trait approach has been supported by studies showing that depressed people are relatively more dependent even when the person is not symptomatic (e.g. Hirschfeld, Klerman, Andreasen, Clayton, & Keller, 1996). Higher levels of dependency traits during the depressive episode may predict less likelihood of or slower recovery (Klein, Harding, Taylor, & Dickstein, 1988). Attempting to further understand the nature of dependency, Clark, Watson, and Mineka (1994) examined its correlates, and reported that dependency appears to be a characterological dimension of inhibited expression, particularly of difficulty expressing hostility and anger. The implications of these findings for excess depression in women are apparent: to the extent that women are relatively more socialised both to orient toward others and to suppress expressions of aggression, they may thereby acquire a vulnerability to depressive experiences.

In addition to dependency, a large quantity of research has linked the personality dimensions of neuroticism and introversion–extroversion to depression (reviewed in Barnett & Gotlib, 1988). In general, neuroticism, characterised by high emotional reactivity, appears to be mood-dependent with only some studies indicating stability during periods of remission from depression (Barnett & Gotlib, 1988). However, introversion—the preference for solitary activities and discomfort in social situations—is consistently associated with depression both during the episode and in remission (e.g. Hirschfeld, Klerman, Clayton, & Keller, 1983; see Barnett & Gotlib, 1988). Introverted behaviours and cognitions would imply that a person might be vulnerable to develop depression, because they may have difficulties in their interpersonal relationships, perhaps experience less enjoyment of social situations and relationships, and have less self-confidence in social occasions. Barnett and Gotlib (1988) note that it may seem paradoxical that some individuals are at once dependent on others for fulfillment of needs for approval and help, while at the same time less likely to feel comfortable and participate in social events. It might be speculated that dependency needs are activated in intimate relations with only one or a few others because social discomfort prevents formation of wide networks of relationships, and thus more demands might be made on such relationships, accompanied by less social support from alternative sources.

Stress and social functioning

Most models of depression are "diathesis-stress" models, positing that stressful life events or circumstances provoke or challenge the person's underlying vulnerabilities, leading to depression. There are several specific ways in which research has demonstrated the importance of interpersonal functioning or social characteristics in predicting individuals' responses to stressors.

Specific vulnerability to interpersonal life events. As noted in Chapter 5, both cognitive (e.g. Beck, 1983) and psychodynamic (e.g. Arieti & Bemporad, 1980; Blatt, 1974) theorists have hypothesised that different subtypes of depression are associated with different life stress vulnerabilities and express somewhat different symptoms. Specifically, one form of vulnerability is the dependent or sociotropic person who is especially likely to base the sense of personal worth and competence on close relations with other people and to become depressed when faced with interpersonal rejection or loss. As noted previously, research has generally supported the link between specific vulnerabilities, related stressors, and depression. If anything the strongest empirical support for the overall model has concerned interpersonal stressors and sociotropy/dependency (e.g. Hammen, Marks, Mayol, & deMayo, 1985; Hammen et al., 1989; Robins & Block, 1988; Robins, 1990; Zuroff & Mongrain, 1987; reviewed in Barnett & Gotlib, 1988; Blatt & Zuroff, 1992; Nietzel & Harris, 1990).

Note that the process is hypothesised to be the same for men and women, but since women may be more likely to subscribe to dependent values and beliefs—and since interpersonal events may be more common than achievement events (Hammen et al., 1985)—such matching may particularly have implications for the preponderance of depression in women. That is, if women are more likely to be socialised to value close connections with others and to be dependent on others' approval and love, they are more vulnerable to depression in the wake of interpersonal losses, conflict, and rejections.

Recently Hammen and colleagues (Hammen et al., 1995) explored the matching of interpersonal events and personal vulnerability to interpersonal experiences from a somewhat different perspective. Reasoning that cognitions about attachment relationships (that is, beliefs about ability to depend on others, fear of abandonment) might mark a particular vulnerability to negative events that threatened attachment, Hammen et al. (1995) tested the association between negative interpersonal events and subsequent depression as moderated by attachment cognitions. As hypothesised, the presence of highly insecure beliefs coupled with high levels of interpersonal stress predicted subsequent depression. In addition, such beliefs and their interaction with interpersonal stressors predicted increases in *nondepressive* symptoms as well, so that the effect was not limited to depressive reactions.

Social support. A considerable body of research indicates that the availability of supportive relationships with others—or perceptions that such support is available—buffers the ill effects of stressful life events (e.g. Billings & Moos, 1985a; Kessler & McLeod, 1985; Paykel & Cooper, 1992; Swindle, Cronkite, & Moos, 1989). A recent large-scale sample of medical and psychiatric patients indicated, for example, that the extent of depressive symptoms decreased over a 2-year period as a function of availability of perceived support, and that if support was available, patients were less likely to develop a new episode (Sherbourne, Hays, & Wells, 1995). Several studies have shown specifically that when a major life event occurs, persons who lack a supportive intimate relationship with another person are significantly more likely to develop depression (Brown & Harris, 1978; Costello, 1982). Research has explored the role of actual supports as well as perceptions of support, and the role of the size of social networks. Additionally, the mechanisms of the effect continue to be explored, with support both for a buffering effect (support reduces the likelihood of depression in the face of stress) and a main effect (both low support and stress independently predict depression). This voluminous research field is beyond the scope of this discussion.

Of particular importance to the prediction of depression, investigators have found both that depressed people have fewer supportive relationships and that depressed persons perceive less support from the relationships that they do have. For instance, depressed people may report having fewer friends or relatives to turn to (reviewed in Gotlib & Hammen, 1992). Moreover, perceived support (the subjective appraisal of the helpfulness or availability of others) is often found to be lower for depressed people than comparison groups (e.g. Billings, Cronkite, & Moos, 1983; Gotlib & Lee, 1989). Such perceptions are not necessarily distorted by the experience of depression; even when no longer symptomatic, depressed individuals have been shown to report restricted networks or perceptions of less support (e.g. Billings & Moos, 1985a, Billings et al., 1983).

The source of limited support among depressed people is not fully understood. It may be due to social skill deficits or other characteristics of the individual as discussed above. As Coyne, Kahn, and Gotlib (1987) have speculated, depressed individuals may alienate those close to them because of their excessive demands for support—a process that elicits rejection that in turn serves to intensify or maintain depression.

Social problem solving.   Several investigators have proposed that deficient problem-solving and coping skills may contribute to depressive reactions to stressors (e.g. Nezu, 1987). Several studies have shown that depressed individuals do indeed display less effective solutions to hypothetical problems (e.g. Gotlib & Asarnow, 1979). Nezu and Ronan (1985; Nezu, 1987) suggested that depressed individuals are particularly deficient in generating and implementing solutions to *social* problems.

However, it is unclear whether depressed persons evidence specifically social problem-solving difficulties or more general deficits in coping responses to stressors. An examination of depressed individuals' coping strategies has found that they are relatively less likely to elect active problem-solving approaches to difficulties, and instead rely more than nondepressed people on avoidant and emotion-focused coping (e.g. Billings & Moos, 1984; Billings, Cronkite, & Moos, 1983)—although when no longer depressed their coping behaviors may not differ significantly from those of control subjects (e.g. Billings & Moos, 1985a). Presence of avoidance coping predicted poorer depressive outcomes and greater likelihood of a recurrence of depression over a 2-year period in a large sample of medical and psychiatric patients (Sherbourne, Hays, & Wells, 1995). As noted in earlier chapters, females in particular have been shown to rely on "ruminative" reactions to their depressive symptoms, intensifying self-focused, passive strategies rather than active problem solving or distraction (Nolen-Hoeksema, 1991).

Generation of interpersonal stressors.   A different strategy for exploring interpersonal factors in vulnerability to depression has been to examine the extent to which individuals contribute to the occurrence of negative life events that are *interpersonal* in nature. As noted in Chapter 5, Hammen (1991b) observed that women with recurrent depression experienced significantly more interpersonal negative events during a 1-year period than groups of women with bipolar or medical disorders or nonpsychiatric controls. Of particular relevance to the present discussion, the unipolar depressed women were especially likely to have experienced conflict events and interpersonal difficulties with a wide variety of others such as friends, spouses, family, employers, and teachers. The tendency of depressed women to contribute to the occurrence of more interpersonal and conflict stressors has recently been replicated in a sample of young women in the community (Daley et al., in press; Davila et al., 1995).

In additional analyses, Davila et al. (1995) found support for the hypothesis that the generation of interpersonal stressors was related not just to depression but also to relatively poor interpersonal problem-solving strategies, as measured by responses to hypothetical events. Poor interpersonal problem solving predicted the later occurrence of elevated levels of interpersonal stressors, which in turn predicted depressive reactions. Thus, deficiencies in the cognitive and behavioural skills needed to conceptualise effective solutions to interpersonal problems may contribute to a self-perpetuating cycle of stressful social relationships and depression.

Recently investigators explored a further mechanism by which interpersonal stressors occur (Potthoff, Holahan, & Joiner, 1995). They reasoned that depressed people often demand considerable reassurance from others, and according to Coyne's (1976) model, such reassurance seeking becomes aversive to others—possibly leading to negative social events. To test their hypotheses they administered (at different times over several weeks) measures of reassurance seeking and minor social stressors (such as being left out of activities, fights or disagreements) and depressive symptoms. The results supported the predictions that increased depressive symptoms resulted from minor social stressors; in turn, such minor social events were higher among those with a previously measured reassurance-seeking style. The authors conclude that such a style is aversive to others, leading to social slights and conflicts which provoke symptoms. These results need to be replicated with clinically depressed individuals, but provide an intriguing glimpse of the operation of "stress generation."

Summary

- Difficulties in social relationships may be a key element of many depressions: disrupted social connectedness may cause depression, and depression disrupts relationships, potentially causing further depression.
- Negative early childhood experiences, in the form of insecure attachment relationships between parent and child and in learning maladaptive skills and cognitions, may contribute to vulnerability to depression.

- Depression affects the family in adverse ways, especially contributing to marital discord, family burden, and poor adjustment in children.
- Depression has a negative impact on others even outside the family, suggesting that depression is aversive to others and contributes to others' rejection of the depressed person.
- Depressed people may have certain maladaptive behaviours and personality traits that affect their relationships even when not depressed, including dependency, introversion, and possibly, dysfunctional social skills and cognitions.
- For various reasons likely to be related both to depression and to underlying attributes, depressed people may contribute to the occurrence of stressful interpersonal events and have relatively deficient supportive relationships with others—contributing to occurrence or perpetuation of depression.

Biological treatments of depression 7

Stephanie experienced two bouts of major depression that each lasted for about six months. During one episode she sought counselling, but discussions of her life difficulties didn't seem to relieve the symptoms of depression, and she dragged herself through the bleak days and endless nights until the depression just seemed to wear away. Recently, when she began to sink into yet another depressive episode, she sought treatment from a medical doctor who prescribed a common antidepressant medication. Within a week her energy improved and she slept more soundly, and within two weeks her mood was definitely better, and she began to feel able to face some of the difficult personal events that had precipitated the depression.

Not surprisingly, the frequency with which depression occurs and causes suffering as well as the evidence that some forms of depression are associated with biological changes, have been two forces that have exerted pressure on medical science for effective treatments. As we discuss in this chapter, there are several well-established biological interventions as well as several more experimental approaches to treatment. This chapter discusses antidepressant medications, electroconvulsive therapy (ECT), light therapy, sleep deprivation, and physical exercise.

Comment on treatment of depression

Before discussing biological or psychotherapy approaches to treating depression, it is important to emphasise a singular fact about treatment in general. The majority of individuals with major depression or dysthymic disorder do not seek treatment for their condition. And of those who do seek help, surveys have generally found that only about 50% of individuals with such disorders seek treatment from a mental health specialist, with others visiting physicians in the general medical sector or seeking assistance from family or friends (Narrow et al., 1993). Unfortunately, as we have seen, the consequences of depression are extremely negative in terms of impaired functioning and impact on others. Moreover, individuals whose depression goes unrecognised and untreated may actually burden the primary care sector and inflate health care costs for medical problems (e.g. Simon, Ormel, VonKorff, & Barlow, 1995).

The reasons for failure to seek treatment for depression are numerous. Commonly depression is unrecognised as such by the individual, who might attribute symptoms to medical conditions or to stress and circumstances—leading either to seeking medical treatment or to the expectation that the distress is simply an aspect of the stress to be endured. Western culture particularly emphasises self-reliance, and many with depression feel guilty about "weakness" and forego seeking help because they believe depression requires firmer will or personal effort—"stiff upper lip" and so forth. Although women are given greater latitude in help seeking, both women and men typically believe that depression is under their own control (if only they were stronger) or that with the help of friends and family, they will get by. Of course, an additional factor may be lack of resources, or negative expectations about the possible outcome of treatment even if it is sought. Depression, of course, magnifies pessimistic beliefs that treatment cannot help.

In view of the general reluctance of individuals to seek treatment for depression, the recent explosion in the availability and use of antidepressant medication may have two desirable outcomes. One, of course, is that more people are getting help for depression. The other is that individuals and their physicians appear to be learning greater understanding of depression and acceptance that it is a condition that needs to be treated.

Antidepressant medications

In the past few years, antidepressants have become widely used to treat mood disorders. Indeed, according to surveys conducted regularly by the US National Center for Health Statistics, the proportion of psychiatrist office visits by patients that included prescription of antidepressant medications increased from about 18% of all such visits in 1980 to 30% in 1989. The number of visits that included prescribing antidepressants increased from 2.5 million in 1980 to 4.7 million in 1989 (Olfson & Klerman, 1993). These investigators note that the use of antianxiety medications remained relatively stable during this period. The surge in use of antidepressants appears to be associated especially with the development of new drugs and increased awareness of their potential usefulness.

Despite their increased use, however, antidepressants continue to be underutilised among depressed outpatients compared with the frequency of depressive disorders, according to a large-scale survey of patients in treatment (Wells, Kayton, Rogers, & Camp, 1994). For instance, Wells and Sturm (1996) found that psychiatrists were prescribing antidepressant medications for only 50% of severely depressed patients and less than 30% of moderately depressed patients. Moreover, even when they are prescribed for patients, they are often administered in subtherapeutic dosages. For instance, the Wells et al. survey found that 39% of those who were prescribed antidepressants received a dose below recommended levels (see also Keller et al., 1982).

Types of antidepressants. Like many drugs used in the treatment of mental disorders, the discovery of antidepressant medications in the 1950s was partly fortuitous, an observed side effect of drugs used to treat medical conditions. Medications that were known to deplete certain neurotransmitters in the brain appeared to cause depression, while those that increased specific neurotransmitters reduced depression. These early effects were focused largely on the monoamine neurotransmitters norepinephrine (noradrenaline), dopamine, and serotonin. Eventually, two classes of medications came to be introduced into widespread use in the 1950s, the *tricyclic antidepressants* (named for their chemical structure) and the *monoamine oxidase inhibitors (MAOIs)*. More recently, newer generation drugs, heterocyclic in chemical structure, have been developed and have achieved considerable popularity (such as Prozac). Table 7.1 lists several of more than twenty currently available antidepressants (and many others are under investigation before release for public use).

Use of antidepressants. Antidepressants are especially recommended for moderate-to-severe levels of depression, although they may also be useful for mild cases (Hellerstein et al., 1993; Joyce & Paykel, 1989). Some medications are initially taken at low dosages and build up to a therapeutic level over time adjusted for the person's needs and reactions, while some of the newer drugs have a standard dosage for everyone that starts immediately. Usually positive effects are not seen for 2 weeks or more, and depressed people need to be informed that they will not recover immediately. Although generally only one medication may be used, occasionally combinations of drugs—including lithium—may be recommended to augment the effectiveness of a particular medication.

TABLE 7.1

Selected antidepressant medications: Chemical and brand names

Generic (chemical) name	Brand name
Tricyclic Antidepressants	
Imipramine	Tofranil
Amitriptyline	Elavil
Clomipramine	Anafranil
Desipramine	Norpramin
Monoamine oxidase inhibitors	
Phenelzine	Nardil
Isocarboxazid	Marplan
"Second generation"heterocyclic drugs	
Trazodone	Desyrel
Maprotiline	Ludiomil
Selective serotonin reuptake inhibitors	
Fluoxetine	Prozac
Sertraline	Zoloft
Paroxetine	Paxil

The treatment of current symptoms is referred to as *acute* treatment, but it is only one phase of the recommended course. Once symptoms have diminished over approximately 6 to 8 weeks of use, *continuation* treatment is recommended for at least 4 to 6 months, and then the medication may be discontinued by tapering off the dosage, as abrupt discontinuation may cause unpleasant side effects. If medication is withdrawn too soon after remission of the acute symptoms, there is a relatively high likelihood of relapse (greater than 50%; Prien & Kupfer, 1986). A third phase of medication treatment, called *maintenance,* is strongly recommended for individuals who have a history of recurrent episodes of depression (American Psychiatric Association, 1994). In contrast to the generally agreed period of treatment for continuation, there is less consensus on the ideal duration of maintenance treatment. Some have recommended that medications be administered indefinitely for those at risk for recurrent or chronic depression, while others argue that the high cost is not warranted (reviewed in Fava & Kaji, 1994; Hirschfeld, 1994).

Mechanisms of action.   The tricyclic drugs have their effects in complex ways, various ones altering functions of norepinephrine, dopamine, serotonin, and related neurotransmitter systems. Depending on their specific mechanisms, they may bind to a receptor site in specific neurons, achieving effects by causing a reaction directly, or by blocking the effects of naturally occurring substances. Alternatively, antidepressant medications may cause the release of more of a particular neurotransmitter, or block the reuptake of a neurotransmitter back into the neuron thereby increasing the amount that is available. In some cases, the medications alter the neurotransmitter receptors, by changing their sensitivity or their numbers. The older tricyclic medications often had effects on several different neurotransmitters. Some of the newer antidepressants are more selective in their mechanisms: they block the reuptake of *serotonin* so that more is available in the synaptic cleft (and are sometimes referred to as SSRIs, or selective serotonin reuptake inhibitors). The MAOIs block the effects of substances that break down the monoamine neurotransmitters, increasing their availability.

For the most part, however, the mechanisms of action are not fully understood, and the effects of antidepressants are more complex than simply increasing amount of a neurotransmitter—otherwise results would be relatively rapid. Instead, antidepressants generally require 2 weeks or more to achieve therapeutic effect. Probably some of the drugs work by altering the densities and sensitivities of certain receptors in specific areas of the brain, or by altering the complex interrelationships among various neurotransmitter systems (McNeal & Cimbolic, 1986).

Effectiveness of antidepressants. There are several issues relevant to effectiveness: do some antidepressants work better than others? How effective are the antidepressants in general? What is known about continuation and maintenance treatment effectiveness? All of the current antidepressant medications are about equally effective. Therefore, the consideration of which drug to take depends on previous response to medications, the type of symptoms displayed, and life circumstances, as well as side effects (Gitlin, 1990). For instance, some of the medications are stimulating while others are sedating. Therefore, someone whose work requires close attention would not want a medication that is sedating and causes drowsiness, whereas someone with an agitated depression would not be comfortable with a stimulating drug. Some of the medications are lethal if taken in an overdose, whereas others are not—thus, suicidal risk may be a consideration. *Individuals* may respond significantly better to one than another, and therefore sometimes a period of trial-and-error is needed to find an effective drug.

How effective are antidepressants in the treatment of depression? Numerous studies comparing the medications to placebos in controlled *blind* trials report effectiveness in the reduction of *acute* depression to be between 50% and 70%, which is 20% to 40% higher than for placebos (reviewed in Thase & Kupfer, 1996). More recently, double-blind studies also have shown antidepressants to reduce symptoms of chronic mild depressions, or dysthymia (e.g. Hellerstein et al., 1993). A fuller discussion of one of the largest clinical trials of medication is presented in Chapter 8, in a discussion of the relative effectiveness of antidepressants and psychotherapy.

Far fewer studies exist to evaluate the effectiveness of *continuation* treatment over a longer period of time. A recent review of such treatment reported that studies of tricyclic antidepressants found that the average risk of relapse was only 22% compared to 50% for patients on placebos (Fava & Kaji, 1994). They also report preliminary results from studies of SSRI drugs, such as fluoxetine (Prozac), suggesting that higher doses of maintenance than acute therapy are more effective in reducing relapse rates, although this conclusion was not reached in Hirschfeld's review (1994). Comparative studies of various classes of drugs during continuation treatment are rare. However, Hirschfeld (1994) reviewed several and concluded that although SSRI and tricyclic antidepressants were equally effective in preventing relapse, the SSRI drugs are a better treatment because they had fewer side effects and therefore might reduce patient reluctance to continue taking them.

Even less information is available on the effectiveness of long-term, or *maintenance*, psychopharmacology. Most of the studies on this topic failed to use appropriate control groups such as randomised, placebo-treated patients, and their period of study was relatively brief. The most extensive study, reported at 3 years by Frank et al. (1990) and at 5 years by Kupfer et al. (1992), found that the tricyclic drug, imipramine, was superior to placebo and significantly reduced rates of recurrence in patients with histories of repeated major depressions. Moreover, Frank et al. (1993) determined that reduced dosages of imipramine were significantly less effective in preventing recurrences during the maintenance phase; those who were treated at the same dosages as during acute treatment did significantly better.

Studies using SSRI drugs have also shown good results in maintenance treatment compared with placebos. However, their durations have been relatively brief (1 or 2 years), thereby limiting definitive conclusions (Fava & Kaji, 1994).

Side Effects. Side effects are also a consideration in choice of medication. Some antidepressants cause dry mouth or blurry vision. Some drugs are sedating (causing drowsiness, being slowed down), and some are stimulating (causing anxiety, tremor, rapid heart beat, insomnia). Weight gain and sexual dysfunction (e.g. erectile difficulties) are common side effects. At the most serious extreme, a few medications may cause seizures in rare cases or cardiac irregularities, or other problems. Constant medical evaluation is important; however, most antidepressant medications do not have known therapeutic levels in the blood that can be monitored. MAOI drugs have a unique and potentially life-threatening side effect; suddenly increased blood pressure, stroke, or even death may occur if the person taking such medications also ingests foods or other drugs containing *tyramine*. Tyramine is an amino acid found in many aged foods such as cheese, smoked or pickled fish or meats, red or fortified wines—and other foods and medications. Thus, people on MAOI drugs must restrict their diets accordingly. Because of the restrictions, MAOIs are usually prescribed only when other medications have been shown to be ineffective for a particular patient.

The "new generation" drugs have become popular because of their relative absence of side effects. In particular, fluoxetine (Prozac) has attracted considerable attention as a potential "wonder drug" (although there is no evidence that it is any more effective than any other antidepressant), with some individuals claiming that it has changed their personalities and their lives. A few years ago Prozac also attracted much media attention because of reports that it sometimes caused suicidal feelings and behaviours. Anti-Prozac publicity became widespread, apparently promoted in part by anti-psychiatry groups such as Scientology.

In response to the news stories that raised questions about Prozac's safety, the Federal Drug Administration's Psychopharmacological Drugs Advisory Committee met to review the issue. Based on analyses of controlled studies, the Committee concluded that there was no evidence of a causal relationship between taking the drug and suicidal behaviour. Similar conclusions were reached in a careful review of studies (Mann & Kapur, 1991). Experts argue that most alleged cases of suicidal behaviour might have been due to prior history of suicidality. Since most antidepressants are actually prescribed by general physicians who lack specialised training in psychiatric disorders (Beardsley, Gardocki, Larson, & Hildalgo, 1988), there may be a risk of inadequate assessment of a patient's suitability for medication treatment.

An additional "side effect" of medications is noncompliance. A sizeable proportion of individuals either discontinue medications or do not follow instructions concerning dosage and timing. Reasons for noncompliance range from unpleasant side effects to psychological concerns about reluctance to use chemicals to control moods or resistance to defining oneself as having a psychiatric problem (e.g. Goodwin & Jamison, 1990). It has been argued that the newer SSRI and heterocyclic medications have far fewer side effects than the MAOIs and tricyclics, and therefore are much better tolerated. To date, however, no studies have demonstrated different rates of compliance with different medications.

Predicting response.   Can we tell who will respond well to antidepressants? There is currently no indicator to predict treatment response. It is sometimes thought that depressed persons with more of the physical symptoms of depression such as appetite and sleep changes, psychomotor retardation, loss of energy and fatigue, might respond best to antidepressants. However, the extent to which these "endogenous" or melancholic subtypes respond best to antidepressants is a matter of controversy. In general, research tends to support the idea that patients with the melancholic subtype of severe depression respond relatively more favourably to antidepressants than do the nonmelancholic depressions, while at less severe (outpatient) levels of depression the melancholic-nonmelancholic medication outcome distinction is far less substantiated (Joyce & Paykel, 1989; Rush & Weissenburger, 1994).

There is no evidence that depressions that seem to have been precipitated by "psychological" causes such as negative life events respond less well to antidepressants than do allegedly "biological" depressions. On the other hand, there may be certain psychological characteristics that predict more favorable response to medication. Peselow et al. (1992) administered the Sociotropy–Autonomy Scale to patients (see Chapter 5 for a discussion of this personality distinction). They found that depressed persons who scored high on Autonomy (need for independence, achievement, and solitude) and low on Sociotropy (dependence on others and need for social contact) responded significantly better to medications than did the highly Sociotropic patients. Moreover, the use of the personality dimension of Sociotropy–Autonomy was a significantly better predictor of drug treatment response than was the classic endogenous (melancholic)—nonendogenous distinction based on symptomatology, although high Autonomy scores tended to be related to endogenous symptoms.

These results suggest good potential for predicting patients who respond better to medications. Possibly the more highly Sociotropic patients may respond better to the interpersonal context of psychotherapy or to therapies with an interpersonal focus. Such a speculation has yet to be tested.

It is also thought that very severe depressions, agitated depression, and depressions with psychotic features do not respond well to antidepressants alone, and may require additional treatment with hospitalisation and possibly, electroconvulsive therapy (ECT). Also, certain kinds of "atypical" depressions, those involving significant personality disorders, and persons with more severe histories of repeated or prolonged episodes, do not respond as well to typical antidepressants (Joyce & Paykel, 1989). As noted, such individuals might be given MAOIs or other combinations of medications. Additionally, chronic depressions may be effectively treated with antidepressants in the sense of reducing severity of symptoms (Hellerstein et al., 1993), but chronic symptoms appear to persist (Kocsis et al., 1988).

Finally, it should be recalled that relatively few depressions arise "endogenously" in the absence of personally significant life difficulties. Consequently, while medications might be useful to reduce the depression which itself is debilitating, they have little effect on the underlying "depressive" circumstances. Thus, many individuals may need psychotherapeutic interventions to deal with such problems. In Chapter 8 the effectiveness of therapies for depression is discussed— including research that has pitted antidepressants and psychotherapy against each other to study their comparative effects.

Antidepressants in treatment of children and adolescents.
Interestingly, despite their general effectiveness with adults, antidepressant medications for youngsters do not appear to be consistently useful. Selected studies using non-blind research designs, using tricyclic antidepressants and serotonin specific reuptake inhibitors (SSRIs) yield generally positive results (Ambrosini, Bianchi, Rabinovich, & Elia, 1993; Apter et al., 1994; Boulos, Kutcher, Gardner, & Young, 1992; Harrington, 1992; Ryan, 1992). However, methodologically superior placebo controlled, double-blind studies have consistently failed to demonstrate superiority of drug over placebo in the treatment of child and adolescent depressive disorders (Geller et al., 1992; Puig-Antich et al., 1987; Simeon, DiNicola, Ferguson & Copping, 1990). Why don't children and adolescents respond as favourably as adults? Generally, the differences are hypothesised to be due to developmental

differences in brain neurochemistry (Ryan, 1992), but these explanations remain hypothetical and speculative. Further controlled studies may be able to identify subgroups of depressed youngsters for whom antidepressants are effective. Caution is especially warranted, however, because of the potentially dangerous side effects of some antidepressants (e.g. cardiac complications) when used with children.

Implications of antidepressant effectiveness for understanding causality. The question arises that if medications are successful in reducing depression, doesn't that prove that depression is caused by disordered biological processes? Although this argument is often mentioned, it is an example of a logical inaccuracy called the *treatment-etiology fallacy*. It is the equivalent of saying that if aspirin cures headaches, headaches must be caused by an absence of aspirin. It is certainly possible that some depressions might originate in a defective neuroregulatory process involving certain neurotransmitters in the brain. However, it is also possible that dysregulation of such neurotransmitter processes itself is caused by depression (or by a further underlying factor that causes depressive reactions). The fact that chemical agents that act on neurotransmitters and lead to relief from depression is most accurately interpreted to indicate that depressive symptoms are mediated by, but not necessarily caused by, defective neurotransmission. Despite the limitations of the etiological argument regarding antidepressants, their success certain enhances and extends the research conducted on biological processes in depression—and might surely help to clarify our understanding of primary causal mechanisms.

Other biological treatments

Additional biological interventions sometimes used to treat depression include electroconvulsive therapy, phototherapy for seasonal affective disorder, and sleep deprivation.

Electroconvulsive Therapy

Electroconvulsive therapy (ECT) often strikes people as a barbaric, inhumane treatment that should be entirely abolished. Indeed, in past decades it was misused, applied to many patient groups without evidence of effectiveness, and caused physical damage to many persons. Accordingly, its use became subjected to stringent restrictions which, along with the increase in use of antidepressants, led to a marked decline from its peak in the 1940s and 1950s as a primary treatment of major depressions. Nowadays its use both in the US and Europe is highly variable according to location, hospital, and patient characteristics, reflecting the ambivalence that many psychiatrists experience about it (e.g. Hermann, Dorwart, Hoover, & Brody, 1995).

Use and effectiveness. ECT has not disappeared for one very good reason. It is extremely effective in the treatment of certain kinds of severe, otherwise untreatable, depressions. It is considered the treatment of choice where there are prominent psychotic features of depression, and especially where severe depression has not responded to medication, and in life-threatening situations where rapid response is needed (Weiner & Coffey, 1988). These authors reviewed controlled and placebo studies of ECT used under medically safe conditions and concluded that it significantly reduces severe depression. Early studies generally indicated that ECT was especially effective for treatment of the melancholic subtype of depression (reviewed in Rush & Weissenburger, 1994). However, recent studies that include more careful control of patient diagnoses fail to support this distinction, suggesting that severely depressed both melancholic and nonmelancholic patients may benefit from ECT (Sackheim & Rush, 1995).

ECT is currently administered under medically safe conditions (with the minimal electrical stimulation sufficient to induce seizure), in which patients are first given sedatives, muscle relaxants, or other agents to control potentially damaging physical side effects. The specific procedures needed to achieve maximum therapeutic success with minimal residual complications have not been established, although it appears that sufficient current must be applied to induce a seizure in order to achieve therapeutic effects. There is controversy, for instance, over the relative advantages of unilateral or bilateral electrical stimulation. Moreover, there is considerable variability in the spacing and total number of ECT treatments, with the typical course averaging 6-9 treatments spaced 2 or 3 times per week. In a recent double-blind study to evaluate the relative efficacy of twice per week vs. 3 times per week administration, Lerer et al. (1995) found negligible differences in clinical outcomes over 4 weeks between the two. However, they observed that the cognitive side effects (such as memory impairment) of twice-per-week ECT were milder, and therefore recommend this frequency as the most advantageous.

How does ECT work? Its mechanisms are not currently understood. However, it is suspected ECT is a powerful anticonvulsive treatment, progressively increasing seizure threshold—and that its anticonvulsive properties, with associated changes in neurotransmitters and other neurobiological characteristics, may be responsible for antidepressant effects (Nobler et al., 1994; Sackheim, 1988). Several studies have specifically examined regional blood flow in the brain associated with ECT, and have found that it generally produces reduced blood flow in certain areas. Nobler et al. (1994), for instance, found that "successful" ECT treatments were associated with significantly more blood flow reductions, especially in the frontal-temporal regions. The authors speculate that depressive episodes may be associated with increased functional activity in specific neural systems, so that reductions of blood flow by ECT may curtail such processes, leading to clinical remission. It is clear that limitations in our knowledge of the functions of the brain obscure definitive conclusions at this time.

Side effects of ECT.   One of the major issues in the use of ECT is whether it causes damage to the recipient, in terms of functions or structure of the brain. Numerous studies of memory functioning reveal that loss of short-term memory for events immediately preceding the ECT is common. However, little evidence exists for long-term memory decrements (Devanand et al., 1994). Moreover, after reviewing studies based on neuroimaging techniques for viewing the brains of ECT recipients, as well as controlled animal studies of neuronal consequences of ECT administration, the authors conclude that there is no evidence that ECT causes structural brain damage (Devanand et al., 1994).

Phototherapy for seasonal mood disorders

Phototherapy, or light therapy, is a treatment for the Seasonal Affective Disorder subtype of depression. Often individuals suffering from SAD do not respond well to antidepressant medications. Therefore, speculating that the disorder may be a "hibernation-like" response resulting from circadian rhythm dysfunction during diminished exposure to light during Winter, investigators reasoned that increasing exposure to bright light might reverse the depressive symptoms. The basic treatment consists of having the depressed person sit near a source of bright (2500 lux) light for a period of time daily. There has been considerable study of how much exposure during each session (e.g. 1 or 2 hours), how many sessions a day (e.g. 1 or 2), and when during the day (early morning, midday, or evening). More recent studies have suggested that time of day is unimportant (e.g. Wirz-Justice et al., 1993; see also Lafer et al., 1994) with good results achieved with either a morning or evening session consisting of 1 hour.

Light therapy has been shown to be effective in controlled studies with up to 70% response rate (e.g. Rosenthal et al., 1985; Wirz-Justice, et al, 1993). Although reductions in depression may be achieved relatively rapidly (within a few days or a week), unfortunately the positive effect seems to be relatively temporary, and depressed people with SAD may need to continue the treatments during low-light months.

The mechanism of action of phototherapy is assumed to relate to circadian rhythm dysregulation. The hypothesis that Winter depressions are triggered by phase delays in the circadian system with respect to the sleep–wake or light–dark cycle would predict that exposure to morning light would achieve antidepressant effects by phase-advancing the circadian rhythm, whereas evening exposure would have no effect. Many studies initially argued for the greater effectiveness of light exposure in the morning than evening. However, recent studies show that time of day is not important, and that successful treatment was unrelated to hormonal markers of circadian phase delay (e.g. Wirz-Justice et al., 1993). Thus, the underlying mechanisms of change remain to be clarified.

Sleep deprivation

Sleep deprivation is an experimental treatment based on the association between sleep disturbances and depression, as well as atypical rapid eye movement (REM) sleep patterns in some depressives. Researchers tried the obvious—keep depressed patients awake during part of the night. More than half of the patients treated with sleep deprivation showed remarkable mood improvement (Wu & Bunney, 1990). However, there are two major problems with this treatment. One is that positive changes are very temporary; more than 80% of unmedicated patients relapsed after a night's sleep or even after naps, as did 59% of the medicated patients. The second problem is that many of the studies reporting positive effects were poorly designed, lacking comparison groups, containing samples with very diverse patient characteristics, and failing to account for patients' expectations of getting better (Leibenluft & Wehr, 1992). Nonetheless, the effects of this low-cost, harmless procedure, suggest that it is worthy of further study.

Effects of physical exercise on depression

Increasing attention has been devoted to "antidepressant" effect of exercise. Although this research is included in this chapter on biological treatments, it must be emphasised at the outset that the actual mechanisms accounting for positive results of exercise might be psychological (rewarding effects of positive activity, distraction, improved self-esteem, changes in cognitions) as much as those due to actual physical changes in energy and physiological arousal. Research has rarely addressed the processes accounting for beneficial effects.

In today's climate of emphasis on physical health and fitness, it is unsurprising to find that normal individuals consider exercise to be a useful way to improve mood. In a large-scale study of methods people use to change a bad mood, exercise was rated as the most successful method among approximately 68 items. Exercise was also rated positively as a method of reducing tension and anxiety and for enhancing energy (Thayer, Newman, & McClain, 1994).

The outcome studies of physical exercise on depression have been somewhat limited in quality, often including nonpatients assessed on mood measures rather than clinical populations—and typically include small samples. Nevertheless, recent studies of clinically depressed patients consistently support the value of exercise in reducing symptomatology (e.g. Bosscher, 1993; Martinsen, 1993). The effects are not dramatic (e.g. Kugler, Seelbach, & Kruskemper, 1994), nor do they suggest that exercise should take the place of psychotherapy or other active treatments. Moreover, as noted, the mechanisms that account for their beneficial effects have not been clarified. Nevertheless, physical exercise deserves further study as a potentially cost-effective treatment adjunct.

Summary

- Antidepressant medications have greatly increased in use in recent years, but continue to be frequently misadministered in terms of dosage and application to suitable cases.
- Antidepressants emerged in the 1950s but only the past several years have new preparations appears that have relatively few side effects.
- There is solid evidence of therapeutic effectiveness of antidepressant medications, although all have about the same level of demonstrated effectiveness, and none have been shown to be superior to psychotherapy developed specifically for treatment of depression.

- Recent treatment guidelines suggest use of antidepressants not only for acute treatment but also for continuation of medication for up to 6 months after recovery to prevent relapse, and for long-term or indefinite maintenance for those with histories of recurrent depression.
- The efficacy of antidepressants is not proof of an underlying biochemical etiology of depression.
- Other biological treatments for depressive disorders include electroconvulsive therapy, phototherapy, sleep deprivation, and possibly, physical exercise.

Psychological treatments of depression 8

Psychotherapy for depression was traditionally regarded as difficult and unrewarding (and often unproductive), because of the relentless negativism, lack of energy, and low motivation of the depressed patients. When depressed, individuals absorbed endless amounts of encouragement and support—or interpretations about the childhood origins of their difficulties—often without apparent relief.

In general, evaluation of traditional insight-oriented psychodynamic treatments has been hampered by unstandardised methods and lack of emphasis on empirical validation. Moreover, contemporary depression theorists view traditional psychoanalytically-based methods as largely unhelpful—relatively passive and focused less on treating depression than on achieving insight into underlying personality problems. More importantly, recent years have seen the development of several theoretically based, systematically tested, and empirically validated psychotherapeutic methods of treating depression. As a result, there are now effective treatments for depression so that it is no longer a disorder for therapists to dread or for which patients feel hopeless about receiving help.

In the sections to follow, two of the most widely used treatment methods are discussed in greater detail, *cognitive-behavioural therapy* and *interpersonal therapy*. Their methods are briefly described, and research is reviewed on their effectiveness, range of application, and mechanisms of change. This focus is not meant to imply that other methods are ineffective—only that they have not been as widely studied or evaluated.

Cognitive-behavioural treatment of depression

Developed by Aaron Beck, a psychoanalytically trained psychiatrist, the theory behind cognitive-behavioural therapy (CBT) emphasises the role of maladaptive cognitions in the origin, maintenance, and worsening of depression (Beck, 1967), as described in Chapter 5. When people think negatively, they feel depressed, and therefore therapy attempts to identify and alter the negative beliefs, expectations, and misinterpretations of reality—while also helping to define and alter dysfunctional behaviours that might be contributing to depression. It should be noted that many of the specific techniques endorsed by CBT draw liberally from diverse applications of behaviour therapy methods, especially those that emphasised the link between depression and reduced access to positive reinforcement (e.g. Lewinsohn, Sullivan, & Grosscup, 1980; Lewinsohn, Antonuccio, Breckenridge, & Teri, 1987), social skills deficiencies (Becker, Heimberg, & Bellack, 1987), and self-regulation problems leading to dysfunctional self-reinforcement (e.g. Rehm, 1977; Rehm et al., 1979). Despite the contributions of these approaches, they are not specifically covered in this chapter because they have not been extensively pursued in empirical studies (but see Gotlib & Hammen, 1992, for a review).

Treatment methods

The essential elements of CBT were described in Beck, Rush, Shaw, and Emery (1979). It is intended to be time-limited, relatively brief (approximately 20 sessions over 16 weeks), active, directive, here-and-now focused on current problems and current dysfunctional thinking. Homework assignments between visits encourage clients to practice skills necessary to master the techniques of the treatment, observe thoughts and behaviour, test hypotheses, and acquire new skills.

Some of the key ingredients of the therapy are behavioural activation, graded task assignments, thought-catching and cognitive restructuring, identification and challenging of underlying maladaptive beliefs, and problem solving and specific behavioural techniques as needed to deal with particular life difficulties. *Behavioural activation* employs the well-known common sense idea that being active leads to rewards that are an antidote to depression. It assists the client in identifying pleasurable or mastery activities and then helps the person overcome obstacles to performing them, followed by accurate assessment of their value. Often depressed individuals fail to participate in previously enjoyable activities because of a loss of interest and pleasure, or they anticipate that activity would be too difficult, take too much energy, or would fail to produce pleasure. The therapist and client collaborate to identify potentially pleasurable or meaningful activities, and then anticipate and deal with possible actual or cognitive obstacles to undertaking them. The client is encouraged to experiment with activity and test the hypothesis that engagement in activities that provide a sense of mastery or pleasure causes improvement in mood. In combination with this technique, *graded task assignments* help clients to engage in successively more rewarding yet demanding activities that lead to increased pleasure or mastery experiences; such activities can also tackle current problems (e.g. lack of rewarding job, relationship difficulties) that contribute to depression. Behavioural activation and graded task assignments are especially likely to be employed to treat the depression syndrome directly, usually at the initial stages of treatment.

Thought-catching of "automatic negative thoughts" is the fundamental tool for changing maladaptive, depressogenic thoughts. Clients are taught to observe the link between thoughts and feelings, and to clarify their own emotion-related thoughts. Using a written form typically divided into 3 columns, individuals keep records of emotion-arousing experiences in Column 1, the automatic negative thoughts associated with them in Column 2, and in the third column, their realistic thoughts or challenges to the maladaptive thoughts. For example, a person might record the event on Column 1: "I asked Arnold to serve on the committee I chair, and he declined" which caused distress. Column 2 contains the automatic thoughts about this event: "He doesn't want to work with me"; "He doesn't respect me"; "I can never command the kind of interest from other people that I want." Column 3 might contain rational replies to these thoughts, such as: "There really is no evidence that he doesn't respect me or want to work with me; in fact, he usually agrees with me or cooperates with me at work"; "Another possible explanation is that he is just too busy this time; that's what he told me, and in fact, he does seem to have a busy schedule"; "My desire to have people show interest in me and give me what I want is normal, but obviously one doesn't always get everything from others."

Several techniques are taught to clients to challenge each negative thought, such as: "Is there a distortion"?; "What's the evidence"?; "Is there another way to look at it?"; and "What if (the worst is really true)?" Usually, one or more of these challenges helps the client to replace the dysfunctional thought with a more realistic one. Often the realistic thoughts lead to specific behavioural activities to try out new ways of behaving, or to collect behavioural data to test one's beliefs.

The negative thoughts are hypothesised to occur at different levels, ranging from surface level interpretations of events ("If he didn't call me it means he doesn't like me"), to deeper, pervasive, core beliefs and assumptions ("If someone doesn't like me it means I'm no good"). Later stages of therapy would be more likely to deal with the deeper level assumptions and schemas. For instance, someone with chronically negative beliefs about self-worth would be encouraged to directly challenge maladaptive beliefs (e.g. "It is not necessary to be valued by everyone for everything I do in order to be a worthwhile person"). Positive attributes that the person might discredit are actively construed as valuable (e.g. "Even if I am not beautiful and brilliant, I am pleasant looking, and have a kind and thoughtful manner with others"). Also, there may be an emphasis on learning specific skills that enhance self-concept, such as improving conversational skills, or mastery of personally relevant goals.

The therapy is intended not only to alleviate the symptoms of depression and resolve immediate difficulties in the client's environment, but also to teach skills that can be used to resolve problems or deal with emerging depressive symptoms. Thus, an important goal of the therapy is to reduce the likelihood of recurrence of depression.

Evaluating outcome of CBT

Outcome studies have addressed various questions: effects of treatment on acute symptoms, relapse prevention or long-term outcomes, effects of severity on outcome, and comparisons between CBT and medications or other psychotherapies.

Acute treatment.   There have been numerous studies of the effectiveness of CBT in reducing acute depression, and they are too numerous to identify individually. Instead, we focus on several reviews or meta-analyses and several large studies. Nietzel, Russell, Hemmings, and Gretter (1987) and Dobson (1989) reported meta-analyses of numerous treatment of depression studies in which the Beck Depression Inventory was the outcome measure. They reported significant clinical improvements due to treatments, and Dobson (1989) concluded that cognitive therapy is significantly better than no therapy, behaviour therapy, or pharmacotherapy or other forms of psychotherapy. The largest meta-analysis to date was reported by Robinson, Berman, and Neimeyer (1990) who reviewed 57 therapies for the treatment of depression. The meta-analyses identified several conclusions. First, treatments for depression overall were superior to no-treatment control groups. However, when such control groups were subdivided into wait-list and placebo controls the effects of treatment were not significant for comparisons with placebo controls. Second, comparisons between types of treatment indicated that cognitive-behavioural interventions were superior to general verbal and to behavioural methods, but did not differ from cognitive-only treatments. Finally, the authors noted that by post-treatment, patients' depression level was typically reduced significantly; however, it remained in the mild depression range.

Several individual studies are noteworthy because of the sample sizes and overall methodological advantages, including careful assessment of symptoms using various standardised methods, random assignment to conditions, and various design features. For instance, the NIMH Treatment of Depression Collaborative Research Program (TDCRP; Elkin et al., 1985) reported results of its multi-site large-scale study. The design compared two brief psychotherapies, cognitive therapy (Beck et al., 1979) and interpersonal psychotherapy (Klerman, Weissman, Rounsaville, & Chevron, 1984), with imipramine plus clinical management, and pill placebo plus clinical management. Two hundred and fifty outpatients with major depression were assigned to one of the four conditions for 16 weeks. Comparative outcomes will be reported in greater detail in a later section, but in terms of reduction of symptoms by the end of the treatment the results were somewhat disappointing. Recovery, defined by minimal symptoms on a psychiatric rating scale for depression, occurred in only 36% of CBT patients, but the rate was higher than for patients assigned to pill placebo treatment (21%).

Hollon and colleagues (1992) assigned 107 patients to CBT or medication or their combination, for 12 weeks of active treatment. Recovery, based on the same criteria as the TDCRP reported above, was attained by 32% of CBT patients, compared with 33% in the drug treatment and 52% in the combined drug-CBT treatment. Thase, Simons, Cahalane, McGeary, and Harden (1991) assigned 59 patients who met criteria for major depression with endogenous features. They received 20 sessions of CBT in a study specifically designed to test the effects of severity on outcome. Across the patient sample as a whole, 71% recovered according to the criteria used in the previous two studies. The authors hypothesise that their stronger effects were due to exclusion of nonendogenous (and possibly more chronically ill) patients, and treatment in a dedicated CBT clinic.

Taken as a whole, the outcome research supports the general effectiveness of cognitive therapy particularly when evaluated as symptom change rather than recovery. Nevertheless, there are additional issues to consider in the following sections: does CBT work better than other treatments including medication, does it work better for less severe depression, and does it succeed in reducing relapse rates over a follow-up period?

CBT compared to other treatments. There are three major comparisons: CBT vs. medications; CBT alone vs. CBT combined with medications; CBT vs. other psychotherapy. As noted in general review and meta-analytic studies, earlier studies of CBT generally found it to be superior to behaviour therapies or pharmacotherapy (e.g. Dobson, 1989; Robinson, Berman, & Neimeyer, 1990). Hollon, Shelton, and Davis (1993) draw somewhat more cautious conclusions about the efficacy of cognitive therapy in comparison to antidepressant medications. Such a comparison is of critical importance, since medications represent the most typical treatment option of persons with clinically significant depression. Hollon et al. (1993) concluded that the designs of most outcome studies comparing cognitive therapy with pharmacotherapy have been inadequate to permit firm conclusions. Specifically, few such comparisons have included pill placebo treatments which would permit a clearer basis for evaluating the effectiveness of medications. In the absence of such controls, it is possible that the drug-treated patients have not been particularly responsive. Moreover, the authors note that few of the medication studies have provided optimal pharmacotherapy in terms of dosage, duration of treatment, or use of supplemental medications. The TDRCP study noted earlier is an exception to the general lack of pill placebo conditions, and in that study the placebo condition—which also included "clinical management" involving brief support and advice to patients along with the pills—did generally worse than the other treatments, but on some measures it was not significantly different in outcomes from the active psychotherapy or medication treatments (Elkin et al., 1989). Recovery rates were superior in the active treatments compared with pill placebo, but outcomes measured by mean scores on depression and functioning measures did not differ significantly across groups. Further studies with placebos are needed to clarify the comparisons between drugs and CBT.

Another possible comparison is between CBT or pharmacotherapy versus the combination of the two. Some of the earlier studies provided mixed results (reviewed in Hollon et al., 1992). Hollon and colleagues (1992) found that combining CBT with medication improved patient responses, compared to either treatment alone—but the effect was not statistically significant. Those investigators suggest that the preponderance of the evidence suggests that there is a modest superiority of the combination of CBT and medication, but that most studies to date may have lacked sufficient sample size to validate the effect. Another possible role for CBT combined with medication was recently proposed by Fava et al. (1994), who administered CBT for residual symptoms that remained after depressed patients had been treated with medication. Following medication treatment, patients were withdrawn from the drugs and assigned to 10 sessions of CBT or "clinical management". CBT was shown to reduce the residual symptoms significantly more than the clinical management condition. Moreover, over a 2-year follow-up, CBT-treated patients had a lower relapse rate (15%) than did the clinical management group (35%), although the difference was not statistically significant in the small samples. The study serves as a preliminary indication that sequential rather than simultaneous CBT-medication treatment might be a useful option to explore further, especially for patients who show incomplete recovery following medication.

The other major comparison studies have pitted CBT against interpersonal psychotherapy (IPT) or psychodynamic-interpersonal therapy. IPT (discussed further in a later section) was compared with CBT, imipramine, and pill placebo (plus clinical management) in the TDRCP as noted earlier. In general, there were few differences between CBT and IPT, and it appeared that both were overall as effective as medication (Elkin et al., 1989). It has been argued, however, that the TDCRP may have obscured important differences across sites of the study that were due to differential competence or preference for one or other of the psychotherapies. For instance, Jacobson and Hollon (1996) note that one site was clearly more experienced in administering CBT than the others, while another site had a strong background in IPT. Therapist "allegiance" and competence, therefore, should be considered before drawing firm conclusions overall about the effectiveness of one or another treatment.

In one additional comparative study, Shapiro et al. (1994) compared CBT with psychodynamic-interpersonal therapy (which used psychodynamic methods such as interpretations with a focus on interpersonal issues) on a sample of 117 depressed patients, and half of the participants were assigned to either 8 or 16 weeks of treatment. Overall, the two psychotherapies were equally effective in symptom reduction.

CBT and level of severity of depression. In an attempt to determine the characteristics of patients who might be especially responsive to CBT, one question is whether psychotherapies are more effective on patients with less severe depression. The TDCRP had reported that, while overall patients responded about equally well to the active treatments, among patients who were most severely depressed, medication was superior to pill placebo and to CBT (Elkin et al., 1989). Among the less depressed, however, there were no differences. The TDCRP results have been reported in some outlets to mean that CBT is no better than pill placebos for the treatment of severe depression. Arguing against that interpretation, Jacobson and Hollon (1996) noted that there was considerable variability across treatment sites, with some of the sites showing effective treatment of severe depression with CBT. Moreover, most other studies have found no differences between more and less severe depression in the effectiveness of CBT. Hollon et al. (1992) tested the same hypothesis in their study, but found no evidence that CBT was less effective than pharmacotherapy in treatment of the more severely depressed. The Shapiro et al. (1994) study similarly found no differences in the effectiveness of CBT among patients differing in severity, although they did observe that more severely depressed patients improved significantly more with 16 sessions rather than the 8-session version of the treatments. Thase and colleagues (1991) found that the more severely depressed patients had a lower percentage symptom change on some measures of outcome of CBT, but in general there were no significant differences between high- and low-depressed groups at the end of treatment on any measures. In view of the somewhat higher symptom levels of the more severely depressed patients at the end of treatment, Thase et al. (1991) suggested that the 16-week treatment may not be optimal for the most severely depressed.

Prevention of relapse/recurrence of depression. Since a key goal of CBT is to teach patients the skills to treat their own depression and deal with problematic circumstances to avoid depressive responding, long-term outcomes are particularly important. Overall, however, all treatments yield somewhat mixed outcomes.

Hollon and Najavits (1988; see also Hollon, Shelton, & Loosen, 1991) reviewed several long-term studies indicating that cognitive therapy has clear superiority to pharmacological treatment in the prevention of relapse/recurrence. They noted that 4 of 5 studies that used follow-ups indicated such superiority, noting that relapse occurs in more than 60% of medication-treated patients without maintenance, compared with 30% for cognitive therapy (e.g. Blackburn, Eunson, & Bishop, 1986; Evans et al., 1992).

In a recent review, however, Hollon, Shelton, and Davis (1993) argue that cognitive therapy has rarely been studied over a long follow-up, and might mostly prevent relapse rather than recurrence. Relapse refers to increase of symptoms before complete remission is attained, whereas recurrence refers to the development of new episodes after a period of sustained remission. It has been speculated that the natural course of a depressive episode may last 6-9 months beyond the remission of symptoms, a period during which the person is vulnerable to relapse. Pharmacotherapy might merely suppress the symptoms in the short term, and if discontinued after remission, would leave the patient open to relapse of symptoms. Thus, cognitive therapy might show superiority compared to what amounts to the premature withdrawal of medication.

The test of long-term effectiveness of treatment would be its effects on recurrence, the development of new episodes over an extended period. To date, however, most studies have not followed-up patients long enough to determine such outcomes. The major exception is the TDCRP, in which patients were studied for 18 months after treatment (Shea, Widiger, & Klein, 1992). The study found that recurrence rates did not differ significantly among the treatment groups, with rates ranging from 33% to 50%. Figure 8.1 indicates that the rates of remaining well among those who recovered were relatively low. In view of the generally disappointing long-term outcomes, the investigators argued that 16 weeks of treatment is insufficient for most depressed patients.

Predictors of effectiveness of CBT. A significant gap in the treatment outcome research on CBT is the identification of patient or clinical characteristics that predict good outcomes. Severity of

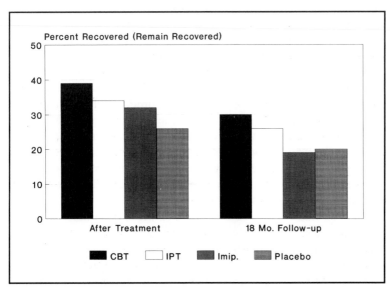

FIG. 8.1. NIMH Treatment of Depression Collaborative Research Program (TDCRP): Outcomes at end of treatment and at 18 months (adapted from Shea et al., 1992).

depression, as indicated earlier, does not seem to predict outcome—other than the observation that the most severely depressed patients tend to improve but continue to have some symptoms following treatment. No studies have evaluated the role of depressive subtypes, although as noted the Thase et al. (1991) study was limited to endogenous depressives, who appeared to have a generally good outcome compared to more mixed patient groups, as reported in the TDCRP. Another important dimension is chronicity of depression. Relatively few studies have evaluated the success of CBT for *dysthymic disorder*, although the handful of small sample studies does seem to indicate positive response to CBT (Markowitz, 1994).

Hollon and Najavits (1988) noted that relatively few studies have investigated predictors of outcome of cognitive therapy. However, in general, outcomes tend to be worse for older female patients who are unemployed, nonendogenous, neurotic, and/or chronically depressed. Other studies indicate that greater Dysfunctional Attitude Scale (DAS) scores predicted worse outcome at termination (Keller, 1983) and at a 1-year follow-up (Simons, Murphy, Levine, & Wetzel, 1986). The TDCRP study attempted to identify individual predictors of outcome (Sotsky et al., 1991). They found that good responses to cognitive therapy were related to lower initial cognitive dysfunction (DAS), briefer duration of the current episode, absence of a family history of affective disorder, later age of onset, and more prior episodes of depression. Simons, Gordon, Monroe, and Thase (1995) recently found that an interaction of DAS and presence of stressful life events predicted response to cognitive-behavioural treatment. Patients did worst who either had high DAS scores and low stress, or low DAS with high stress. The authors speculate that these patterns reflect two different conditions under which cognitive therapy is less effective: one in which the person has high levels of dysfunctional attitudes that are rigid and resistant to change; and the other in which high stress (in the absence of exaggerated dysfunctional cognitions) may reflect realistically difficult stressors that brief therapy cannot resolve. Taken together, the few studies suggest that presence of high levels of cognitive dysfunction do *not* indicate preferential response to cognitive therapy; in fact, if anything, high levels of cognitive dysfunction may predict poor outcome.

Applications of cognitive therapy

The review and meta-analysis studies reported above typically aggregated their analyses across widely different subject populations. For instance, cognitive therapy for depression — in its various forms —

has been applied to depressed elderly populations (e.g. Beutler et al., 1987; Gallagher & Thompson, 1982; Steuer et al., 1984), as well as to juvenile populations (Lewinsohn, Clarke, Hops, & Andrews, 1990, and see later). While cognitive therapy has been most commonly studied in treatments of outpatients, it has also been shown to be more effective (in combination with standard medication treatment) for *inpatients* than standard treatment alone in proportions of treatment responders and maintenance of gains during 6- and 12-month follow-ups (Miller, Norman, & Keitner, 1989). It has been applied to individuals mostly, but also to marital couples, and in groups (and comparisons of group and individual therapy formats have led to discrepant conclusions: e.g. Nietzel, Russell, Hemmings, & Gretter, 1987; Robinson et al., 1990). In a recent study, cognitive-behavioural therapy for depressed spouses performed as well as behavioural marital therapy for couples in alleviating depression (Jacobson et al., 1991). Moreover, the two groups had approximately the same relapse rates (10-15%) at a 1-year follow-up (Jacobson et al., 1993). Cognitive therapy for depression has even been administered by computer and shown to be as effective as therapist-administered treatment, and both treatments were superior to a waiting-list control (Selmi et al., 1990). Recently, Thase et al. (1994) evaluated CBT for male and female patients, and found no differences in overall outcome—although female patients tended to have more severe depression that resulted in somewhat poorer outcomes, while male patients attended fewer therapy sessions than did the women.

Mechanisms of change in cognitive-behavioural therapy

A small number of studies have investigated various components of CBT in an effort to determine its most effective ingredients. Teasdale and Fennell (1982) showed that *changing* chronically depressed patients' distorted thoughts led to improved mood, compared to a control condition in which simply *exploring* the thoughts did not. Persons and Burns (1985) tested the effects of changing automatic negative thoughts and the quality of the patient-therapist relationship in a small sample of anxious and depressed patients. They found a highly significant relationship between the amount of change in negative thoughts and mood change, and also a significant association between mood change and quality of relationship. The two therapeutic ingredients made separate and additive contributions to mood change. DeRubeis and Feeley (1990) explored the predictors of change in 25 depressed patients treated with cognitive therapy. Raters made judgments of the extent to which the therapists created facilitative conditions (e.g. warmth, empathy), developed a positive therapeutic alliance, and adhered to methods of cognitive therapy. The latter ratings were subdivided into two categories, representing "concrete" symptom-focused methods, or "abstract" discussions of principles. Only the specific, concrete interventions predicted improvement; neither abstract discussions nor traditional therapist-client relationship characteristics were related to change.

A recent large-scale study designed to evaluate the components of CBT casts doubt on some of the assumptions of the effective ingredients. Jacobson et al. (1996) randomly assigned 150 depressed outpatients to treatments based on components of CBT: behavioural activation, behavioural activation plus modification of automatic negative thoughts, or "full" CBT which consisted of behavioural activation, modification of negative thoughts, plus changing core dysfunctional schemas. At the end of treatment as well as at a 6-month follow-up, there were no differences between the groups. The behavioural activation component, for example, was as successful in reducing depression and altering negative thinking as was the full CBT. The authors suggest that the behavioural activation component presents a powerful treatment that might be simpler to learn and administer than full CBT—but its success calls into question some of the assumptions of the cognitive-behavioural model. They acknowledge, however, that long-term relapse prevention is the real test of full CBT, and await results from their 2-year follow-up.

The role of cognitive change.   The theory on which CBT is based hypothesises that cognitive change is a mechanism that drives symptom reduction. Several studies have examined general changes in cognition as related to therapy outcome. Rush et al. (1982) found that cognitions did mediate change for cognitive therapy patients but not for those treated with tricyclic antidepressants. On the other hand, Simons, Garfield, and Murphy (1984) and Zeiss, Lewinsohn, and Munoz (1979) found that cognitive changes were as likely to occur in noncognitive interventions as in cognitive therapy. Similarly, the NIMH TDCRP study failed to find mode-specific differences in outcome measures in the different treatment groups (Imber et al., 1990). That is, the Dysfunctional Attitude Scale —a putative measure of the operative mechanism of cognitive therapy —was as likely to show changes in the medication or interpersonal therapy groups as in cognitive therapy.

One interpretation of the nonspecificity of cognitive change in cognitive therapy is that cognitions do not mediate change. Such an interpretation would certainly undercut the primary assumption of cognitive therapy. However, Hollon, DeRubeis, and Evans (1987) argue that such an interpretation is premature in that the analyses fail to make a distinction between cognitions as consequences of therapy and as causal determinants of outcome (causal specificity vs. consequential specificity). Hollon et al. (1987) argue for the plausibility of a causal specificity/consequential nonspecificity model: cognitive therapy produces cognitive changes that cause changes in depression (that in turn also alter cognitive processes), whereas other outcomes of other modalities are not mediated by cognitive changes, even though mood changes they produce may alter cognitions. As Hollon and colleagues (1987) point out, some of the previous studies such as Simons et al. (1984) cannot rule out the possibility that cognitive variables were mediators in one treatment method and consequences of change in the other. Indeed, it is very difficult to develop tests of the competing roles of cognition. Cross-sectional analyses of equivalently powerful treatments make it very difficult to distinguish cause from effect, especially when the depressive symptoms and the mechanisms of effective treatment are reciprocally related. Hollon et al. (1987) urge the use of causal modelling analyses as one way to provide greater clarity concerning mechanisms of change.

An alternative strategy to address the issue was reported by DeRubeis and Feeley (1990), based on the Hollon et al. (1987) study comparing cognitive therapy and imipramine. DeRubeis and Feeley measured the amount of cognitive change (on several questionnaire measures such as the Dysfunctional Attitude Scale, the Hopelessness Scale, and the Attribution Style Questionnaire) from pretreatment to mid-treatment. Regression analyses were then used to predict change in depression from mid-treatment to post-treatment as a function of cognitive change. The results indicated significant group by cognitive change interactions, with the CBT group, but not the medication treatment group, showing changes in depression as a function of cognitive change. The authors conclude that the cognitive processes did play a mediating role in symptom change in cognitive therapy, but that it was not a causally sufficient role. The imipramine treatment group showed as much depression reduction as did the cognitive therapy, but its effects apparently were not mediated by cognitive change. The authors speculate that cognitive therapy is effective to the extent that clients learn to monitor and alter cognitions, apply these techniques and see change occur. Thus early cognitive change predicts further cognitive activity leading to symptom change. On the other hand, pharmacotherapy-treated subjects may alter their cognitions initially (such as beliefs that pills produce change) but that such early cognitive change does not produce later cognitive activity and symptom change.

A question that is related to the issue of cognitive mechanisms of change is whether successful therapy actually alters the core, dysfunctional schemas of depressed patients. Whisman, Miller, Norman, and Keitner (1991) examined cognitions and symptom levels during 6- and 12-month follow-ups in a sample of depressed patients who had been treated as inpatients. Patients who had received cognitive therapy in addition to standard medication and milieu therapy reported significantly less cognitive bias and hopelessness, and lower DAS scores at the 6-month assessment, compared to those having standard treatment only. Notably, however, the groups did not differ on concurrent symptom levels. The authors interpret the results to indicate specific effects due to cognitive therapy, and speculate that such changes may help to explain the success of cognitive therapy in lowering relapse rates during follow-ups.

Barber and DeRubeis (1989) discuss several possible mechanisms of change originally described by Hollon, Evans, and DeRubeis (1988). One model is "accommodation", meaning that cognitive therapy effects a change in the basic cognitive schemata, either in content or process or both. A second possible model of change is "activation–deactivation" in which the maladaptive schemas are not *changed*, but are deactivated while more adaptive schemas are activated. The third model of change is "compensatory skills," the one favoured by Barber and DeRubeis (1989). According to this model, cognitive therapy does not alter the tendency to think in depressive ways, but rather provides a set of skills that help individuals deal with the thoughts when they do arise. The authors indicate that no research has actually evaluated the various possible change mechanisms, but that results of various studies are more logically consistent with the latter. Brewin (1996) provides a review and theoretical discussion of potential mechanisms of change in cognitive-behavioural therapy, distinguishing between those that modify conscious beliefs and those that change unconscious representations in memory.

Interpersonal psychotherapy

Klerman, Weissman, Rounsaville, and Chevron (1984) describe interpersonal psychotherapy (IPT) for depression, based generally on the interpersonal therapy model of Harry Stack Sullivan, founded on the assumption that depression can result from, and lead to, difficulties in the interpersonal relationships among depressed persons and their significant others. IPT, therefore, attempts both to alleviate depressive symptoms and to improve interpersonal functioning by "clarifying, refocusing, and renegotiating the interpersonal context associated with the onset of depression" (Weissman & Klerman, 1990).

Treatment methods

IPT is a brief, weekly time-limited therapy of 12 to 16 weeks, administered individually. Three general phases are described. The first few sessions are devoted to assessment and forming treatment goals. During this phase the patient is taught the "sick role," learning about depression as an illness and receiving encouragement to continue regular activities but without the expectation of performing normally. The second phase identifies and targets interpersonal problems thought to contribute to the depression, and the third, or termination, phase focuses on consolidating what has been learned and anticipating using the skills during times of future difficulty. The therapy is oriented toward the here-and-now, rather than the early origins of depressive vulnerabilities or interpersonal difficulties.

Improving the depressed patient's interpersonal functioning is accomplished by exploring with the patient one or more of the following problem areas commonly associated with the onset of depression: grief, role disputes, role transition, or interpersonal deficits. Information is gathered concerning the patient's functioning in these areas. Klerman et al. (1984) discuss specific goals and procedures to deal with each of the four problem areas. *Grief* refers to abnormal bereavement (distorted, delayed, or chronic) and the need to resolve loss by accurate perception and by replacing some of the lost activities or resources. *Role disputes* and *role transitions* refer to difficulties with others in managing or changing important areas of functioning and self-definition, such as marital conflict, occupational difficulties, dealing with a child moving out of the home, and the like. The therapy aims at identification of the problem, clarification of expectations, negotiation of disputes, and improvement of communication. *Interpersonal deficits* refer to relatively depression-related problems in interpersonal functioning, such as communication or forming friendships; therapy helps the person identify the problem and its consequences and acquire new behaviours. In general, IPT therapists make use of nondirective exploration, encourage expression of affect, teach the patient more effective methods of interpersonal communication, and attempt to alter depressive behaviours through insight, providing information, and role-playing.

As an example of IPT, a woman might report depression occurring in the context of dealing with a rebellious teenage daughter; she feels upset because the teenager is disrespectful and disobedient, and the mother cannot control her actions, causing great worry. The woman also feels that her husband ignores the problem and does not support her emotionally or behaviourally with this conflict. IPT would draw a link between the depression and the woman's goals and disputes in the parental role. Through exploration, support, and problem-solving activity, the therapy helps the woman to see the extent to which her own self-esteem is tied to the approval of her daughter and the daughter's achievements. The mother is encouraged to have realistic expectations for her child's behaviour, and to pursue alternative means of bolstering her own self-esteem (such as working outside the home). She is aided in developing reasonable standards of conduct for her daughter, and consistency in disciplining the girl (instead of being lenient as a way to avoid the child's anger at her).

Evaluating the outcome of IPT

A number of studies have now been conducted examining the efficacy of IPT in the treatment of acute major depression. DiMascio et al. (1979) and Weissman et al. (1979) have demonstrated that IPT is as effective as pharmacotherapy in reducing depressive symptomatology, and is more effective than pharmacotherapy in improving interpersonal functioning. Furthermore, at a 1-year follow-up, patients who had received IPT alone or in combination with pharmacotherapy demonstrated significantly better social functioning than did patients who had received only pharmacotherapy (Weissman et al., 1981). As discussed in greater detail earlier, data from the NIMH Treatment of Depression Collaborative Research Program indicated that IPT was as effective as cognitive therapy and pharmacotherapy in the reduction of depressive symptoms; moreover, patients treated by IPT achieved more rapid gains in interpersonal functioning (Elkin et al., 1989). Interestingly, IPT also had the lowest attrition rate in the study.

With respect to long-term outcomes, as noted earlier, IPT and CBT were approximately equal in percentage of patients who relapsed during the follow-up of the TDCRP, and somewhat superior to medication alone (Shea, Widiger, & Klein, 1992). Frank et al. (1990) tested the use of IPT for the *maintenance* of gains after successful medication treatment, in one of the only maintenance psychotherapy studies reported. Patients were assigned to one of 5 maintenance treatments: monthly IPT alone, monthly IPT combined with high-dosage continuation medication, IPT plus placebo, or placebo alone. The results showed that at 3 years, mean survival time without relapse was greatest for patients in the combined IPT plus medication, and even patients who received only monthly IPT stayed well almost twice as long as patients receiving only placebos (Frank et al., 1990).

Foley et al. (1989) recently reported results of a study designed to compare the effects of IPT conducted with and without the explicit involvement of the depressed person's spouse. Foley et al. (1989) randomly assigned 18 depressed outpatients to either individual IPT or to a newly developed couple format version of IPT. In sessions with the spouse, the functioning of the couple is assessed in 5 general areas: communication, intimacy, boundary management, leadership, and attainment of socially appropriate goals. Treatment was focused on bringing about improved functioning in these areas. Foley et al. (1989) found that the inclusion of the spouse in cases where there are ongoing marital disputes was well received by patients and, even in their small sample, resulted in marginally greater improvement in the marital relationship than did the standard individual format for IPT. On the other hand, both formats produced significant and comparable reductions in symptoms of depression.

In a recent review of the use of IPT, Weissman and Markowitz (1994) indicate that it is being applied to dysthymic disorder, geriatric depressed patients, depressed primary care patients, and even bipolar patients. Since it is not as well-studied as CBT, however, little evidence exists to evaluate the mechanisms of therapeutic action, or the clinical predictors of effectiveness.

Treating children and adolescents

In common with much of the research on depression in children and adolescents, the research is less extensive than with adults, and also its major focus has concerned downward extensions of methods of treatment originally applied to adults. Nevertheless, despite these limitations, there is agreement on the importance of developing effective methods of intervention—and indeed, of prevention.

The treatment procedures that have been empirically evaluated have been based on cognitive and behavioural techniques initially applied to depressed adults—procedures that themselves were derived from presumed etiological mechanisms of maladaptive cognitions and behaviours. Most approaches to treating children and adolescents target several areas of functioning as common difficulties contributing to depressive symptoms in youngsters. These include social and academic difficulties, social problem-solving difficulties including the management of emotions, maladaptive family relationships, poor self-esteem or other dysfunctional cognitions about the self and others. Several of the best-developed methods include specific methods of working with parents, both as a method of increasing their involvement in the child's treatment as well as serving as a focus of intervention where the parent–child or family relationships are themselves contributing to depression.

Cognitive-behavioural treatment of depression in children

Based on methods derived from Beck's treatment of adult depressed patients, Kevin Stark and colleagues have developed a comprehensive programme for children (Stark, Rouse, & Kurowski, 1994). The programme is based on the assumption that depression arises from skills deficits and from cognitive dysfunction; children and their parents are therefore engaged in a psychoeducational process aimed at acquiring more adaptive skills and cognitive problem-solving techniques. The authors encourage the use of a group format, because it enhances learning of social processes and also provides feedback and reinforcement from peers. Stark and colleagues identify interventions for mood disturbance, maladaptive behaviours, cognitive interventions, and parent treatment. These procedures are described more fully by the authors (Stark et al., 1994).

Evaluation of cognitive-behavioural interventions for depressed children. A handful of studies has examined the efficacy of brief, structured treatments for depression in children. An earlier version of Stark's programme described above was evaluated in 29 children ages 9-12 who scored relatively high on a self-report measure of depression administered in schools (Stark, Reynolds, & Kaslow, 1987). The goal of the study was to develop and compare interventions for children based on two models of adult depression. Self-control therapy (Rehm, 1977) proposed that depression results from maladaptive cognitions and behaviours related to processes of setting goals and standards, monitoring performance, and assigning reinforcement. Children were taught cognitive and behavioural skills for setting realistic standards, monitoring, accurately evaluating and interpreting the causes of good and bad outcomes, and providing appropriate positive rewards for success. In the comparison treatment, children were taught behavioural problem solving that included pleasant activity scheduling as well as problem-solving skills. Following 12 sessions administered over a 5-week period, compared with children assigned to a waiting list control, those in both of the active treatments showed significantly improved depression scores that were maintained over an 8-week follow-up.

Kahn, Kehle, Jenson, and Clark (1990) compared 3 brief (approximately 12 sessions) treatments with a waiting-list control group; 68 moderately depressed children in a school setting were randomly assigned. One treatment was cognitive behavioural, consisting of skills for recognising and modifying dysfunctional thoughts and dealing with problem solving and social skills deficits. A second treatment was based on relaxation training and the link between distress and anxiety. The third treatment was called self-modelling, and primarily addressed social skills deficits by creating video tapes of the child performing adaptive social skills in different contexts and encouraging the child to view the tapes. The treatments were successful in reducing depressive symptoms and increasing self-esteem—especially the cognitive-behavioural and relaxation treatments.

In general, research clearly indicates the need for further studies, particularly with clinical populations with evaluations of functioning over a meaningful follow-up. Such studies also need to evaluate the specific ingredients that might be relatively more successful, such as parent training, relaxation training, social skills training and the like. The limited success of the brief treatments nevertheless encourages investigators to pursue structured, cognitive-behavioural interventions.

Interventions with depressed adolescents

Two treatment programmes are briefly noted, one a mixture of cognitive and behavioural techniques, and the other based on the adult interpersonal psychotherapy (IPT) adapted for adolescents.

The Oregon Coping with Depression (CWD) Course

for adolescents. This programme, based on Lewinsohn's cognitive-behavioural model of depression, is an adaptation of the adult Coping with Depression course (Lewinsohn, Steinmetz, Atonuccio, & Teri, 1984). The programme is administered in the form of a course with workbooks, and includes a parent training component. A key focus is on learning effective skills, the lack of which represents maladaptive coping with aversive events and leads to depression. Thus, learning problem-solving skills of various kinds is hypothesised to reduce depression in the short term, but also prevent further episodes in the future. Methods are described in Hops and Lewinsohn (1994), and Lewinsohn, Clarke, Hops, and Andrews (1990).

Youngsters attend classes twice a week for 8 weeks in groups of 4 to 8 adolescents meeting with a group leader. Homework assignments are given regularly, and workbooks provide readings, tasks, and forms to be used for homework. The course includes several specific goals and related tasks or methods. The modules covered in the course include self-monitoring and self-reinforcement training, social skills training (such as conversation techniques, planning social activities), behavioural activation, anxiety reduction, reducing depressogenic cognitions, communication, and problem-solving skills training. A parent-programme includes parents attending a weekly 2-hour session in which they learn the steps that their child is learning, with information on how to encourage the youth's practicing of relevant skills during the course. Parents are also taught the same communication, negotiation, and problem-solving skills the adolescents learn and attend the joint sessions noted above in order to work on issues salient to their particular family.

Empirical evaluation of the Oregon programme.   Lewinsohn et al. (1990) recruited 59 adolescents aged 14–18, who met diagnostic criteria for major, minor, or intermittent depression. The youngsters were randomly assigned to one of 3 conditions: the CWD course for adolescents only; the CWD course for both adolescents and their parents as already described; and a waiting-list control group. Compared to the waiting-list group, the two treatment groups improved significantly on measures of depression, and maintained the gains over a 2-year follow-up. In comparisons between the parent–adolescent and adolescent-only forms of treatment, the parent–adolescent group generally did better, but the differences were not generally significantly different. The parents who were in the programme saw their youngsters more positively at the end of treatment, however. Also, the investigators note that the version of the programme that was evaluated did not include the two parent–child joint sessions. As a result of their belief that the parent-involvement programme is important, they have subsequently strengthened it by including those sessions. A subsequent analysis of the treatment outcomes as a function of severity of depression indicated that the CWD course was equally effective with both mildly and severely depressed youngsters (Rohde, Lewinsohn, & Seeley, 1994).

To date, the only additional empirically evaluated study of depression treatment in adolescents is a project by Reynolds and Coats (1986). They tested a cognitive-behavioural programme for 30 adolescents selected for elevated depression scores administered in their schools. The youngsters were assigned to either 10-session cognitive-behavioural therapy, relaxation training, or a waiting-list control group. Both of the active treatments were superior to the waiting-list control in reducing depression symptoms, but the two treatments did not differ from each other. The major disadvantage of the study was the use of a nonclinical population, so that the generalisability to more severely depressed youngsters is unknown.

Interpersonal psychotherapy for adolescents (IPT-A). Recently, Moreau, Mufson, Weissman, and Klerman (1991) adapted the IPT for adults for use with depressed adolescents. The major adaptations include a focus on the interpersonal problems typically encountered by teenagers within the domains of role disputes and role transitions, bereavement, and interpersonal deficiencies. In addition, they added a fifth area of interpersonal problems, single-parent families, because it is an area often associated with difficult challenges for youth. To date, the IPT-A programme has not been empirically evaluated, although clinical trials are underway.

Prevention of depression in children and adolescents. In view of the risk that elevated symptoms of depression often foretell the development of depressive episodes, Clarke et al. (1995) developed a preventive intervention based on the Coping with Depression programme. Fifteen sessions of 45 minutes each were administered in groups 3 times per week. Adolescents (mean age about 15 years) were selected for high self-reported depression scores on a screening questionnaire. The programme, called the Coping with Stress course, focused largely on cognitive techniques to identify and challenge dysfunctional thoughts. After treatment and over a 12-month follow-up period, those who participated in the course had a significantly lower rate of developing a depression diagnosis (14.5%) compared with those in the control group (25.7%).

Other prevention efforts have mostly involved depressive symptoms rather than prevention of disorders. The few controlled outcome studies include a school-based intervention to enhance academic competence among first-grade children (Kellam et al. 1994) and a school-based programme to teach adaptive cognitions and coping styles to elementary-aged children who are at risk because of high depressive symptoms and/or exposure to parental conflict (Jaycox, Reivich, Gillham, & Seligman, 1994; Seligman, Reivich, Jaycox, & Gillham, 1995). So far these studies report promising results, but their generalisation to clinically significant depression remains to be shown. Finally, Beardslee et al. (1995) have presented preliminary results of an intervention with children at risk for depression due to parental affective disorder. Their intervention consisted of a psycho-educational family-centered approach, in which there was a strong emphasis on a cognitive component; that is, teaching families what depression is, what they can do to encourage resiliencies in their youngsters, and an experiential component emphasising the need for families to understand together the impact of the adversity they've undergone together (i.e. episodes of parental depression). In the recent pilot study, effects of this intervention were compared to a control condition involving parents receiving the cognitive information in a lecture format without direct involvement of the children. Parents reported significant behaviour and attitude changes more frequently in the family-based intervention than in the lecture intervention at 6-month post-intervention (Beardslee et al., 1993) and also 3 years post-intervention (Beardslee et al., 1995).

Summary

- Cognitive-behavioural treatment of depression stresses changing maladaptive cognitions, as well as behavioural methods to reduce depression and to improve dysfunctional skills and problem solving.
- CBT is significantly more effective than no treatment, and appears to equal medication and interpersonal therapy in reducing depression in the acute phase; it may be more successful than medication in long-term prevention of relapse and recurrence though all treatments are somewhat disappointing given that most patients show a return of depression.
- The active ingredients that make CBT successful are unclear given mixed research findings; it remains to be seen whether underlying dysfunctional cognitions are actually altered.
- Interpersonal psychotherapy for depression is based on more traditional methods of exploration and insight, with a particular focus on interpersonal problems as the cause of depression.
- IPT appears to be successful compared to no treatment, and to be the equal of medication and CBT in achieving short-term results. IPT is the only treatment to date that has shown maintenance effects, supporting the value of infrequent sessions over time to prevent recurrences after successful medication treatment.

- Numerous unresolved issues remain, among them whether combined medication and psychotherapy is superior to either alone, whether CBT or IPT work as well with severe depression as does medication, and what individual characteristics predict good response to psychotherapy.
- Both CBT and IPT have been extended to treat depression in child and adolescent populations, and several studies have attempted prevention of depression. Limited evidence is available suggesting effectiveness, but further study is needed.

Further reading

Brown, G.W., & Harris, T.O. (1978). *Social origins of depression*. London: Free Press.

Beck, A.T. (1976). *Cognitive therapy and the emotional disorders*. New York: International Universities Press.

Blatt, S.J., & Zuroff, D. (1992). Inter-personal relatedness and self-definition: Two prototypes for depression. *Clinical Psychological Review, 12*, 527–562.

Coyne, J.C., Burchill, S.A.L., & Stiles, W.B. (1991). An interactional perspective on depression. In C.R. Snyder & D.R. Forsyth (Eds.), *Handbook of social and clinical psychology: The health perspective* (pp.327–349). New York: Pergamon.

Goodwin, F.K., & Jamison, K.R., Eds. (1990). *Manic-depressive illness*. New York: Oxford University Press.

Haaga, D.A., Ernst, D., & Dyck, M.J. (1991). Empirical status of cognitive theory of depression. *Psychological Bulletin, 110*, 215–236.

Hammen, C.L. (1991). *Depression runs in families: The social context of risk and resilience in children of depressed mothers*. New York: Springer-Verlag.

Hammen, C.L., & Rudolph, K. (1996). Childhood depression. In E.J. Mash & R.A. Barkley (Eds.), *Child psychopathology*. (pp.153–195). New York: Guilford.

Hollon, S.D., Shelton, R.C., & Davis, D.D. (1993). Cognitive therapy for depression: Conceptual issues and clinical efficacy. *Journal of Consulting and Clinical Psychology, 61*, 270–275.

Kaslow, N.J., Deering, C.G., & Racusin, G.R. (1994). Depressed children and their families. *Clinical Psychology Review, 14*, 39–59.

Nolen-Hoeksema, S.N., & Girgus, J.S. (1994). The emergence of gender differences in depression during adolescence. *Psychological Bulletin, 115*, 424–443.

Paykel, E.S. (Ed.) (1992). *Handbook of affective disorders* (2nd Ed.). New York: Guilford.

Seligman, M.E., Reivich, K., Jaycox, L., & Gillham, J. (1995). *The optimistic child*. Boston, MA: Houghton-Mifflin.

Teasdale, J.D., & Barnard, P.J. (1993). *Affect, cognition and change: Re-modelling depressive thought*. Hove, UK: Lawrence Erlbaum Associates Ltd.

Thase, M.E., & Howland, R. (1995). Biological processes in depression: An updated review and integration. In E.E. Beckham & W.R. Leber (Eds.), *Handbook of depression* (2nd ed., pp.213–279). New York: Guilford.

References

Abramson, L.Y., & Alloy, L.B. (1992). A consensus conference without our consensus. *Psychological Inquiry, 3,* 225–277.

Abramson, L.Y., Alloy, L.B., & Metalsky, G.I. (1989). Hopelessness depression: A theory-based subtype of depression. *Psychological Review, 96,* 358–372.

Abramson, L.Y., Seligman, M.E.P., & Teasdale, J.D. (1978). Learned helplessness in humans: Critique and reformulation. *Journal of Abnormal Psychology, 87,* 49–74.

Akiskal, H.S. (1982). Factors associated with incomplete recovery in primary depressive illness. *Journal of Clinical Psychiatry, 43,* 266–271.

Akiskal, H.S., Maser, J.D., Zeller, P.J., Endicott, J., Coryell, W., Keller, M.B., Warshaw, M., Clayton, P.J., & Goodwin, F.K. (1995). Switching from "unipolar" to bipolar II: An 11–year prospective study of clinical and temperamental predictors in 559 patients. *Archives of General Psychiatry, 52,* 114–123.

Allgood-Merten, B., Lewinsohn, P.M., & Hops, H. (1990). Sex differences and adolescent depression. *Journal of Abnormal Psychology, 99,* 55–63.

Alloy, L.B., & Abramson, L.Y. (1979). Judgment of contingency in depressed and nondepressed students: Sadder but wiser? *Journal of Experimental Psychology: General, 108,* 441–485.

Ambrosini, P., Bianchi, M., Rabinovich, H., & Elia, J. (1993). Antidepressant treatments in children and adolescents: I. Affective disorders. *Journal of the American Academy of Child and Adolescent Psychiatry, 32,* 1–6.

American Psychiatric Association. (1994). *Diagnostic and statistical manual of mental disorders* (4th ed.). Washington, DC: Author.

Anderson, C.A., & Hammen, C.L. (1993). Psychosocial outcomes of children of unipolar depressed, bipolar, medically ill, and normal women: A longitudinal study. *Journal of Consulting and Clinical Psychology, 61,* 448–454.

Andrews, B., & Brown, G.W. (1988). Social support, onset of depression and personality: An exploratory analysis. *Social Psychiatry and Psychiatric Epidemiology, 23,* 99–108.

Andrews, B., & Brown, G.W. (1995). Stability and change in low self-esteem: The role of psychosocial factors. *Psychological Medicine, 25,* 23–31.

Andrews, B., Brown, G.W., & Creasey, L. (1990). Intergenerational links between psychiatric disorder in mothers and daughters: The role of parenting experiences. *Journal of Child Psychology and Psychiatry, 31,* 1115–1129.

Andrews, B., Valentine, E.R., & Valentine, J.D. (1994). Depression and eating disorders following abuse in childhood in two generations of women. *British Journal of Clinical Psychology, 33,* 1–16.

Aneshensel, C.S., Frerichs, R.R., & Clark, V.A. (1981). Family roles and sex differences in depression. *Journal of Health and Social Behavior, 22,* 379–393.

Angold, A., & Costello, E.J. (1993). Depressive comorbidity in children and adolescents: Empirical, theoretical, and methodological issues. *American Journal of Psychiatry, 150,* 1779–1791.

Angold, A., & Rutter, M. (1992). Effects of age and pubertal status on depression in a large clinical sample. *Development and Psychopathology, 4,* 5–28.

Angst, J. (1984, April). *A prospective study on the course of affective disorders.* Paper presented at the National Institute of Mental Health Consensus Development Conference, Washington, DC.

Angst, J., Baastrup, P.C., Grof, P., Hippius, H., Poeldinger, W., & Weiss, P. (1973). The course of monopolar depression and bipolar psychoses. *Psychiatrie, Neurologie et Neurochirurgie, 76,* 246–254.

Anthony, J.C., Folstein, M., Romanoski, A.J., Von Korff, M.R., Nestadt, G.R., Chahal, R., Merchant, A., Brown, C.H., Shapiro, S., Kramer, M., & Gruenberg, E.M. (1985). Comparison of the Lay Diagnostic Interview Schedule and a standardized psychiatric diagnosis. *Archives of General Psychiatry, 42,* 667–675.

APA Task Force on Laboratory Tests in Psychiatry. (1987). The dexamethasone suppression test: An overview of its current status in psychiatry. *American Journal of Psychiatry, 144,* 1253–1262.

Apter, A., Ratzoni, G., King, R., Weizman, A., Iancu, I., Binder, M., & Riddle, M. (1994). Fluvoxamine open-label treatment of adolescent inpatients with obsessive compulsive disorder or depression. *Journal of the American Academy of Child and Adolescent Psychiatry, 33,* 342–348.

Arieti, S., & Bemporad, J. (1980). The psychological organization of depression. *American Journal of Psychiatry, 137,* 1360–1365.

Armsden, G.C., McCauley, E., Greenberg, M.T., Burke, P.M., & Mitchell, J.R. (1990). Parent and peer attachment in early adolescent depression. *Journal of Abnormal Child Psychology, 18,* 683–697.

Asarnow, J.R., & Bates, S. (1988). Depression in child psychiatric inpatients: Cognitive and attributional patterns. *Journal of Abnormal Child Psychology, 16,* 601–615.

Asarnow, J.R., Goldstein, M.J., Tompson, M., & Guthrie, D. (1993). One-year outcomes of depressive disorders in child psychiatric in-patients: Evaluation of the prognostic power of a brief measure of expressed emotion. *Journal of Child Psychology and Psychiatry, 34,* 129–137.

Aseltine, R.H., Gore, S., & Colten, M.E. (1994). Depression and the social developmental context of adolescence. *Journal of Personality and Social Psychology, 67,* 252–263.

Barber, J.P., & DeRubeis, R.J. (1989). On second thought: Where the action is in cognitive therapy for depression. *Cognitive Therapy and Research, 13,* 441–457.

Barlow, D.H. (1988). *Anxiety and its disorders: The nature and treatment of anxiety and panic.* New York: Guilford.

Barnett, P.A., & Gotlib, I.H. (1988). Psychosocial functioning and depression: Distinguishing among antecedents, concomitants, and consequences. *Psychological Bulletin, 104,* 97–126.

Beardslee, W.R., Salt, P., Porterfield, K., Rothberg, P.C., van de Velde, P., Swatling, S., Hoke, L., Moilanen, D.L., & Wheelock, I. (1993). Comparison of preventive interventions for families with parental affective disorder. *Journal of the American Academy of Child and Adolescent Psychiatry, 32,* 254–263.

Beardslee, W.R., Schultz, L.H., & Selman, R.L. (1988). Level of social-cognitive development, adaptive functioning, and DSM-III diagnoses in adolescent offspring of parents with affective disorders: Implication of the development of the capacity for mutuality. *Developmental Psychology, 23,* 807–815.

Beardslee, W.R., Wright, E., Rothberg, P.C., Salt, P., & Versage, E. (1995). *Response of families to two preventive intervention strategies: Long-term differences in behavior and attitude change.* Manuscript submitted for publication.

Beardsley, R.S., Gardocki, G.J., Larson, D.B., & Hidalgo, J. (1988). Prescribing of psychotropic medication.

Bebbington, P.E. (1987). Marital status and depression: A study of English national admission statistics. *Acta Psychiatrica Scandanavica, 75,* 640–650.

Bebbington, P.E., Hurry, J., & Tennant, C.T. (1988). Adversity and the symptoms of depression. *International Journal of Social Psychiatry, 34,* 163–171.

Beck, A.T. (1967). *Depression: Clinical, experimental, and theoretical aspects.* New York: Harper & Row.

Beck, A.T. (1983). Cognitive therapy of depression: New perspectives. In P.J. Clayton & J.E. Barrett (Eds.), *Treatment of depression: Old controversies and new approaches.* New York: Raven.

Beck, A.T., Brown, G.P., Steer, R.A., Eidelson, J.I., & Riskind, J.H. (1987). Differentiating anxiety and depression: A test of the cognitive content-specificity hypothesis. *Journal of Abnormal Psychology, 96,* 179–183.

Beck, A.T., & Freeman, A. (1990). *Cognitive therapy of personality disorders.* New York: Guilford.

Beck, A.T., Rush, A.J., Shaw, B., & Emery, G. (1979). *Cognitive therapy of depression.* New York: Guilford.

Beck, A.T., Steer, R.A., Epstein, N.B., & Brown, G.P. (1990). Beck Self-Concept Test. *Psychological Assessment, 2,* 191–197.

Beck, A.T., Steer, R.A., & Garbin, M.G. (1988). Psychometric properties of the Beck Depression Inventory: Twenty-five years of evaluation. *Clinical Psychology Review, 8,* 77–100.

Beck, A.T., Ward, C.H., Mendelsohn, M., Mock, J., & Erbaugh, J. (1961). An inventory for measuring depression. *Archives of General Psychiatry, 4,* 561–571.

Becker, R.E., Heimberg, R.G., & Bellack, A.S. (1987). *Social skills training treatment for depression.* New York, Pergamon.

Belle, D. (1990). Poverty and women's mental health. *American Psychologist, 45,* 385–389.

Belsher, G., & Costello, C.G. (1988). Relapse after recovery from unipolar depression: A critical review. *Psychological Bulletin, 104,* 84–96.

Berman, A.L., & Jobes, D. (1991). *Adolescent suicide: Assessment and intervention.* Washington, DC: American Psychological Association.

Bernet, C.Z., Ingram, R.E., & Johnson, B.R. (1993). Self-esteem. In C.G. Costello (Ed.), *Symptoms of depression* (pp.141–159). New York: Wiley.

Berti Ceroni, G., Neri, C., & Pezzoli, A. (1984). Cronicity in major depression: A naturalistic prospective study. *Journal of Affective Disorders, 7,* 123–132.

Beutler, L.E., Scogin, F., Kirkish, P., Schretlen, D., Corbishley, A., Hamblin, D., Meredith, K., Potter, R., Bamford, C.R., & Levenson, A.I. (1987). Group cognitive therapy and alprazolam in the treatment of depression in older adults. *Journal of Consulting and Clinical Psychology, 55,* 550–556.

Bifulco, A.T., Brown, G.W., & Adler, Z. (1991). Early sexual abuse and clinical depression in adult life. *British Journal of Psychiatry, 159,* 115–122.

Bifulco, A.T., Brown, G.W. & Harris, T.O. (1987). Childhood loss of parent, lack of adequate parental care and adult depression: A replication. *Journal of Affective Disorders, 12,* 115–128.

Billings, A.G., Cronkite, R.C., & Moos, R.H. (1983). Social–environmental factors in unipolar depression: Comparisons of depressed patients and nondepressed controls. *Journal of Abnormal Psychology, 93,* 119–133.

Billings, A.G., & Moos, R.H. (1982). Psychosocial theory and research on depression: An integrative framework and review. *Clinical Psychology Review, 2,* 213–237.

Billings, A.G., & Moos, R.H. (1983). Comparisons of children of depressed and nondepressed parents: A social-environment perspective. *Journal of Abnormal Child Psychology, 11,* 463–485.

Billings, A.G., & Moos, R.H. (1984). Coping, stress, and social resources among adults with unipolar depression. *Journal of Personality and Social Psychology, 46,* 877–891.

Billings, A.G., & Moos, R.H. (1985a). Life stressors and social resources affect posttreatment outcomes among depressed patients. *Journal of Abnormal Psychology, 94,* 140–153.

Billings, A.G., & Moos, R.H. (1985b). Psychosocial processes of remission in unipolar depression: Comparing depressed patients with matched community controls. *Journal of Consulting and Clinical Psychology, 53,* 314–325.

Blackburn, I.M., Eunson, K, & Bishop, S. (1986). A two-year naturalistic follow-up of depressed patients treated with cognitive therapy, pharmaco-therapy, and a combination of both. *Journal of Affective Disorders, 10,* 67–75.

Blackburn, I.M., Jones, S., & Lewin, R.J.P. (1986). Cognitive style in depression. *British Journal of Clinical Psychology, 25,* 241–251.

Bland, R.C., Newman, S.C., & Orn, H. (1986). Recurrent and nonrecurrent depression: A family study. *Archives of General Psychiatry, 43,* 1085–1089.

Blatt, S.J. (1974). Levels of object representation in anaclitic and introjective depression. *Psychoanalytic Study of the Child, 29,* 107–157.

Blatt, S.J., & Homann, E. (1992). Parent–child interaction in the etiology of dependent and self-critical depression. *Clinical Psychology Review, 12,* 47–91.

Blatt, S.J., Quinlan, D.M., Chevron, E., McDonald, C., & Zuroff, D.C. (1982). Dependency and self-criticism: Psychological dimensions of depression. *Journal of Consulting and Clinical Psychology, 50,* 113–124.

Blatt, S.J., Wein, S.J., Chevron, E., & Quinlan, D.M. (1979). Parental representations and depression in normal young adults. *Journal of Abnormal Psychology, 88,* 388–397.

Blatt, S.J., & Zuroff, D.C. (1992). Interpersonal relatedness and self-definition: Two prototypes for depression. *Clinical Psychology Review, 12,* 527–562.

Blazer, D.G., Kessler, R.C., McGonagle, K.A., & Swartz, M.S. (1994). The prevalence and distribution of major depression in a national community sample: The national comorbidity survey. *American Journal of Psychiatry, 151,* 979–986.

Blazer, D.G., Swartz, M., Woodbury, M., Manton, K.G., Hughes, D., & George, L.K. (1988). Depressive symptoms and depressive diagnoses in a community population. *Archives of General Psychiatry, 45,* 1078–1084.

Blehar, M.C., Weissman, M.M., Gerson, E.S., & Hirschfeld, R.M.A. (1988). Family and genetic studies of affective disorders. *Archives of General Psychiatry, 45,* 289–292.

Bornstein, R.F. (1992). The dependent personality: Developmental, social, and clinical perspectives. *Psychological Bulletin, 112,* 3–23.

Bosscher, R. (1993). Running and mixed physical exercises with depressed psychiatric patients. *International Journal of Sport Psychology, 24,* 170–184.

Boulos, C., Kutcher, S., Gardner, D., & Young, E. (1992). An open naturalistic trial of fluoxetine in adolescents and young adults with treatment-resistant major depression. *Journal of Child and Adolescent Psychopharmacology, 2*, 103–111.

Bower, G.H. (1981). Mood and memory. *American Psychologist, 36*, 129–148.

Bowlby, J. (1978). *Attachment and loss: Vol. 2. Separation: Anxiety and anger.* Harmondsworth, UK: Penguin.

Bowlby, J. (1981). *Attachment and loss: Vol. 3. Loss: Sadness and depression.* Harmondsworth, UK: Penguin.

Bradley, B., & Mathews, A. (1983). Negative self-schemata in clinical depression. *British Journal of Clinical Psychology, 22*, 173–182.

Breslau, N., Davis, G.C., & Prabucki, K. (1988). Depressed mothers as informants in family history research: Are they accurate? *Psychiatry Research, 24*, 345–359.

Brewin, C.R. (1996). Theoretical foundations of cognitive–behavioral therapy for anxiety and depression. *Annual Review of Psychology, 47*, 33–57.

Brewin, C.R., Andrews, B., & Gotlib, I.H. (1993). Psychopathology and early experience: A reappraisal of retrospective reports. *Psychological Bulletin, 113*, 82–98.

Brewin, C.R., Firth-Cozens, J., Furnham, A., & McManus, C. (1992). Self-criticism in adulthood and recalled child experience. *Journal of Abnormal Psychology, 101*, 561–566.

Broadhead, W.E., Blazer, D.G., George, L.K., & Tse, C.K. (1990). Depression, disability days, and days lost from work in a prospective epidemiologic survey. *Journal of the American Medical Association, 264*, 2524–2528.

Brooks-Gunn, J, & Warren, M.P. (1989). Biological and social contributions to negative affect in young adolescent girls. *Child Development, 60*, 40–55.

Brown, D.R., Ahmed, F., Gary, L.E., & Milburn, N.G. (1995). Major depression in a community sample of African Americans. *American Journal of Psychiatry, 152*, 373–378.

Brown, G.R., & Anderson, B. (1991). Psychiatric morbidity in adult inpatients with childhood histories of sexual and physical abuse. *American Journal of Psychiatry, 148*, 55–61.

Brown, G.W., Andrews, B., Harris, T.O., Adler, Z., & Bridge, L. (1986). Social support, self-esteem, and depression. *Psychological Medicine, 16*, 813–831.

Brown, G.W., Bifulco, A.T., & Harris, T.O. (1987). Life events, vulnerability and onset of depression: Some refinements. *British Journal of Psychiatry, 150*, 30–42.

Brown, G.W., & Harris, T.O. (1978). *Social origins of depression: A study of psychiatric disorders in women.* New York: Free Press.

Brown, G.W., & Harris, T.O. (1989). Depression. In G.W. Brown & T.O. Harris (Eds.), *Life events and illness* (pp.49–93). New York: Guilford.

Brown, G.W., & Harris, T.O. (1993). Aetiology of anxiety and depressive disorders in an inner-city population: 1. Early adversity. *Psychological Medicine, 23*, 143–154.

Brown, G.W., Harris, T.O., & Hepworth, C. (1994). Life events and endogenous depression: A puzzle re-examined. *Archives of General Psychiatry, 51*, 525–534.

Brown, G.W., Ni Bhrolchain, M., & Harris, T.O. (1979). Psychotic and neurotic depression: III. Aetiological and background factors. *Journal of Affective Disorders, 1*, 195–211.

Bruce, M.L., Takeuchi, D.T., & Leaf, P.J. (1991). Poverty and psychiatric status: Longitudinal evidence from the New Haven Epidemiologic Catchment Area Study. *Archives of General Psychiatry, 48*, 470–474.

Buchwald, A.M. & Rudick-Davis, D. (1993). The symptoms of major depression. *Journal of Abnormal Psychology, 102*, 197–205.

Burbach, D.J., & Borduin, C.M. (1986). Parent–child relations and the etiology of depression: A review of methods and findings. *Clinical Psychology Review, 6*, 133–153.

Burke, K.C., Burke, J.D., Rae, D., & Regier, D.A. (1991). Comparing age at onset of major depression and other psychiatric disorders by birth cohorts in five US community populations. *Archives of General Psychiatry, 48,* 789–795.

Burke, K.C., Burke, J.D., Regier, D.A., & Rae, D.S. (1990). Age at onset of selected mental disorders in five community populations. *Archives of General Psychiatry, 47,* 511–518.

Burnam, M.A., Stein, J.A., Golding, J.M., Seigel, J.M., Sorenson, S.B., Forsythe, A.B., & Telles, C.A. (1988). Sexual assault and mental disorders in a community population. *Journal of Consulting and Clinical Psychology, 56,* 843–850.

Burns, D.D. (1980). *Feeling good: The new mood therapy.* New York: William Morrow.

Carlson, G.A., & Cantwell, D.P. (1980). Unmasking masked depression in children and adolescents. *American Journal of Psychiatry, 137,* 445–449.

Carlson, G.A., & Kashani, J.H. (1988). Phenomenology of major depression from childhood through adulthood: Analysis of three studies. *American Journal of Psychiatry, 145,* 1222–1225.

Carroll, B.J., Feinberg, M., Greden, J.F., Tarika, J., Albala, A.A., Haskett, R.F., James, N.M., Kronfol, Z., Lohr, N., Steiner, M., de Vigne, J.P., & Young, E. (1981). A specific laboratory test for the diagnosis of melancholia: Standardization, validation, and clinical utility. *Archives of General Psychiatry, 38,* 15–22.

Chakrabarti, S., Kulhara, P., & Verma, S.K. (1992). Extent and determinants of burden among families of patients with affective disorders. *Acta Psychiatrica Scandinavica, 86,* 247–252.

Cicchetti, D., & Schneider-Rosen, K. (1986). An organizational approach to childhood depression. In M. Rutter, C.E. Izard, & P.E. Read (Eds.), *Depression in young people* (pp.71–134). New York: Guilford.

Clark, D.A., Beck, A.T., Brown, G.P. (1989). Cognitive mediation in general psychiatric outpatients: A test of the content-specificity hypothesis. *Journal of Personality and Social Psychology, 56,* 958–964.

Clark, D.C., & Fawcett, J. (1992). Review of empirical risk factors for evaluation of the suicidal patient. In B.M. Bongar (Ed.), *Suicide: Guidelines for assessment, management, and treatment* (pp.16–48). New York: Oxford University Press.

Clark, D.M., & Teasdale, J.D. (1982). Diurnal variation in clinical depression and accessibility of memories of positive and negative experiences. *Journal of Abnormal Psychology, 91,* 87–95.

Clark, L.A., Watson, D., & Mineka, S. (1994). Temperament, personality, and the mood and anxiety disorders. *Journal of Abnormal Psychology, 103,* 103–116.

Clarke, G., Hawkins, W., Murphy, M., Sheeber, L., Lewinsohn, P.M., & Seeley, J.R. (1995). Targeted prevention of unipolar depressive disorder in an at-risk sample of high school adolescents: A randomized trial of a group cognitive intervention. *Journal of the American Academy of Child and Adolescent Psychiatry, 34,* 312–321.

Clarke, G., Lewinsohn, P.M., & Hops, H. (1990). *Adolescent coping with depression course.* Eugene, OR: Castalia Press.

Cloitre, M., Katz, M.M., & Van Praag, H.M. (1993). Psychomotor agitation and retardation. In C.G. Costello (Ed.), *Symptoms of depression* (pp.207–226). New York: Wiley.

Coffey, C.E., Wildinson, W.E., Weiner, R.D., Parashos, I.A., Djang, W.T., Webb, M.C., Figiel, G.S., & Spritzer, C.E. (1993). Quantitative cerebral anatomy in depression: A controlled magnetic resonance imaging study. *Archives of General Psychiatry, 50,* 7–16.

Cohen, P., Cohen, J., Kasen, S., Velez, C.N., Hartmark, C., Johnson, J., Rojas, M., Brook, J., & Streuning, E.L. (1993). An epidemiological study of disorders in late childhood and adolescence: I. Age and gender-specific prevalence. *Journal of Child Psychology and Psychiatry, 34,* 851–867.

Cohn, J.F., Matias, R., Tronick, E., Connell, D., & Lyons-Ruth, K. (1986). Face-to-face interactions of depressed mothers and their infants. In E. Tronick & T. Field (Eds.), *Maternal depression and infant disturbance.* (New Directions for Child Development, No. 34, pp.31–46). San Francisco: Jossey-Bass.

Cole, D.A., & McPherson, A.E. (1993). Relation of family subtypes to adolescent depression: Implementing a new family assessment strategy. *Journal of Family Psychology, 7,* 119–133.

Compas, B.E. (1987). Stress and life events during childhood and adolescence. *Clinical Psychology Review, 7,* 275–302.

Compas, B.E., & Grant, K. (1993, March). *Stress and adolescent depressive symptoms: Underlying mechanisms and processes.* Paper presented at the biennial meeting of the Society for Research in Child Development, New Orleans, LA.

Compas, B.E., Slavin, L.A., Wagner, B.M., & Vannatta, K. (1986). Relationship of life events and social support with psychological dysfunction among adolescents. *Journal of Youth and Adolescents, 15,* 205–221.

Cooper, P.J., & Goodyer, I. (1993). A community study of depression in adolescent girls: Estimates of symptom and syndrome prevalence. *British Journal of Psychiatry, 163,* 369–374.

Copeland, J.R. (1984). Reactive and endogenous depressive illness and five-year outcome. *Journal of Affective Disorders, 6,* 153–162.

Cornell, D.G., Milden, R.S., & Shimp, S. (1985). Stressful life events associated with endogenous depression. *Journal of Nervous and Mental Disease, 173,* 470–476.

Coryell, W., Akiskal, H.S., Leon, A.C., Winokur, G., Maser, J.D., Mueller, T., & Keller, M.B. (1994). The time course of nonchronic major depressive disorder: Uniformity across episodes and samples. *Archives of General Psychiatry, 51,* 405–410.

Coryell, W., Endicott, J., & Keller, M.B. (1990). Outcome of patients with chronic affective disorder: A five-year follow-up. *American Journal of Psychiatry, 147,* 1627–1633.

Coryell, W., Endicott, J., & Keller, M.B. (1991). Predictors of relapse into major depressive disorder in a nonclinical population. *American Journal of Psychiatry, 148,* 1353–1358.

Coryell, W., Endicott, J., & Keller, M.B. (1992). Major depression in a nonclinical sample: Demographic and clinical risk factors for first onset. *Archives of General Psychiatry, 49,* 117–125.

Coryell, W., Scheftner, W., Keller, M.B., Endicott, J., Maser, J.D., & Klerman, G.L. (1993). The enduring psychological consequences of mania and depression. *American Journal of Psychiatry, 150,* 720–727.

Coryell, W., Endicott, J., Maser, J.D., Keller, M.B., Leon, A.C., & Akiskal, H.S. (1995). Long-term stability of polarity distinctions in the affective disorders. *American Journal of Psychiatry, 152,* 385–390.

Coryell, W., Winokur, G., Shea, T., Maser, J.D., Endicott, J., & Akiskal, H.S. (1994). The long-term stability of depressive subtypes. *American Journal of Psychiatry, 151,* 199–204.

Costello, C.G. (1982). Social factors associated with depression: A retrospective community study. *Psychological Medicine, 12,* 329–339.

Costello, E.J., Costello, A.J., Edelbrock, C., Burns, B.J., Dulcan, M.K., Brent, D., & Janiszewski, S. (1988). Psychiatric disorders in pediatric primary care:

Prevalence and risk factors. *Archives of General Psychiatry, 45,* 1107–1116.

Cox, A.D., Puckering, C., Pound, A., & Mills, M. (1987). The impact of maternal depression in young children. *Journal of Child Psychology and Psychiatry and Allied Disciplines, 28,* 917–928.

Coyne, J.C. (1976). Depression and the response of others. *Journal of Abnormal Psychology, 85,* 186-193.

Coyne, J.C. (1992). Cognition in depression: A paradigm in crisis. *Psychological Inquiry, 3,* 232–235.

Coyne, J.C., Kahn, J., & Gotlib, I.H. (1987). Depression. In T. Jacob (Ed.), *Family interaction and psychopathology: Theories, methods, and findings. Applied clinical psychology* (pp.509–533). New York: Plenum.

Coyne, J.C., Kessler, R.C., Tal, M., Turnbull, J., Wortman, C.B., Greden, J.F. (1987). Living with a depressed person. *Journal of Consulting and Clinical Psychology, 55,* 347–352.

Crook, T., & Eliot, J. (1980). Parental death during childhood and adult depression. *Psychological Bulletin, 87,* 252–259.

Crook, T., Raskin, A., & Eliot, J. (1981). Parent–child relationships and adult depression. *Child Development, 52,* 950–957.

Cross-National Collaborative Group (1992). The changing rate of major depression: Cross-national comparisons. *Journal of the American Medical Association, 268,* 3098–3105.

Curry, J.F., & Craighead, W.E. (1990). Attributional style in clinically depressed and conduct disordered adolescents. *Journal of Consulting and Clinical Psychology, 58,* 109–115.

Cutler, S.E., & Nolen-Hoeksema, S.N. (1991). Accounting for sex differences in depression through female victimization: Childhood sexual abuse. *Sex Roles, 24,* 425–438.

Daley, S.E., Hammen, C.L., Burge, D., Davila, J., Paley, B., Lindberg, N., & Herzberg, D. (in press). Predictors of the generation of stressful life events: A longitudinal study of late adolescent women. *Journal of Abnormal Psychology.*

Daniels, D., & Moos, R.H. (1990). Assessing life stressors and social resources among adolescents: Applications to depressed youth. *Journal of Adolescent Research, 5,* 268–289.

Davila, J., Hammen, C.L., Burge, D., Daley, S.E., & Paley, B. (1995). Poor inter-personal problem solving as a mechanism of stress generation in depression among adolescent women. *Journal of Abnormal Psychology, 104,* 592–600.

Delgado, P.L., Price, L.H., Miller, H.L., Salomon, R.M., Aghajanian, G.K., Heninger, G.R., & Charney, D.S. (1994). Serotonin and the neurobiology of depression. *Archives of General Psychiatry, 51,* 865–874.

DeMulder, E.K., & Radke-Yarrow, M. (1991). Attachment with affectively ill and well mothers: Concurrent behavioral correlates. *Development and Psychopathology, 3,* 227–242.

Dent, J., & Teasdale, J.D. (1988). Negative cognition and the persistence of depression. *Journal of Abnormal Psychology, 97,* 29–34.

Depue, R.A., & Monroe, S.M. (1986). Conceptualization and measurement of human disorder and life stress research: The problem of chronic disturbance. *Psychological Bulletin, 99,* 36–51.

DeRubeis, R.J., & Feeley, M. (1990). Determinants of change in cognitive therapy for depression. *Cognitive Therapy and Research, 14,* 469–482.

Devanand, D.P., Dwork, A.J., Hutchinson, E.R., Bolwig, T.G., & Sackeim, H.A. (1994). Does ECT alter brain structure? *American Journal of Psychiatry, 151,* 957–970.

DiMascio, A., Weissman, M.M., Prusoff, B.A., Neu, C., Zwilling, M., & Klerman, G.L. (1979). Differential symptom reduction by drugs and psychotherapy in acute depression. *Archives of General Psychiatry, 36*, 1450–1456.

Dobson, K.S. (1989). A meta-analysis of the efficacy of cognitive therapy for depression. *Journal of Consulting and Clinical Psychology, 57*, 414– 419.

Dobson, K.S., & Segal, Z.V. (1992). Reflections on consensus building and cognitive models of depression. *Psychological Inquiry, 3*, 278–282.

Dobson, K.S., & Shaw, B.F. (1986). Cognitive assessment with major depressive disorders. *Cognitive Therapy and Research, 10*, 13–29.

Dobson, K.S., & Shaw, B.F. (1987). Specificity and stability of self-referent encoding in clinical depression. *Journal of Abnormal Psychology, 96*, 34–40.

Dohr, K.B., Rush, A.J., & Bernstein, I.H. (1989). Cognitive biases in depression. *Journal of Abnormal Psychology, 98*, 263–267,

Dohrenwend, B.P., Shrout, P.E., Link, B.G., Martin, J., & Skodol, A.E. (1986). Overview and initial results from a risk-factor study of depression and schizophrenia. In J.E. Barrett (Ed.), *Mental disorder in the community: Progress and challenges.* New York: Guilford.

Dolan, R.J., Calloway, S.P., Fonagy, P., De Souza, F.V.A., & Wakeling, A. (1985). Life events, depression, and hypothalamic-pituitary-adrenal axis function. *British Journal of Psychiatry, 147*, 429–433.

Downey, G., & Coyne, J.C. (1990). Children of depressed parents: An integrative review. *Psychological Bulletin, 108*, 50–76.

Dykman, B.M., Abramson, L.Y., Alloy, L.B., & Hartlage, S. (1989). Processing of ambiguous and unambiguous feedback by depressed and nondepressed college students: Schematic biases and their implications for depressive realism. *Journal of Personality and Social Psychology, 56*, 431–445.

Dykman, B.M., Horowitz, L.M., Abramson, L.Y., & Usher, M. (1991). Schematic and situational determinants of depressed and nondepressed students' interpretation of feedback. *Journal of Abnormal Psychology, 100*, 45–55.

Eaves, G., & Rush, A.J. (1984). Cognitive patterns in symptomatic and remitted unipolar major depression. *Journal of Abnormal Psychology, 93*, 31–40.

Eckenrode, J., & Gore, S. (1981). Stressful events and social supports: The significance of context. In B. Gottlieb (Ed.), *Social networks and social support* (pp.63–68). Beverly Hills, CA: Sage.

Elkin, I., Parloff, M.B., Hadley, S.W., & Autry, J.H. (1985). National Institute of Mental Health treatment of depression collaborative research program. *Archives of General Psychiatry, 42*, 305–316.

Elkin, I., Shea, T., Watkins, J.T., Imber, S.D., Sotsky, S.M., Collins, J.F., Glass, D.R., Pilkonis, P.A., Leber, W.R., Docherty, J.P., Fiester, S.J., & Parloff, M.B. (1989). National Institute of Mental Health treatment of depression collaborative research program. *Archives of General Psychiatry, 46*, 971–982.

Endicott, J., Spitzer, R.L. (1978). A diagnostic interview: The Schedule for Affective Disorders and Schizophrenia. *Archives of General Psychiatry, 35*, 837–844.

Evans, M.D., Hollon, S.D., DeRubeis, R.J., Piasecki, J.M., Grove, W.M., Garvey, M.J., & Tuason, V.B. (1992). Differential relapse following cognitve therapy and pharmacotherapy for depression. *Archives of General Psychiatry, 49*, 802–808.

Fadden, G., Bebbington, P.E., & Kuipers, L. (1987). Caring and its burdens: A study of the spouses of depressed patients. *British Journal of Psychiatry, 151*, 660–667.

Faedda, G.L., Tondo, L., Teicher, M.H., Baldessarini, R.J., Gelbard, H.A., & Floris, G.F. (1993). Seasonal mood disorders: Patterns of seasonal recurrence in mania and depression. *Archives of General Psychiatry, 50,* 17–23.

Fava, G.A., Grandi, S., Zielezny, M., Canestrari, R., & Morphy, M.A. (1994). Cognitive-behavioral treatment of residual symptoms in primary major depressive disorder. *American Journal of Psychiatry, 151,* 1295–1299.

Fava, M., & Kaji, J. (1994). Continuation and maintenance treatments of major depressive disorder. *Psychiatric Annals, 24,* 281–290.

Fechner-Bates, S., Coyne, J.C., & Schwenk, T.L. (1994). The relationship of self-reported distress to depressive disorders and other psychopathology. *Journal of Consulting and Clinical Psychology, 62,* 350–559.

Feldman, L.A. & Gotlib, I.H. (1993). Social dysfunction. In C.G. Costello (Ed.), *Symptoms of depression* (pp.85–112). New York: Wiley.

Fiske, S.T., & Linville, P.W. (1980). What does the schema concept buy us? *Personality and Social Psychology Bulletin, 6,* 543–557.

Fleming, J.E., & Offord, D.R. (1990). Epidemiology of childhood depressive disorders: A critical review. *Journal of the American Academy of Child and Adolescent Psychiatry, 29,* 571–580.

Fleming, J.E., Offord, D.R., & Boyle, M.H. (1989). Prevalence of childhood and adolescent depression in the community: Ontario Child Health Study. *British Journal of Psychiatry, 155,* 647–654.

Foley, S.H., Rounsaville, B.J., Weissman, M.M., Sholomskas, D., & Chevron, E. (1989). Individual versus conjoint interpersonal psychotherapy for depressed patients with marital disputes. *International Journal of Family Psychiatry, 10,* 29–42.

Ford, D.E., & Kamerow, D.B. (1989). Epidemiologic study of sleep disturbances and psychiatric disorders: An opportunity for prevention? *Journal of the American Medical Association, 262,* 1479–1484.

Fowler, R.C., Rich, C.L., & Young, D. (1986). San Diego suicide study: II. Substance abuse in young cases.*Archives of General Psychiatry, 43,* 962–965.

Frank, E., Anderson, B., Reynolds, C.F., Ritenour, A., & Kupfer, D.J. (1994). Life events and the Research Diagnostic Criteria endogenous subtype: A confirmation of the distinction using the Bedford College methods. *Archives of General Psychiatry, 51,* 519–524.

Frank, E., Kupfer, D.J., & Perel, J.M. (1989). Early recurrence in unipolar depression. *Archives of General Psychiatry, 46,* 397–400.

Frank, E., Kupfer, D.J., Perel, J.M., Cornes, C.L., Jarrett, D.J., Mallinger, A.G., Thase, M.E., McEachran, A.B., & Grochocinski, V.J. (1990). Three-year outcomes for maintenance therapies in recurrent depression. *Archives of General Psychiatry, 47,* 1093–1099.

Frank, E., Kupfer, D.J., Perel, J.M., Cornes, C.L., Jarrett, D.B., Mallinger, A.G., Thase, M.E., McEachran, A.B., & Grochociniski, V.J. (1993). Comparison of full-dose vs. half-dose pharmacotherapy in the maintenance treatment of recurrent depression. *Journal of Affective Disorders, 27,* 139–145.

Frasure-Smith, N., Lesperance, F., & Talajic, M. (1993). Depression following myocardial infarction: Impact on 6-month survival. *Journal of the American Medical Association, 270,* 1819–1825.

Gallagher, D.E., & Thompson, L.W. (1982). Treatment of major depressive disorder in older adult outpatients with brief psychotherapies. *Psychotherapy: Theory, Research, and Practice, 19,* 482–490.

Garber, J., Kriss, M.R., Koch, M., & Lindholm, L. (1988). Recurrent depression in adolescents: A follow-up study. *Journal of the American Academy of Child and Adolescent Psychiatry, 27,* 49–54.

Garrison, C.Z., Jackson, K.L., Marstellar, F., McKeown, R.E., & Addy, C. (1990). A longitudinal study of depressive symptomatology in young adolescents. *Journal of the American Academy of Child and Adolescent Psychiatry, 29,* 581–585.

Garside, R.F., Kay, D.W.K., Wilson, I.C., Deaton, I.D., & Roth., M. (1971). Depressive syndromes and the classification of patients. *Psychological Medicine, 1,* 333–338.

Geller, B., Cooper, T.B., Graham, D., Fetner, H., Marstellar, F., & Wells, J. (1992). Pharmacokinetically designed double-blind placebo-controlled study of nortriptyline in 6- to 12-year-olds with major depressive disorder. *Journal of the American Academy of Child and Adolescent Psychiatry, 31,* 34–44.

Gerlsma, C., Emmelkamp, P.M.G., & Arrindell, W.A. (1990). Anxiety, depression, and perception of early parenting: A meta-analysis. *Clinical Psychology Review, 10,* 251–277.

Gershon, E.S. (1990). Genetics. In F.K. Goodwin & K.R. Jamison (Eds.), *Manic-depressive illness.* New York: Oxford University Press.

Giles, D.E., Jarrett, R., Biggs, M., Guzick, D., & Rush, A.J. (1989). Clinical predictors of recurrence in depression. *American Journal of Psychiatry, 146,* 764–767.

Giles, D.E., Jarrett, R., Rush, A.J., Biggs, M., & Roffwarg, H.P. (1993). Prospective assessment of electroencelographic sleep in remitted major depressives. *Psychiatry Research, 46,* 269–284.

Giles, D.E., Roffwarg, H.P., Dahl, R.E., & Kupfer, D.J. (1992). EEG sleep abnormalities in depressed children: A hypothesis. *Psychiatry Research, 41,* 53–63.

Girgus, J.S., Nolen-Hoeksema, S.N., & Seligman, M.E.P. (1989, August). *Why do sex differences in depression emerge during adolescence?* Paper presented at the 97th Annual Convention of the American Psychological Association, New Orleans, LA.

Gitlin, M.J. (1990). *The psychotherapist's guide to psychopharmacology.* New York: Free Press.

Gitlin, M.J., & Pasnau, R.O. (1989). Psychiatric syndromes linked to reproductive function in women: A review of current knowledge. *American Journal of Psychiatry, 146,* 1413–1422.

Gold, P.W., Goodwin, F.K., & Chrousos, G.P. (1988). Clinical and biochemical manifestations of depression: Relation to the neurobiology of stress. *The New England Journal of Medicine, 319,* 348–419.

Goldstein, R.B., Black, D.W., Nasrallah, A., & Winokur, G. (1991). The prediction of suicide: Sensitivity, specificity, and predictive value of a multivariate model applied to suicide among 1906 patients with affective disorders. *Archives of General Psychiatry, 48,* 418–422.

Goodyer, I., & Cooper, P.J. (1993). A community study of depression in adolescent girls: II. The clinical features of identified disorder. *British Journal of Psychiatry, 163,* 374–380.

Gordon, D., Burge, D., Hammen, C.L., Adrian, C., Jaenicke, C., & Hiroto, D. (1989). Observations of interactions of depressed women with their children. *American Journal of Psychiatry, 146,* 50–55.

Gotlib, I.H. (1984). Depression and general psychopathology in university students. *Journal of Abnormal Psychology, 93,* 19–30.

Gotlib, I.H., & Asarnow, R.F. (1979). Interpersonal and impersonal problem-solving skills in mildly and clinically depressed university students. *Journal of Consulting and Clinical Psychology, 47,* 86–95.

Gotlib, I.H., & Beatty, M.E. (1985). Negative responses to depression: The role of attributional style. *Cognitive Therapy and Research, 9,* 91–103.

Gotlib, I.H., & Hammen, C.L. (1992). *Psychological aspects of depression: Toward a cognitive-interpersonal integration.* Chichester, UK: Wiley.

Gotlib, I.H., & Lee, C.M. (1990). Children of depressed mothers: A review and directions for future research. In C.D. McCann & N.S. Endler (Eds.), *Depression: New directions in theory, research, and practice* (pp.187–208). Toronto: Wall & Thompson.

Gotlib, I.H., Lewinsohn, P.M., & Seeley, J.R. (1995). Symptoms versus a diagnosis of depression: Differences in psychosocial functioning. *Journal of Consulting and Clinical Psychology, 65,* 90–100.

Gotlib, I.H., Lewinsohn, P.M., Seeley, J.R., Rohde, P., & Redner, J.E. (1993). Negative cognitions and attributional style in depressed adolescents: An examination of stability and specificity. *Journal of Abnormal Psychology, 102,* 607–615.

Gotlib, I.H., & McCann, C.D. (1984). Construct accessibility and depression: An examination of cognitive and affective factors. *Journal of Personality and Social Psychology, 47,* 427–439.

Gotlib, I.H., & Meltzer, S.J. (1987). Depression and the perception of social skill in dyadic interaction. *Cognitive Therapy and Research, 11,* 41–53.

Gotlib, I.H., Mount, J.H., Cordy, N.I., & Whiffen, V.E. (1988). Depression and perceptions of early parenting: A longitudinal investigation. *British Journal of Psychiatry, 152,* 24–27.

Gotlib, I.H., & Whiffen, V.E. (1989). Depression and marital functioning: An examination of specificity and gender differences. *Journal of Abnormal Psychology, 98,* 23–30.

Gotlib, I., Whiffen, V.E., Wallace, P., & Mount, J.H. (1991). A prospective investigation of postpartum depression: Factors involved in onset and recovery. *Journal of Abnormal Psychology, 100,* 122–132.

Greenberg, R.P., Greenberg, M.D., Bornstein, R.F., & Fisher, S. (1992). A meta-analysis of antidepressant outcome under "blinder" conditions. *Journal of Consulting and Clinical Psychology, 60,* 664–669.

Group for the Advancement of Psychiatry. (1989). *Suicide and ethnicity in the United States.* New York: Brunner/Mazel.

Haaga, D., Dyck, M., & Ernst, D., (1991). Empirical status of cognitive therapy of depression. *Psychological Bulletin, 110,* 215–236.

Hamilton, E.B., & Abramson, L.Y. (1983). Cognitive patterns and major depressive disorder: A longitudinal study in a hospital setting. *Journal of Abnormal Psychology, 92,* 173–184.

Hamilton, E.B., Hammen, C.L., Minasian, G., & Jones, M. (1993). Communication styles of children of mothers with affective disorders, chronic medical illness, and normal controls: A contextual perspective. *Journal of Abnormal Child Psychology, 21,* 51–63.

Hamilton, M. (1960). A rating scale for depression. *Journal of Neurology, Neurosurgery and Psychiatry, 12,* 56–62.

Hammen, C.L. (1991a). *Depression runs in families: The social context of risk and resilience in children of depressed mothers.* New York: Springer-Verlag.

Hammen, C.L. (1991b). The generation of stress in the course of unipolar depression. *Journal of Abnormal Psychology, 100,* 555–561.

Hammen, C.L. (1992). Cognitions and depression: Some thoughts about new directions. *Psychological Inquiry, 3,* 247–250.

Hammen, C.L. (1995). Stress and depression: Research findings on the validity of an endogenous subtype of depression. *Directions in Psychiatry, 15*, 1–8.

Hammen, C.L., Adrian, C., Gordon, D., Burge, D., Jaenicke, C., & Hiroto, D. (1987). Children of depressed mothers: Maternal strain and symptom predictors of dysfunction. *Journal of Abnormal Psychology, 96*, 190–198.

Hammen, C.L., Burge, D., Burney, E., & Adrian, C. (1990). Longitudinal study of diagnoses in children of women with unipolar and bipolar affective disorder. *Archives of General Psychiatry, 47*, 1112–1117.

Hammen, C.L., Burge, D., Daley, S.E., Davila, J., Paley, B., & Rudolph, K.D. (1995). Interpersonal attachment cognitions and prediction of symptomatic responses to interpersonal stress. *Journal of Abnormal Psychology, 104*, 436–443.

Hammen, C.L., & Compas, B.E. (1994). Unmasking unmasked depression in children and adolescents: The problem of comorbidity. *Clinical Psychology Review, 14*, 585–603.

Hammen, C.L., Davila, J., Brown, G.P., Gitlin, M.J., & Ellicott, A. (1992). Stress as a mediator of the effects of psychiatric history on severity of unipolar depression. *Journal of Abnormal Psychology, 101*, 45–52.

Hammen, C.L., Ellicott, A., Gitlin, M.J., & Jamison, K.R. (1989). Sociotropy/autonomy and vulnerability to specific life events in unipolar and bipolar patients. *Journal of Abnormal Psychology, 98*, 154–160.

Hammen, C.L., & Krantz, S.E. (1985). Measures of psychological processes in depression. In E.E. Beckham & W.R. Leber (Eds.), *Handbook of depression: Treatment, assessment, and research* (pp.408–444). Homewood, IL: Dorsey.

Hammen, C.L., Marks, T., Mayol, A., & deMayo, R. (1985). Depressive self-schemas, life stress, and vulnerability to depression. *Journal of Abnormal Psychology, 94*, 308–319.

Hammen, C.L., & Peters, S.D. (1978). Interpersonal consequences of depression: Responses to men and women enacting a depressed role. *Journal of Abnormal Psychology, 87*, 322–332.

Hammen, C.L., & Rudolph, K.D. (1996). Childhood depression. In E.J. Mash & R.A. Barkley (Eds.), *Child psychopathology* (pp.153–195). New York: Guilford.

Harlow, H.F., & Suomi, S.J. (1974). Induced depression in monkeys. *Behavioral Biology, 12*, 273–296.

Harrington, R. (1992). Annotation: The natural history and treatment of child and adolescent affective disorders. *Journal of Child Psychology and Psychiatry, 33*, 1287–1302.

Harrington, R., Fudge, H., Rutter, M., Pickles, A., & Hill, J. (1990). Adult outcomes of childhood and adolescent depression: Psychiatric status. *Archives of General Psychiatry, 47*, 465–473.

Harris, T., Brown, G.W., & Bifulco, A.T. (1986). Loss of parent in childhood and adult psychiatric disorder: The role of lack of adequate parental care. *Psychological Medicine, 16*, 641–659.

Haslam, N., & Beck, A.T. (1994). Subtyping major depression: A taxometric analysis. *Journal of Abnormal Psychology, 103*, 686–692.

Hays, R.D., Wells, K.B., Sherbourne, C.D., Rogers, W., & Spritzer, K. (1995). Functioning and well-being outcomes of patients with depression compared with chronic general medical illnesses. *Archives of General Psychiatry, 52*, 11–19.

Hedlund, S., & Rude, S.S. (1995). Evidence of latent depressive schemas in formerly depressed individuals. *Journal of Abnormal Psychology, 104*, 517–525.

Hellerstein, D.J., Yanowitch, P., Rosenthal, J., Samstag, L.W., Maurer, M., Kasch, K., Burrows, L., Poster, M., Cantillon, M., & Winston, A. (1993). A randomized double-blind study of fluoxetine versus placebo in the treatment of dysthymia. *American Journal of Psychiatry, 150*, 1169–1175.

Henriksson, M.M., Aro, H.M., Marttunen, M.J., Heikkinen, M.E, Isometsa, E.T., Kuoppasalmi, K.I., & Lonnqvist, J.K. (1993). Mental disorders and comorbidity in suicide. *American Journal of Psychiatry, 150*, 935–940.

Henriques, J.B., & Davidson, R.J. (1990). Regional brain electrical asymmetries discriminate between previously depressed and healthy control subjects. *Journal of Abnormal Psychology, 99*, 22–31.

Henriques, J.B., & Davidson, R.J. (1991). Left frontal hypoactivation in depression. *Journal of Abnormal Psychology, 100*, 535–545.

Hermann, R.C., Dorwart, R.A., Hoover, C.W., & Brody, J. (1995). Variation in ECT use in the United States. *American Journal of Psychiatry, 152*, 869–875.

Hinchliffe, M., Hooper, D., & Roberts, F.J. (1978). *The melancholy marriage.* New York: Wiley.

Hirsch, B.J., Moos, R.H., & Reischl, T.M. (1985). Psychosocial adjustment of adolescent children of a depressed, arthritic, or normal parent. *Journal of Abnormal Psychology, 94*, 154–164.

Hirschfeld, R.M.A. (1994). Guidelines for the long-term treatment of depression. *Journal of Clinical Psychiatry, 55*, 61–69.

Hirschfeld, R.M.A., Klerman, G.L., Andreasen, N.C., Clayton, P.J., & Keller, M.B. (1986). Psycho-social predictors of chronicity in depressed patients. *British Journal of Psychiatry, 148*, 648–654.

Hirschfeld, R.M.A., Klerman, G.L., Clayton, P.J., & Keller, M.B. (1983). Personality and depression: Empirical findings. Archives of General Psychiatry, 40, 993–998.

Hokanson, J.E., Hummer, J.T., & Butler, A.C. (1991). Interpersonal perceptions by depressed college students. *Cognitive Therapy and Research, 15*, 443–457.

Hokanson, J.E., Rubert, M.P., Welker, R.A., Hollander, G.R., & Hedeen, C. (1989). Interpersonal concomitants and antecedents of depression among college students. *Journal of Abnormal Psychology, 98*, 209–217.

Holahan, C.J., & Moos, R.H. (1991). Life stressors, personal and social resources, and depression: A 4-year structural model. *Journal of Abnormal Psychology, 100*, 31–38.

Hollon, S.D., DeRubeis, R.J., & Evans, M.D. (1987). Causal mediation of change in treatment for depression: Discriminating between nonspecificity and noncausality. *Psychological Bulletin, 102*, 139–149.

Hollon, S.D., DeRubeis, R.J., Evans, M.D., & Wiemer, M.J. (1992). Cognitive therapy and pharmacotherapy for depression: Singly and in combination. *Archives of General Psychiatry, 49*, 774–781.

Hollon, S.D., Evans, M.D., & DeRubeis, R.J. (1988). Preventing relapse following treatment for depression: The cognitive pharmacotherapy project. In T.M. Field, P.M. McCabe, & N. Schneiderman (Eds.), *Stress and coping across development.* (pp.227–243). Hillsdale, NJ: Lawrence Erlbaum Associates Inc.

Hollon, S.D., Evans, M.D., & DeRubeis, R.J. (1990). Cognitive mediation of relapse prevention following treatment for depression: Implications of differential risk. In R.E. Ingram (Ed.), *Contemporary psychological approaches to depression* (pp.117–136). New York: Plenum.

Hollon, S.D., Kendall, P.C., & Lumry, A. (1986). Specificity of depressotypic cognitions in clinical depression. *Journal of Abnormal Psychology, 95*, 52–59.

Hollon, S.D., & Najavits, L. (1988). Review of empirical studies on cognitive therapy. In A. Frances & R. Hales (Eds.), *Review of psychiatry* (Vol.7, pp.643–666). Washington, DC: American Psychiatric Press.

Hollon, S.D., Shelton, R.C., & Davis, D. (1993). Cognitive therapy for depression: Conceptual issues and clinical efficacy. *Journal of Consulting and Clinical Psychology, 61*, 270–275.

Hollon, S.D., Shelton, R.C., & Loosen, P.T. (1991). Cognitive therapy and pharmacotherapy for depression. *Journal of Consulting and Clinical Psychology, 59*, 88–99.

Holmes, S.J., & Robins, L.N. (1987). The influence of childhood disciplinary experience on the development of alcoholism and depression. *Journal of Child Psychology and Psychiatry, 28*, 399–415.

Holmes, S.J., & Robins, L.N. (1988). The role of parental disciplinary practices in the development of depression and alcoholism. *Psychiatry, 51*, 24–35.

Holsboer, F. (1992). The hypothalamic-pituitary-adrenocortical system. In E.S. Paykel (Ed.), *Handbook of affective disorders* (2nd ed., pp.267–287). New York: Guilford.

Hooley, J.M., Orley, J., & Teasdale, J.D. (1986). Levels of expressed emotion and relapse in depressed patients. *British Journal of Psychiatry, 148*, 642–647.

Hooley, J.M., & Teasdale, J.D. (1989). Predictors of relapse in unipolar depressives: Expressed emotion, marital distress, and perceived criticism. *Journal of Abnormal Psychology, 98*, 229–237.

Hops, H., & Lewinsohn, P.M. (1994). A course for the treatment of depression among adolescents. In K. Craig, & K.S. Dobson (Eds.), *Anxiety and depression in adults and children* (pp.230–245). Thousand Oaks, CA: Sage.

Hops, H., Lewinsohn, P.M., Andrews, J.A., & Roberts, R.E. (1990). Psychosocial correlates of depressive symptomatology among high school students. *Journal of Clinical Child Psychology, 19*, 211–220.

Horwath, E., Johnson, J., Klerman, G.L., & Weissman, M.M. (1992). Depressive symptoms as relative and attributable risk factors for first-onset major depression. *Archives of General Psychiatry, 49*, 817–823.

Howes, M.J., Hokanson, J.E., & Loewenstein, D.A. (1985). Induction of depressive affect after prolonged exposure to a mildly depressed individual. *Journal of Personality and Social Psychology, 49*, 1110–1113.

Imber, S.D., Pilkonis, P.A., Sotsky, S.M., Elkin, I., Watkins, J.T., Collins, J.F., Shea, M.T., Leber, W.R., & Glass, D.R. (1990). Mode-specific effects among three treatments for depression. *Journal of Consulting and Clinical Psychology, 58*, 352–359.

Ingram, R.E. (1990). Self-focused attention in clinical disorders: Review and a conceptual model. *Psychological Bulletin, 107*, 156–176.

Jacobsen, F.M., Wehr, T.A., Sack, D.A., James, S.P., & Rosenthal, N.E. (1986). Seasonal affective disorder: A review of the syndrome and its public health implications. *American Journal of Public Health, 77*, 57–60.

Jacobson, N.S., Dobson, K.S., Fruzzetti, A.E., Schmaling, K.B., & Salusky, S. (1991). Marital therapy as a treatment for depression. *Journal of Consulting and Clinical Psychology, 59*, 547–557.

Jacobson, N.S., Dobson, K.S., Truax, P.A., Addis, M.E., Koerner, K., Gollan, J.K., Gortner, E., & Prince, S.E. (1996). A component analysis of cognitive behavioral treatment for depression. *Journal of Consulting and Clinical Psychology, 64*, 295–304.

Jacobson, N.S., Fruzzetti, A.E., Dobson, K.S., Whisman, M.A., & Hops, H. (1993). Couple therapy as a treatment for depression: II. The effects of relationship quality and therapy on depressive relapse. *Journal of Consulting and Clinical Psychology, 61,* 516–519.

Jacobson, N.S., & Hollon, S.D. (1996). Cognitive behavior therapy vs. pharmacotherapy: Now that the jury's returned its verdict, it's time to present the rest of the evidence. *Journal of Consulting and Clinical Psychology, 64,* 74–80.

Jaenicke, C., Hammen, C.L., Zupan, B., Hiroto, D., Gordon, D., Adrian, C., & Burge, D. (1987). Cognitive vulnerability in children at risk for depression. *Journal of Abnormal Child Psychology, 15,* 559–572.

Jaycox L.H., Reivich, K.J., Gillham J., & Seligman M.E.P. (1994). Prevention of depressive symptoms in school children. *Behavior Research Therapy, 32,* 801–816.

Jensen, P., Roper, M., Fisher, P., Piacentini, J., Canino, G., Richters, J., Rubio-Stipec, M., Dulcan, M.K., Goodman, S., Davies, M., Rae, D., Shaffer, D., Bird, H., Lahey, B., & Shwab-Stone, M. (1995). Test–retest reliability of the Diagnostic Interview Schedule for Children (DISC 2.1). *Archives of General Psychiatry, 52,* 61–71.

Johnson, J., Weissman, M.M., & Klerman, G.L. (1992). Service utilization and social morbidity associated with depressive symptoms in the community. *Journal of the American Medical Association, 267,* 1478–1483.

Joyce, P.R., & Paykel, E.S. (1989). Predictors of drug response in depression. *Archives of General Psychiatry, 46,* 89–99.

Kahn, J., Kehle,T., Jenson, W., & Clark, E. (1990). Comparison of cognitive-behavioral, relaxation, and self-modeling interventions for depression among middle-school students. *School Psychology Review, 19,* 196–211.

Kahn, J., Coyne, J.C., & Margolin, G. (1985). Depression and marital disagreement: The social construction of despair. *Journal of Social and Personal Relationships, 2,* 447–461.

Kandel, D.B., & Davies, M. (1986). Adult sequelae of adolescent depressive symptoms. *Archives of General Psychiatry, 43,* 255–262.

Kaplan, B.J., Beardslee, W.R., & Keller, M.B. (1987). Intellectual competence in children of depressed parents. *Journal of Clinical Child Psychology, 16,* 158–163.

Kashani, J.H., & Carlson, G.A. (1987). Seriously depressed preschoolers. *American Journal of Psychiatry, 144,* 348–350.

Kashani, J.H., Holcomb, W.R., & Orvaschel, H. (1986). Depression and depressive symptoms in preschool children from the general population. *American Journal of Psychiatry, 143,* 1138–1143.

Kashani, J.H., Rosenberg, T.K., & Reid, J.C. (1989). Developmental perspectives in child and adolescent depressive symptoms in a community sample. *American Journal of Psychiatry, 146,* 871–875.

Kaslow, N.J., Deering, C.G., & Racusin, G.R. (1994). Depressed children and their families. *Clinical Psychology Review, 14,* 39–59.

Kasper, S., Wehr, T.A., Bartko, J.J., Gaist, P.A., & Rosenthal, N.E. (1989). Epidemiological findings of seasonal changes in mood and behavior: A telephone survey of Montgomery County, Maryland. *Archives of General Psychiatry, 46,* 823–833.

Kay, D.W.K., Garside, R.F., Beamish, P., & Roy, J.R. (1969). Endogenous and neurotic syndromes of depression: A factor analytic study of 104 cases: Clinical features. *British Journal of Psychiatry, 115,* 377–388.

Keitner, G.I., Ryan, C.E., Miller, I.W., Kohn, R., Bishop, D.S., & Epstein, N.B. (1995). Role of the family in recovery and major depression. *American Journal of Psychiatry, 152,* 1002–1008.

Kellam S.G., Rebok G.W., Mayer L.S., Ialongo N., & Kalodner C.R. (1994).

Depressive symptoms over first grade and their response to a developmental epidemiologically based preventive trial aimed at improving achievement. *Development and Psychopathology 6,* 463–481.

Keller, K.E. (1983). Dysfunctional attitudes and cognitive therapy for depression.*Cognitive Therapy and Research, 7,* 437–444.

Keller, M.B. (1985). Chronic and recurrent affective disorders: Incidence, course, and influencing factors. In D. Kemali & G. Recagni (Eds.), *Chronic treatments in neuropsychiatry.* New York: Raven.

Keller, M.B. (1988). Diagnostic issues and clinical course of unipolar illness. In A. Frances & R. Hales (Eds.), *Review of psychiatry* (Vol.7, pp.188–212). Washington, DC: American Psychiatric Press.

Keller, M.B., Beardslee, W.R., Lavori, P.W., Wunder, J., Dorer, D.L., & Samuelson, H. (1988). Course of major depression in non-referred adolescents: A retrospective study. *Journal of Affective Disorders, 15,* 235–243.

Keller, M.B., Klerman, G.L., Lavori, P.W., Fawcett, J.A., Coryell, W., Endicott, J. (1982). Treatment received by depressed patients. *Journal of the American Medical Association, 248,* 1848–1855.

Keller, M.B., Lavori, P.W., Endicott, J., Coryell, W., & Klerman, G.L. (1983). "Double depression": Two-year follow-up. *American Journal of Psychiatry, 140,* 689–694.

Keller, M.B., Lavori, P.W., Mueller, T.I., Endicott, J., Coryell, W., Hirschfeld, R.M.A., & Shea, T. (1992). Time to recovery, chronicity, and levels of psychopathology in major depression. *Archives of General Psychiatry, 49,* 809–816.

Keller, M.B., Lavori, P.W., Rice, J., Coryell, W., & Hirschfeld, R.M.A. (1986). The persistent risk of chronicity in recurrent episodes of nonbipolar major depressive disorder: A prospective follow-up. *American Journal of Psychiatry, 143,* 24–28.

Keller, M.B., Shapiro, R.W., Lavori, P.W., & Wolfe, N. (1982). Recovery in major depressive disorder: Analysis with the life table and regression models. *Archives of General Psychiatry, 39,* 905–910.

Kendall, P.C., Hollon, S., Beck, A., Hammen, C.L., & Ingram, R.E. (1987). Issues and recommendations regarding use of the Beck Depression Inventory. *Cognitive Therapy & Research, 11,* 289–299.

Kendler, K.S., Kessler, R.C., Neale, M.C., Heath, A.C., & Eaves, L.J. (1993). The prediction of major depression in women: Toward an integrated etiologic model. *American Journal of Psychiatry, 150,* 1139–1148.

Kendler, K.S., Kessler, R.C., Walters, E.E., MacLean, C., Neale, M.C., Heath, A.C., & Eaves, L.J. (1995). Stressful life events, genetic liability, and onset of an episode of major depression in women. *American Journal of Psychiatry, 152,* 833–842.

Kendler, K.S., Neale, M.C., Kessler, R.C., Heath, A.C., & Eaves, L.J. (1992). A population-based twin study of major depression in women. *Archives of General Psychiatry, 49,* 257–266.

Kendler, K.S., Neale, M.C., Kessler, R.C., Heath, A.C., & Eaves, L.J. (1993). A longitudinal twin study of 1–year prevalence of major depression in women. *Archives of General Psychiatry, 50,* 843–852.

Kessler, R.C., & Magee, W.J. (1993). Childhood adversities and adult depression: Basic patterns of association in a US national survey. *Psychological Medicine, 23,* 679–690.

Kessler, R.C., & McLeod, J.D. (1985). Social support and mental health in community samples. In S. Cohen & S.L. Syme (Eds.), *Social support and health* (pp.219–240). Orlando, FL: Academic Press.

Kiloh, L.G., Andrews, G., Neilson, M., & Bianchi, G.N. (1972). The relationship of the syndromes called endogenous and neurotic depression. *British Journal of Psychiatry, 121*, 183–196.

Klein, D.N., Clark, D.C., Dansky, L., & Margolis, E.T. (1988). Dysthymia in the offspring of parents with primary unipolar affective disorder. *Journal of Abnormal Psychology, 97*, 265–274.

Klein, D.N., Harding, K., Taylor, E.B., & Dickstein, S. (1988). Dependency and self-criticism in depression: Evaluation in a clinical population. *Journal of Abnormal Psychology, 97*, 399–404.

Klein, D.N., & Miller, G.A. (1993). Depressive personality in nonclinical subjects. *American Journal of Psychiatry, 150*, 1718–1724.

Klein, D.N., Riso, L.P., Donaldson, S.K., Schwartz, J.E., Anderson, R.L., Ouimette, P.C., Lizardi, H., & Aronson, T.A. (1995). Family study of early-onset dysthymia. *Archives of General Psychiatry, 52*, 487–496.

Klein, D.N., Taylor, E.B., Dickstein, S., & Harding, K. (1988a). Primary early-onset dysthymia: Comparison with primary nonbipolar nonchronic major depression on demographic, clinical, familial, personality, and socioenvironmental characteristics and short-term outcome. *Journal of Abnormal Psychology, 97*, 387–398.

Klein, D.N., Taylor, E.B., Harding, K., & Dickstein, S. (1988b). Double depression and episodic major depression: Demographic, clinical, familial, personality, and socio-environmental characteristics and short-term outcomes. *American Journal of Psychiatry, 145*, 1226–1231.

Kleinman, A. (1991, April). *Culture and DSM-IV: Recommendation for the introduction and for the overall structure.*
Paper presented at the National Institute of Mental Health-sponsored Conference on Culture and Diagnosis, Pittsburgh, PA.

Klerman, G.L., & Weissman, M.M. (1989). Increasing rates of depression. *Journal of the American Medical Association, 261*, 2229–2235.

Klerman, G.L., Weissman, M.M., Rounsaville, B.J., & Chevron, E. (1984). *Interpersonal psychotherapy of depression.* New York: Basic Books.

Klinger, E. (1993). Loss of interest. In C.G. Costello (Ed.), *Symptoms of depression* (pp.43–62). New York: Wiley.

Kobak, R.R., Sudler, N., & Gamble, W. (1991). Attachment and depressive symptoms during adolescence: A developmental pathways analysis. *Development and Psychopathology, 3*, 461–474.

Kocsis, J.H., Frances, A.J., Voss, C.B., Mann, J.J., Mason, B.J., & Sweeney, J. (1988). Imipramine treatment for chronic depression. *Archives of General Psychiatry, 45*, 253–257.

Kovacs, M. (1983, October 12–15). *DSM-III: The diagnosis of depressive disorders in children: An interim appraisal.* Paper presented at the American Psychiatric Association Invitational Workshop, DSM-III: An Interim Appraisal, Washington, DC.

Kovacs, M., Akiskal, H.S., Gatsonis, C., & Parrone, P.L. (1994). Childhood-onset dysthymic disorder: Clinical features and prospective naturalistic outcome. *Archives of General Psychiatry, 51*, 365–374.

Kovacs, M., Feinberg, T.L., Crouse-Novak, M.A., Paulauskas, S.L., & Finkelstein, R. (1984). Depressive disorders in childhood: I. A longitudinal prospective study of chracteristics and recovery. *Archives of General Psychiatry, 41*, 229–237.

Kraepelin, E. (1921). *Manic-depressive insanity and paranoia.* New York: Arno.

Kugler, J., Seelbach, H., & Kruskemper, G. (1994). Effects of rehabilitation exercise programmes on anxiety and depression in coronary patients: A meta-analysis. *British Journal of Clinical Psychology, 33*, 401–410.

Kupfer, D.J., Frank, E., Perel, J.M., Cornes, C.L., Mallinger, A.G., Thase, M.E., McEachran, A.B., & Grochocinski, V.J. (1992). Five-year outcome for maintenance therapies in recurrent depression. *Archives of General Psychiatry, 49*, 769–773.

Kupfer, D.J., & Thase, M.E. (1983). The use of the sleep laboratory in the diagnosis of affective disorders. *Psychiatric Clinic of North America, 5*, 3–25.

Lafer, B., Sachs, G.S., Labbate, L.A., Thibault, A., & Rosenbaum, J.F. (1994). Phototherapy for seasonal affective disorder: A blind comparison of three different schedules. *American Journal of Psychiatry, 151*, 1081–1083.

Larson, R.W., Raffaelli, M., Richards, M.H., Ham, M., & Jewell, L. (1990). Ecology of depression in late childhood and early adolescence: A profile of daily states and activities. *Journal of Abnormal Psychology, 99*, 92–102.

Lauer, C., Schreiber, W., Holsboer, F., & Krieg, J.C. (1995). In quest of identifying vulnerability markers for psychiatric disorders by all-night polysomnography. *Archives of General Psychiatry, 52*, 145–153.

Lazarus, R.S., & Folkman, S. (1984). *Stress, appraisal, and coping.* New York: Springer.

Lee, C.M., & Gotlib, I.H. (1989a). Clinical status and emotional adjustment of children of depressed mothers. *American Journal of Psychiatry, 146*, 478–483.

Lee, C.M., & Gotlib, I.H. (1989b). Maternal depression and child adjustment: A longitudinal analysis. *Journal of Abnormal Psychology, 98*, 78–85.

Leibenluft, E., & Wehr, T.A. (1992). Is sleep deprivation useful in the treatment of depression? *American Journal of Psychiatry, 149*, 159–168.

Lerer, B., Shapira, B., Calev, A., Tubi, N., Drexler, H., Kindler, S., Lidsky, D., & Schwartz, J.E. (1995). Antidepressant and cognitive effects of twice- versus three-times weekly ECT. *American Journal of Psychiatry, 152*, 564–570.

Lewinsohn, P.M., Antonuccio, D.O., Breckenridge, J., & Teri, L. (1987). *The coping with depression course: A psychoeducational intervention for unipolar depression.* Eugene, OR: Castalia.

Lewinsohn, P.M., Clarke, G., Hops, H., & Andrews, J.A. (1990). Cognitive-behavioral treatment for depressed adolescents. *Behavior Therapy, 21*, 385–401.

Lewinsohn, P.M., Clarke, G., Seeley, J.R., & Rohde, P. (1994). Major depression in community adolescents: Age at onset, episode duration, and time to recurrence. *Journal of the American Academy of Child & Adolescent Psychiatry, 33*, 809–818.

Lewinsohn, P.M., Duncan, E., Stanton, A.K., & Hautzinger, M. (1986). Age at first onset for nonbipolar depression. *Journal of Abnormal Psychology, 95*, 378–383.

Lewinsohn, P.M., Fenn, S., S., Stanton, A.K., & Franklin, J. (1986). Relation of age at onset to duration of episode in unipolar depression. *Journal of Psychology and Aging, 1*, 63–68.

Lewinsohn, P.M., Hoberman, H., & Rosenbaum, M. (1988). A prospective study of risk factors for unipolar depression. *Journal of Abnormal Psychology, 97*, 251–264.

Lewinsohn, P.M., Hops, H., Roberts, R.E., Seeley, J.R., & Andrews, J.A. (1993). Adolescent psychopathology: I. Prevalence and incidence of depression and other DSM-III-R disorders in high school students. *Journal of Abnormal Psychology, 102*, 133–144.

Lewinsohn, P.M., Roberts, R.E., Seeley, J.R., Rohde, P., Gotlib, I.H., & Hops, H. (1994). Adolescent psychopathology: II. Psychosocial risk factors for depression. *Journal of Abnormal Psychology, 103*, 302-315.

Lewinsohn, P.M., Rohde, P., & Seeley, J.R. (1994). Psychosocial risk factors for future adolescent suicide attempts. *Journal of Consulting and Clinical Psychology, 62*, 297-305.

Lewinsohn, P.M., Rohde, P., & Seeley, J.R. (1995). Adolescent psychopathology: III. The clinical consequences of comorbidity. *Journal of the American Academy of Child and Adolescent Psychiatry, 34*, 510-519.

Lewinsohn, P.M., Rohde, P., Seeley, J.R., & Fischer, S.A. (1993). Age-cohort changes in the lifetime occurrence of depression and other mental disorders. *Journal of Abnormal Psychology, 102*, 110-120.

Lewinsohn, P.M., Rohde, P., Seeley, J.R., & Hops, H. (1991). Comorbidity of unipolar depression: I. Major depression with dysthymia. *Journal of Abnormal Psychology, 100*, 205-213.

Lewinsohn, P.M., & Rosenbaum, M. (1987). Recall of parental behavior by acute depressives, and nondepressives. *Journal of Personality and Social Psychology, 52*, 611-619.

Lewinsohn, P.M., Steinmetz, J.L., Antonuccio, D.O., & Teri, L. (1984). Group therapy for depression: The coping with depression course. *International Journal of Mental Health, 13*, 8-13.

Lewinsohn, P.M., Steinmetz, J.L., Larson, D.W., & Franklin, J. (1981). Depression-related cognitions: Antecedent or consequence? *Journal of Abnormal Psychology, 90*, 213-219.

Lewinsohn, P.M., Sullivan, J.M., & Grosscup, S.J. (1980). Changing reinforcing events: An approach to the treatment of depression. *Psychotherapy: Theory, Research, and Practice, 47*, 322-334.

Lewinsohn, P.M., Zeiss, A., & Duncan, E. (1989). Probability of relapse after recovery from an episode of depression. *Journal of Abnormal Psychology, 98*, 107-116.

Lizardi, H., Klein, D.N., Ouimette, P.C., Riso, L.P., Anderson, R.L., & Donaldson, S.K. (1995). Reports of the childhood home environment in early-onset dysthymia and episodic major depression. *Journal of Abnormal Psychology, 104*, 132-139.

Lloyd, C. (1980a). Life events and depressive disorder reviewed: 1. Events as predisposing factors. *Archives of General Psychiatry, 37*, 529-535.

Lloyd, C. (1980b). Life events and depressive disorder reviewed: 2. Events as precipitating factors. *Archives of General Psychiatry, 37*, 541-548.

Lyons-Ruth, K., Zoll, D., Connell, D., & Grunebaum, H.U. (1986). The depressed mother and her one-year-old infant: Environment, interaction, attachment, and infant development. In E. Tronick & T. Field (Eds.), *Maternal depression and infant disturbance*, (New Directions for Child Development, No. 34, pp.31-46). San Francisco: Jossey-Bass.

Lyubomirsky, S., & Nolen-Hoeksema, S.N. (1995). Effects of self-focused rumination on negative thinking and interpersonal problem solving. *Journal of Personality and Social Psychology, 69*, 176-190.

Mann, J.J., & Kapur, S. (1991). The emergence of suicidal ideation and behavior during antidepressant pharmacotherapy. *Archives of General Psychiatry, 48*, 1027-1033.

Manning, M. (1994). *Undercurrents: A therapist's reckoning with her own depression*. San Francisco: Harper.

Manson, S.M. (1991, April). *Culture and the DSM-IV: Implications for the diagnosis of mood and anxiety disorders*. Paper presented at the National Institute of

Mental Health-sponsored Conference on Culture and Diagnosis, Pittsburgh, PA.

Maris, R.W., Berman, A.L., Maltsberger, J.T., & Yufit, R.I. (1992). *Assessment and prediction of suicide*. New York: Guilford.

Markowitz, J.C. (1994). Psychotherapy of dysthymia. *American Journal of Psychiatry, 151*, 1114–1121.

Martinsen, E. (1993). Therapeutic implications of exercise for clinically anxious and depressed patients. *International Journal of Sport Psychology, 24*, 185–199.

McCauley, E., Myers, K., Mitchell, J.R., Calderon, R., Schloredt, K., & Treder, R. (1993). Depression in young people: Initial presentation and clinical course. *Journal of the American Academy of Child and Adolescent Psychiatry, 32*, 714–722.

McGlashan, T.H. (1989). Comparison of adolescent- and adult-onset unipolar depression. *American Journal of Psychiatry, 146*, 1208–1211.

McGuffin, P., Katz, R., & Bebbington, P.E. (1988a). The Camberwell Collaborative Depression Study: II. Investigation of family members. *British Journal of Psychiatry, 152*, 766–774.

McGuffin, P., Katz, R., & Bebbington, P.E. (1988b). The Camberwell Collaborative Depression Study: III. Depression and adversity in the relatives of depressed probands. *British Journal of Psychiatry, 152*, 775–782.

McGuffin, P., Katz, R., Watkins, S., & Rutherford, J. (1996). A hospital-based twin register of the heritability of DSM-IV unipolar depression. *Archives of General Psychiatry, 53*, 129–136.

McIntosh, J.L. (1992). Suicide of the elderly. In B. Bonger (Ed.), *Suicide: Guidelines for assessment, management, and treatment* (pp.106–124). New York: Oxford University Press.

McNeal, E.T., & Cimbolic, P. (1986). Antidepressants and biochemical theories of depression. *Psychological Bulletin, 99*, 361–374.

Mendels, J., & Cochrane, C. (1968). The nosology of depression: The endogenous-reactive concept. *American Journal of Psychiatry, 124*, 1–11.

Merikangas, K.R., Weissman, M.M., Prusoff, B.A., & John, K. (1988). Assortative mating and affective disorders: Psychopathology in offspring. *Psychiatry, 51*, 48–57.

Miller, I.W., Norman, W.H., & Keitner, G.I. (1989). Cognitive-behavioral treatment of depressed inpatients: Six- and twelve-month follow-up. *American Journal of Psychiatry, 146*, 1274–1279.

Miranda, J., & Persons, J.B. (1988). Dysfunctional attitudes are mood-state dependent. *Journal of Abnormal Psychology, 97*, 76–79.

Miranda, J., Persons, J.B., & Byers, C. (1990). Endorsement of dysfunctional beliefs depends on current mood state. *Journal of Abnormal Psychology, 99*, 237–241.

Mitchell, J.R., McCauley, E., Burke, P.M., & Moss, S.J. (1988). Phenomenology of depression in children and adolescents. *Journal of the American Academy of Child and Adolescent Psychiatry, 27*, 2–20.

Monroe, S.M., & Simons, A.D. (1991). Diathesis-stress theories in the context of life-stress research: Implications for the depressive disorders. *Psychological Bulletin, 110*, 406–425.

Monroe, S.M., Simons, A.D., & Thase, M.E. (1992). Social factors and the psychobiology of depression: Relations between life stress and rapid eye movement sleep latency. *Journal of Abnormal Psychology, 101*, 528–537.

Monroe, S.M., Thase, M.E., Hersen, M., Himmelhoch, J.M., & Bellack, A.S. (1985). Life events and the endogenous–nonendogenous distinction in the treatment and posttreatment course of depression. *Comprehensive Psychiatry, 26*, 175–186.

Moran, P.W., & Lambert, M.J. (1983). A review of current assessment tools for monitoring changes in depression. In M.J. Lambert, E.R. Christensen, & S.S. DeJulio (Eds.), *The assessment of psychotherapy outcome* (pp.304–355). New York: Wiley.

Moreau, D., Mufson, L., Weissman, M.M., & Klerman, G.L. (1991). Interpersonal psychotherapy for adolescent depression: Description of modification and preliminary application. *Journal of the American Academy of Child and Adolescent Psychiatry, 30,* 642–651.

Murphy, J.M., Monson, R.R., Olivier, D.C., Sobol, A.M., & Leighton, A.H. (1987). Affective disorders and mortality. *Archives of General Psychiatry, 44,* 473–480.

Murray, L. (1992). The impact of postnatal depression on infant development. *Journal of Child Psychology and Psychiatry, 33,* 543–561.

Narrow, W., Regier, D.A., Rae, D., Manderscheid, R., & Locke, B.Z. (1993). Use of services by persons with mental and addictive disorders. *Archives of General Psychiatry, 50,* 95–107.

Nelson, G. (1982). Parental death during childhood and adult depression: Some additional data. *Social Psychiatry, 17,* 37–42.

Nezlek, J.B., Imbrie, M., & Shean, G.D. (1994). Depression and everyday social interaction. *Journal of Personality and Social Psychology, 67,* 1101–1111.

Nezu, A.M. (1987). A problem-solving formulation of depression: A literature review and proposal of a pluralistic model. *Clinical Psychology Review, 7,* 121–144.

Nezu, A.M., Nezu, C.M., & Perri, M.G. (1989). *Problem-solving therapy for depression: Theory, research, and clinical guidelines.* New York: Wiley.

Nezu, A.M., & Ronan, G.F. (1985). Life stress, current problems, problem solving, and depressive symptoms: An integrative model. *Journal of Consulting and Clinical Psychology, 53,* 693–697.

Nietzel, M.T., & Harris, M.J. (1990). Relationship of dependency and achievement/autonomy to depression. *Clinical Psychology Review, 10,* 279–297.

Nietzel, M.T., Russell, R., Hemmings, K., & Gretter, M. (1987). Clinical significance of psychotherapy for unipolar depression: A meta-analytic approach to social comparison. *Journal of Consulting and Clinical Psychology, 55,* 156–161.

Nobler, M.S., Sackeim, H.A., Prohovnik, I., Moeller, J.R., Mukherjee, S., Schnur, D.B., Prudic, J., & Devanand, D.P. (1994). Regional cerebral blood flow in mood disorders, III. *Archives of General Psychiatry, 51,* 884–897.

Nolen-Hoeksema, S.N. (1987). Sex differences in unipolar depression: Evidence and theory. *Psychological Bulletin, 101,* 259–282.

Nolen-Hoeksema, S.N. (1990). *Sex differences in depression.* Stanford: Stanford University Press.

Nolen-Hoeksema, S.N. (1991). Responses to depression and their effects on the duration of depressive episodes. *Journal of Abnormal Psychology, 100,* 569–582.

Nolen-Hoeksema, S.N., & Girgus, J.S. (1994). The emergence of gender differences in depression during adolescence. *Psychological Bulletin, 115,* 424–443.

Nolen-Hoeksema, S.N., Morrow, J., & Fredrickson, B.L. (1993). Response styles and the duration of episodes of depressed mood. *Journal of Abnormal Psychology, 102,* 20–28.

Nolen-Hoeksema, S.N., Parker, L.E., & Larson, J. (1994). Ruminative coping with depressed mood following loss. *Journal of Personality and Social Psychology, 67,* 92–104.

Nurnberger, J., & Gershon, E.S. (1984). Genetics of affective disorders. In R. Post & J. Ballenger (Eds.), *Neurobiology of mood disorders* (pp.76–101). Baltimore: Williams & Wilkins.

O' Hara, M.W. (1986). Social support, life events, and depression during pregnancy and the puerperium. *Archives of General Psychiatry, 43*, 569–573.

O' Hara, M.W., Schlechte, J.A., Lewis, D.A., & Varner, M.W. (1991). Controlled prospective study of postpartum mood disorders: Psychological, environmental, and hormonal variables. *Journal of Abnormal Psychology, 100*, 63–73.

O' Hara, M.W., Zekoski, E.M., Philipps, L.H., & Wright, E.J. (1990). Controlled prospective study of postpartum mood disorders: Comparison of childbearing and nonchildbearing women. *Journal of Abnormal Psychology, 99*, 3–15.

Olfson, M., & Klerman, G.L. (1993). Trends in the prescription by office-based psychiatrists. *American Journal of Psychiatry, 150*, 571–577.

Orvaschel, H., Walsh-Allis, G., & Ye, W. (1988). Psychopathology in children of parents with recurrent depression. *Journal of Abnormal Child Psychology, 16*, 17–28.

Paykel, E.S., & Cooper, Z. (1992). Life events and social stress. In E.S. Paykel (Ed.), *Handbook of affective disorders* (2nd ed., pp.149–170). London: Guilford.

Paykel, E.S., Rao, B.M., & Taylor, C.N. (1984). Life stress and symptom pattern in out-patient depression. *Psychological Medicine, 14*, 559–568.

Persons, J.B., & Burns, D.D. (1985). Mechanisms of action of cognitve therapy: The relative contributions of technical and interpersonal interventions. *Cognitive Therapy and Research, 9*, 539–551.

Peselow, E.D., Robins, C.J., Sanfilipo, M.P., Block, P., & Fieve, R.R. (1992). Sociotropy and autonomy: Relationship to antidepressant drug treatment response and the endogenous–nonendogenous dichotomy. *Journal of Abnormal Psychology, 101*, 479–486.

Petersen, A.C., Sarigiani, P.A., & Kennedy, R.E. (1991). Adolescent depression: Why more girls? *Journal of Youth and Adolescence, 20*, 247–271.

Peterson, C. (1991). The meaning and measurement of explanatory style. *Psychological Inquiry, 2*, 1–10.

Pfohl, B., Sherman, B., Schlechte, J.A., & Stone, R. (1985). Pituitary-adrenal axis rhythm disturbances in psychiatric depression. *Archives of General Psychiatry, 42*, 897–903.

Philipps, L.H.C., & O'Hara, M.W. (1991). Prospective study of postpartum depression: 4½-year follow-up of women and children. *Journal of Abnormal Psychology, 100*, 151–155.

Powell, K.B., & Miklowitz, D.J. (1994). Frontal lobe dysfunction in the affective disorders. *Clinical Psychology Review, 14*, 525–546.

Post, R.M. (1992). Transduction of psychosocial stress into the neurobiology of recurrent affective disorder. *American Journal of Psychiatry, 149*, 999–1010.

Potthoff, J.G., Holahan, C.J., & Joiner, T.E. (1995). Reassurance seeking, stress generation, and depressive symptoms: An integrative model. *Journal of Personality and Social Psychology, 68*, 664–670.

Pound, A., Cox, A.D., Puckering, C., & Mills, M. (1985). The impact of maternal depression on young children. In J.E. Stevenson (Ed.), *Recent research in developmental psychopathology (pp.3–10)*. Oxford: Pergamon.

Prien, R.F. (1988). Somatic treatment of unipolar depressive disorder. In A. Frances & R. Hales (Eds.), *Review of psychiatry* (Vol.7, pp.213–234). Washington, DC: American Psychiatric Press.

Prien, R.F., & Kupfer, D.J. (1986). Continuation drug therapy for major depressive episodes: How long should it be maintained? *American Journal of Psychiatry, 143*, 18–23.

Puig-Antich, J., Chambers, W., & Tabrizi, M.A. (1983). The clinical assessment of current depressive episodes in children and adolescents: Interview with parents and children. In B.P. Cantwell & G.A. Carlson (Eds.), *Affective disorders in childhood and adolescence* (pp.157–180). New York: SP Medical & Scientific Books.

Puig-Antich, J., Goetz, R., Hanlon, C., Davies, M., Thompson, J., Chambers, W., Tabrizi, M.A., & Weitzman, E. (1982). Sleep architecture and REM sleep measures in prepubertal children with major depression. *Archives of General Psychiatry, 39,* 932–939.

Puig-Antich, J., Kaufman, J., Ryan, N.D., Williamson, D.E., Dahl, R.E., Lukens, E., Todak, G., Ambrosini, P., Rabinovich, H., & Nelson, B. (1993). The psychosocial functioning and family environment of depressed adolescents. *Journal of the American Academy of Child and Adolescent Psychiatry, 32,* 244–253.

Puig-Antich, J., Perel, J.M., Lupatkin, W., Chambers, W., Tabrizi, M.A., King, J., Goetz, R., Davies, M., & Stiller, R. (1987). Imipramine in prepubertal major depressive disorders. *Archives of General Psychiatry, 44,* 81–89.

Pyszczynski T., & Greenberg, J. (1987). Self-regulatory perseveration and the depressive self-focusing style: A self-awareness theory of reactive depression. *Psychological Bulletin, 102,* 122–138.

Radke-Yarrow, M., Cummings, E.M., Kuczynski, L., & Chapman, M. (1985). Patterns of attachment in two- and three-year-olds in normal families and families with parental depression. *Child Development, 56,* 884–893.

Rao, U., Dahl, R.E., Ryan, N.D., Birmaher, B., Williamson, D.E., Giles, D.E., Rao, R., Kaufman, J., & Nelson, B. (1996). The relationship between longitudinal clinical course and sleep and cortisol changes in adolescent depression. *Biological Psychiatry, 40,* 474–484.

Rao, U., Ryan, N.D., Birmaher, B., Dahl, R.E., Williamson, D.E., Kaufman, J., Rao, R., & Nelson, B. (1995). Unipolar depression in adolescents: Clinical outcomes in adulthood. *Journal of the American Academy of Child and Adolescent Psychiatry, 34,* 566–578.

Regier, D.A., Boyd, J.H., Burke, J.D., Rae, D.S., Myers, J.K, Kramer, M., Robins, L.N., George, L.K., Karno, M., & Locke, B.Z. (1988). One-month prevalence of mental disorders in the United States. *Archives of General Psychiatry, 45,* 977–986.

Rehm, L.P. (1977). A self-control model of depression. *Behavior Therapy, 8,* 787–804.

Rehm, L.P., Fuchs, C.Z., Roth, D.M., Kornblith, S.J., & Romano, J.M. (1979). A comparison of self-control and assertion skills treatments of depression. *Behavior Therapy, 10,* 429–442.

Rende, R., & Plomin, R. (1992). Diathesis-stress models of psychopathology: A quantitative genetic perspective. *Applied and Preventive Psychology, 1,* 177–182.

Reynolds, C.F., & Kupfer, D.J. (1987). Sleep research in affective illness: State of the art circa 1987. *Sleep, 10,* 199–215.

Reynolds, W.M., & Coats, K.I. (1986). A comparison of cognitive-behavioral therapy and relaxation training for the treatment of depression in adolescents. *Journal of Consulting and Clinical Psychology, 54,* 653–660.

Ribeiro, S.C.M., Tandon, R., Grunhaus, L., & Greden, J.F. (1993). The DST as a predictor of outcome in depression: A meta-analysis. *American Journal of Psychiatry, 150,* 1618–1629.

Roberts, J.E., & Monroe, S.M. (1994). A multidimensional model of self-esteem in depression. *Clinical Psychology Review, 14,* 161–181.

Robins, C.J. (1990). Congruence of personality and life events in depression. *Journal of Abnormal Psychology, 99,* 393–397.

Robins, C.J., & Block, P. (1988). Personal vulnerability, life events, and depressive symptoms: A test of a specific interational model. *Journal of Personality and Social Psychology, 54*, 847–852.

Robins, L.N., Helzer, J.E., Croughan, J., & Ratcliff, K.S. (1981). National Institute of Mental Health Diagnostic Interview Schedule: Its history, characteristics, and validity. *Archives of General Psychiatry, 38*, 381–389.

Robinson, L., Berman, J., & Neimeyer, R. (1990). Psychotherapy for the treatment of depression: A comprehensive review of controlled outcome research. *Psychological Bulletin, 108*, 30–49.

Rockett, I.R.H., & Smith, G.S. (1989). Homicide, suicide, motor vehicle crash, and fall mortality: United States' experience in comparative perspective. *American Journal of Public Health, 79*, 1396–1400.

Rohde, P., Lewinsohn, P.M., & Seeley, J.R. (1990). Are people changed by the experience of having an episode of depression? A further test of the scar hypothesis. *Journal of Abnormal Psychology, 99*, 264–271.

Rohde, P., Lewinsohn, P.M., & Seeley, J.R. (1991). Comorbidity of unipolar depression: II. Comorbidity with other mental disorders in adolescents and adults. *Journal of Abnormal Psychology, 100*, 214–222.

Rohde, P., Lewinsohn, P.M., & Seeley, J.R. (1994). Response of depressed adolescents to cognitive-behavioral treatment: Do differences in initial severity clarify the comparison of treatments? *Journal of Consulting and Clinical Psychology, 62*, 851–854.

Rose, D.T., Abramson, L.Y., Hodulik, C.J., Halberstadt, L., & Leff, G. (1994). Heterogeneity of cognitive style among depressed inpatients. *Journal of Abnormal Psychology, 103*, 419–429.

Rosenfarb, I.S., Becker, J., & Khan, A. (1994). Perceptions of parental and peer attachments with mood disorders. *Journal of Abnormal Psychology, 103*, 637–644.

Rosenthal, N.E., Sack, D.A., Carpenter, C.J., Parry, B.L., Mendelson, W.B., & Wehr, T.A. (1985). Antidepressant effects of light in seasonal affective disorder. *American Journal of Psychiatry, 142*, 163–170.

Rush, A.J., Beck, A.T., Kovacs, M., Weissenburger, J.E., & Hollon, S.D. (1982). Comparison of the effects of cognitive therapy and pharmacotherapy on hopelessness and self-concept. *American Journal of Psychiatry, 139*, 862–866.

Rush, A.J., & Weissenburger, J.E. (1994). Melancholic symptom features and DSM-IV. *American Journal of Psychiatry, 151*, 489–498.

Rutter, M., & Quinton, P. (1984). Parental psychiatric disorder: Effects on children. *Psychological Medicine, 14*, 853–880.

Ryan, N.D. (1992). The pharmacologic treatment of child and adolescent depression. *Psychiatric Clinics of North America, 15*, 29–40.

Ryan, N.D., Puig-Antich, J., Ambrosini, P., Rabinovich, H., Robinson, D., Nelson, B., Iyengar, S., & Twomey, J. (1987). The clinical picture of major depression in children and adolescents. *Archives of General Psychiatry, 44*, 854–861.

Ryan, N.D., Williamson, D.E., Iyengar, S., Orvaschel, H., Reich, T., Dahl, R.E., & Puig-Antich, J. (1992). A secular increase in child and adolescent onset affective disorder. *Journal of the American Academy of Child and Adolescent Psychiatry, 31*, 600–605.

Sackheim, H.A. (1988). Mechanisms of action of electroconvulsive therapy. In A. Frances & R. Hales (Eds.), *Review of Psychiatry* (Vol.7, pp.436–457). Washington, DC: American Psychiatric Press.

Sackheim, H.A., & Rush, A.J. (1995). Melancholia and response to ECT. *American Journal of Psychiatry, 152*, 1242–1243.

Sanderson, W., Beck, A., & Beck, J. (1990). Syndrome comorbidity in patients with major depression or dysthymia: Prevalence and temporal relationships. *American Journal of Psychiatry, 147,* 1025–1028.

Sands, J.R., & Harrow, M. (1994). Psychotic unipolar depression at follow-up: Factors related to psychosis in the affective disorders. *American Journal of Psychiatry, 151,* 995–1000.

Sargeant, J.K., Bruce, M.L., Florio, L., & Weissman, M.M. (1990). Factors associated with 1–year outcome of major depression in the community. *Archives of General Psychiatry, 47,* 519–526.

Schildkraut, J.J. (1965). The catecholamine hypothesis of affective disorders: A review of supporting evidence. *American Journal of Psychiatry, 122,* 509–522.

Schleifer, S.J., Keller, S.E., Bond, R.N., Cohen, J., & Stein, M. (1989). Major depressive disorder and immunity. *Archives of General Psychiatry, 46,* 81–87.

Segal, Z.V., & Dobson, K.S. (1992). Cognitive models of depression: Report from a consensus development conference. *Psychological Inquiry, 3,* 219–224.

Segal, Z.V., Gemar, M., Truchon, C., Guirguis, M., & Horowitz, L.M. (1995). A priming methodology for studying self-representation in major depressive disorder. *Journal of Abnormal Psychology, 104,* 205–213.

Segal, Z.V., Hood, J.E., Shaw, B.F., & Higgins, E.T. (1988). A structural analysis of the self-schema construct in major depression. *Cognitive Therapy and Research, 12,* 471–485.

Segal, Z.V., & Ingram, R.E. (1994). Mood priming and construct activation in tests of cognitive vulnerability to unipolar depression. *Clinical Psychology Review, 14,* 663–695.

Segal, Z.V., Shaw, B.F., Vella, D.D., & Katz, R. (1992). Cognitive and life stress predictors of relapse in remitted unipolar depressed patients: A test of the congruency hypothesis. *Journal of Abnormal Psychology, 101,* 26–36.

Segal, Z.V., Truchon, C., Horowitz, L.M., Gemar, M., & Guirguis, M. (1995). A priming methodology for studying self-representation in major depressive disorder. *Journal of Abnormal Psychology, 104,* 205–213.

Segrin, C., & Abramson, L.Y. (1994). Negative reactions to depressive behaviors: A communication theories analysis. *Journal of Abnormal Psychology, 103,* 655–668.

Seligman, M.E.P. (1975). *Helplessness: On depression, development and death.* San Francisco: Freeman.

Seligman, M.E.P., Castellon, C., Cacciola, J., Schulman, P., Luborsky, L., Ollove, M., & Downing, R. (1988). Explanatory style changes during cognitive therapy for unipolar depression. *Journal of Abnormal Psychology, 97,* 13–18.

Selmi, P.M., Klein, M.H., Greist, J.H., Sorrell, S.P., & Erdman, H.P. (1990). Computer-administered cognitive-behavioral therapy for depression. *American Journal of Psychiatry, 147,* 51–56.

Shapiro, D.A., Barkham, M., Rees, A., Hardy, G.E., Reynolds, S., & Startup, M. (1994). Effects of treatment duration and severity of depression on the effectiveness of cognitive-behavioral and psychodynamic-interpersonal psychotherapy. *Journal of Consulting and Clinical Psychology, 62,* 522–534.

Shaw, B.F., Vallis, T.M., & McCabe, S.B. (1985). The assessment of the severity and symptom patterns in depression. In E.E. Beckham & W.R. Leber (Eds.), *Handbook of depression: Treatment, assessment, and research* (pp.372–409). Homewood, IL: Dorsey.

Shea, M.T., Pilkonis, P.A., Beckham, E., Collins, J.F., Elkin, I., Sotsky, S.M., & Docherty, J.P. (1990). Personality disorders and treatment outcome in the NIMH treatment of depression collaborative research program. *American Journal of Psychiatry, 98,* 468–477.

Shea, M.T., Widiger, T.A., & Klein, M.H. (1992). Comorbidity of personality disorders and depression: Implications for treatment. *Journal of Consulting and Clinical Psychology, 60,* 857–868.

Shelton, R.C., Hollon, S.D., Purdon, S.E., & Loosen, P.T. (1991). Biological and psychological aspects of depression. *Behavior Therapy, 22,* 201–228.

Sherbourne, C.D., Hays, R.D., & Wells, K.B. (1995). Personal and psychosocial risk factors for physical and mental health outcomes and course of depression among depressed patients. *Journal of Consulting and Clinical Psychology, 63,* 345–355.

Shrout, P.E., Link, B.G., Dohrenwend, B.P., Skodol, A.E., Stueve, A., & Mirttznik, J. (1989). Characterizing life events as risk factors for depression: The role of fateful loss events. *Journal of Abnormal Psychology, 98,* 460–467.

Siever, L.J., & Davis, K.L. (1985). Overview: Toward a dysregulation hypothesis of depression. *American Journal of Psychiatry, 142,* 1017–1031.

Silverman, J.S., Silverman, J.A., & Eardley, D.A. (1984). Do maladaptive attitudes cause depression? *Archives of General Psychiatry, 41,* 28–30.

Simeon, J., DiNicola, V., Ferguson, H., & Copping, W. (1990). Adolescent depression: A placebo-controlled fluoxetine treatment study and follow-up. *Progress in Neuropsycho-pharmacology and Biological Psychiatry, 14,* 791–795.

Simon, G., Ormel, J., VonKorff, M., & Barlow, W. (1995). Health care costs associated with depressive and anxiety disorders in primary care. *American Journal of Psychiatry, 152,* 352–357.

Simons, A.D., Garfield, S.L., & Murphy, G.E. (1984). The process of change in cognitive therapy and pharmacotherapy: Changes in mood and cognitions. *Archives of General Psychiatry, 41,* 45–51.

Simons, A.D., Gordon, J.S., Monroe, S.M., & Thase, M.E. (1995). Toward an integration of psychologic, social, and biologic factors in depression: Effects on outcome and course of cognitive therapy. *Journal of Consulting and Clinical Psychology, 63,* 369–377.

Simons, A.D., Murphy, G.E., Levine, J.L., & Wetzel, R.D. (1986). Cognitive therapy and pharmacotherapy for depression: Sustained improvement over one year. *Archives of General Psychiatry, 43,* 43–48.

Simons, A.D., & Thase, M.E. (1992). Biological markers, treatment outcome, and 1-year follow-up in endogenous depression: Electroencephalographic sleep studies and response to cognitive therapy. *Journal of Consulting and Clinical Psychology, 60,* 392–401.

Skodol, A.E., Schwartz, S., Dohrenwend, B.P., Levav, I., & Shrout, P.E. (1994). Minor depression in a cohort of young adults in Israel. *Archives of General Psychiatry, 51,* 542–551.

Smith, A.L., & Weissman, M.M. (1992). Epidemiology. In E.S. Paykel (Ed.), *Handbook of affective disorders* (pp.111–129). New York: Guilford.

Sorenson, S.B., Rutter, C.M., & Aneshensel, C.S. (1991). Depression in the community: An investigation into age of onset. *Journal of Consulting Clinical Psychology, 59,* 541–546.

Sotsky, S.M., Glass, D.R., Shea, T., Pilkonis, P.A., Collins, J.J., Elkin, I., Watkins, J.T., Imber, S.D., Leber, W.R., Moyer, J., & Oliveri, M.E. (1991). Patient predictors of response to psychotherapy and pharmacotherapy: Findings in the NIMH treatment of depression collaborative research program. *American Journal of Psychiatry, 148,* 997–1008.

Spitzer, R.L., Williams, J.B.W., Gibbon, M., & First, M.B. (1990). *User's guide for the Structured Clinical Interview for DSM-III-R*. Washington, DC: American Psychiatric Press.

Stark, K.D. (1990). *Childhood depression: School-based intervention*. New York: Guilford.

Stark, K.D., Humphrey, L.L., Crook, K., & Lewis, K. (1990). Perceived family environments of depressed and anxious children: Child's and maternal figure's perspective. *Journal of Abnormal Child Psychology, 18*, 527–547.

Stark, K.D., Reynolds, W.M., & Kaslow, N.J. (1987). A comparison of the relative efficacy of self-control therapy and a behavioral problem-solving therapy for depression in children. *Journal of Abnormal Child Psychology, 15*, 91–113.

Stark, K.D., Rouse, L., & Kurowski, C. (1994). Psychological treatment approaches for depression in children. In W.M. Reynolds & H. Johnston, (Eds.), *Handbook of depression in children and adolescents* (pp.275–307). New York: Plenum.

Starkstein, S.E., & Robinson, R.G. (1991). The role of the frontal lobes in affective disorder following stroke. In H.L. Levin, H.M. Eisenberg, & A.L. Benton (Eds.), *Frontal lobe function and dysfunction* (pp.288–303). New York: Oxford University Press.

Starkstein, S.E., & Robinson, R.G. (1992). Neuropsychiatric aspects of cerebral vascular disorders. In S.C. Yudofsky & R.E. Hales (Eds.), *The American psychiatric press textbook of neuropsychiatry*. Washington, DC: American Psychiatric Press.

Stephens, R.S., Hokanson, J.E., & Welker, R.A. (1987). Responses to depressed interpersonal behavior: Mixed reactions in a helping role. *Journal of Personality and Social Psychology, 52*, 1274–1282.

Steuer, J., Mintz, J., Hammen, C.L., Jarvik, L., McCarley, T., Motoike, P., & Rosen, R. (1984). Cognitive-behavioral and psychodynamic group psychotherapy in treatment of geriatric depression. *Journal of Consulting and Clinical Psychology, 52*, 180–189.

Strack, S., & Coyne, J.C. (1983). Social confirmation of dysphoria: Shared and private reactions to depression. *Journal of Personality and Social Psychology, 44*, 798–806.

Strober, M., Lampert, C., Schmidt, S., & Morrell, W. (1993). The course of major depressive disorder in adolescents: Recovery and risk of manic switching in a 24-month prospective, naturalistic follow-up of psychotic and nonpsychotic subtypes. *Journal of the American Academy of Child and Adolescent Psychiatry, 32*, 34–42.

Styron, W. (1990). *Darkness visible: A memoir of madness*. New York: Random House.

Suomi, S.J. (1991a). Early stress and adult emotional reactivity in rhesus monkeys. *The childhood environment and adult disease* (pp.171–188). Chichester, UK: Wiley (Ciba Foundation Symposium).

Suomi, S.J. (1991b). Primate separation models of affective disorders. In J. Madden IV (Ed.), *Neurobiology of learning, emotion and affect* (pp.195–213). New York: Raven.

Sweeney, P.D., Anderson, K., & Bailey, S. (1986). Attributional style in depression: A meta-analytic review. *Journal of Personality and Social Psychology, 50*, 974–991.

Swindle, R.W., Cronkite, R.C., & Moos, R.H. (1989). Life stressors, social resources, coping, and the 4-year course of unipolar depression. *Journal of Abnormal Psychology, 98*, 468–477.

Teasdale, J.D. (1983). Negative thinking in depression: Cause, effect, or reciprocal relationship? *Advances in Behaviour Research and Therapy, 5*, 3–25.

Teasdale, J.D. (1985). Psychological treatments for depression: How do they work? *Behaviour Research and Therapy, 23*, 157–165.

Teasdale, J.D. (1988). Cognitive vulnerability to persistent depression. *Cognition and Emotion, 2*, 247–274.

Teasdale, J.D., & Dent, J. (1987). Cognitive vulnerability to depression: An investigation of two hypotheses. *British Journal of Psychiatry, 26*, 113–126.

Teasdale, J.D., & Fennell, M.J.V. (1982). Immediate effects on depression of cognitive therapy interventions. *Cognitive Therapy and Research, 6*, 343–352.

Teasdale, J.D., Taylor, M.J., Cooper, Z., Hayhurst, H., & Paykel, E.S. (1995). Depressive thinking: Shifts in construct accessibility or in schematic mental models? *Journal of Abnormal Psychology, 104*, 500–507.

Tennant, C.T., Bebbington, P.E., & Hurry, J. (1980). Parental death in childhood and risk of adult depressive disorder: A review. *Psychological Medicine, 10*, 289–299.

Thase, M.E., Frank, E., & Kupfer, D.J. (1985). Biological processes in major depression. In E.E. Beckham & W.R. Leber (Eds.), *Depression: Basic mechanisms, diagnosis, and treatment* (pp.816–913). New York: Dow Jones/Irwin.

Thase, M.E., & Kupfer, D.J. (1996). Recent developments in the pharacotherapy of mood disorders. *Journal of Consulting and Clinical Psychology, 64*, 646–659.

Thase, M.E., Reynolds III, C.F., Frank, E., Simons, A.D., McGeary, J., Fasiczka, A.L., Garamoni, G.G., Jennings, R., & Kupfer, D.J. (1994). Do depressed men and women respond similarly to cognitive behavior therapy? *American Journal of Psychiatry, 151*, 500–505.

Thase, M.E., Simons, A.D., Cahalane, J.F., McGeary, J., & Harden, T. (1991). Severity of depression and response to cognitive behavior therapy. *American Journal of Psychiatry, 148*, 784–789.

Thase, M.E., Simons, A.D., McGeary, J., Cahalane, J.F., Hughes, C., Harden, T., & Friedman, E. (1992). Relapse after cognitive behavior therapy of depression: Potential implications for longer courses of treatment. *American Journal of Psychiatry, 149*, 1046–1052.

Thayer, R., Newman, J.R., & McClain, T. (1994). Self-regulation of mood: Strategies for changing a bad mood, raising energy, and reducing tension. *Journal of Personality and Social Psychology, 67*, 910–925.

Thoits, P.A. (1983). Dimensions of life events that influence psychological distress: An evaluation and synthesis of the literature. In H.B. Kaplan (Ed.), *Psychosocial stress: Trends in theory and research* (pp.33–103). New York: Academic Press.

Thornicroft, G., & Sartorius, N. (1993). The course and outcome of depression in different cultures: 10-year follow-up of the WHO Collaborative Study on the Assessment of Depressive Disorders. *Psychological Medicine, 23*, 1023–1032.

Torgersen, S. (1986). Genetic factors in moderately severe and mild affective disorders. *Archives of General Psychiatry, 43*, 222–226.

Toth, S., Manly, J.T., & Cicchetti, D. (1992). Child maltreatment and vulnerability to depression. *Development and Psychopathology, 4*, 97–112.

Troutman, B.R., & Cutrona, C.E. (1990). Nonpsychotic postpartum depression among adolescent mothers. *Journal of Abnormal Psychology, 99*, 69–78.

United States Department of Health and Human Services (1991). *Health, United States, 1991*. Washington, DC: Public Health Service.

Verhulst, F.C., & Van der Ende, J. (1992). Six-year developmental course of internalizing and externalizing problem behaviors. *Journal of the American Academy of Child and Adolescent Psychiatry, 31*, 924–931.

Von Korff, M.R., Ormel, J., Katon, W., & Lin, E.H. (1992). Disability and depression among high utilizers of health care: A longitudinal analysis. *Archives of General Psychiatry, 49,* 91–100.

Wallace, J., & O'Hara, M.W. (1992). Increases in depressive symptomatology in the rural elderly: Results from a cross-sectional and longitudinal study. *Journal of Abnormal Psychology, 101,* 398–404.

Warner, V., Weissman, M.M., Fendrich, M., Wickramaratne, P., & Moreau, D. (1992). The course of major depression in the offspring of depressed parents. *Archives of General Psychiatry, 49,* 795–801.

Watts, F.N. (1993). Problems of memory and concentration. In C.G. Costello (Ed.), *Symptoms of depression* (pp.113–140). New York: Wiley.

Weiner, R.D., & Coffey, C.E. (1988). Indications for use of electroconvulsive therapy. In A. Frances & R. Hales (Eds.), *Review of psychiatry* (Vol.7, pp.458–481). Washington, DC: American Psychiatric Press

Weisberg, R.W. (1994). Genius and madness? A quasi-experimental test of the hypothesis that manic-depression increases creativity. *Psychological Science, 5,* 361–367.

Weissman, M.M. (1988). Psychopathology in the children of depressed parents: Direct interview studies. In D.L. Dunner & E.S. Gershon, *Relatives at risk for mental disorders,* pp.143–159. New York: Raven.

Weissman, M.M., & Klerman, G.L. (1977). Sex differences in the epidemiology of depression. *Archives of General Psychiatry, 34,* 98–111.

Weissman, M.M., & Klerman, G.L. (1990). Interpersonal psychotherapy for depression. In B.B. Wolman & G. Stricker (Eds.), *Depressive disorders: Facts, theories, and treatment methods* (pp.379–395). New York: Wiley.

Weissman, M.M., Klerman, G.L., Prusoff, B.A., Sholomskas, D., & Padian, N. (1981). Depressed outpatients: Results one year after treatment with drugs and/or interpersonal psychotherapy. *Archives of General Psychiatry, 38,* 51–55.

Weissman, M.M., Leaf, P., & Bruce, M.L. (1987). Single parent women: A community study. *Social Psychiatry, 22,* 29–36.

Weissman, M.M., & Markowitz, J.C. (1994). Interpersonal psychotherapy. *Archives of General Psychiatry, 51,* 599–606.

Weissman, M.M., & Olfson, M. (1995). Depression in women: Implications for health care research. *Science, 269,* 799–801.

Weissman, M.M., Prusoff, B.A., DiMascio, A., Neu, C., Goklaney, M., & Klerman, G.L. (1979). The efficacy of drugs and psychotherapy in the treatment of acute depressive episodes. *American Journal of Psychiatry, 136,* 555–558.

Weissman, M.M., Wickramarante, P., Warner, V., John, K., Prusoff, B.A., Merikangas, K.R., & Gammon, D. (1987). Assessing psychiatric disorders in children: Discrepancies between mothers' and children's reports. *Archives of General Psychiatry, 44,* 747–753.

Weller, R., Weller, E., Fristad, M., & Bowes, J. (1991). Depression in recently bereaved prepubertal children. *American Journal of Psychiatry, 148,* 1536–1540.

Wells, K.B., & Sturm, R. (1996). Informing the policy process: From efficacy to effectiveness data on pharmacotherapy. *Journal of Consulting and Clinical Psychology, 64,* 638–645.

Wells, K.B., Burnam, A., Rogers, W., Hays, R.D., & Camp, P. (1992). The course of depression in adult outpatients. *Archives of General Psychiatry, 49,* 688–749.

Wells, K.B., Kayton, W., Rogers, B., & Camp, P. (1994). Use of minor tranquilizers and antidepressant medications by depressed outpatients: Results from the medical outcomes study. *American Journal of Psychiatry, 151,* 694–700.

Wells, K.B., Stewart, A., Hays, R.D., Burnam, A., Rogers, W., Daniels, M., Berry, S., Greenfield, S., & Ware, J. (1989). The functioning and well-being of depressed patients. *Journal of the American Medical Association, 262,* 914–919.

Whiffen, V.E., & Gotlib, I.H. (1989a). Infants of postpartum depressed mothers: Temperament and cognitive status. *Journal of Abnormal Psychology, 98,* 274–279.

Whiffen, V.E., & Gotlib, I.H. (1989b). Stress and coping in maritally satisfied and dissatisfied couples. *Journal of Social and Personal Relationships, 6,* 327–344.

Whiffen, V.E. & Gotlib, I.H. (1993). Comparison of postpartum and nonpostpartum depression: Clinical presentation, psychiatric history, and psychosocial functioning. *Journal of Consulting and Clinical Psychology, 61,* 485–494.

Whisman, M.A., Miller, I.W., Norman, W.H., & Keitner, G.I. (1991). Cognitive therapy with depressed inpatients: Specific effects on dysfunctional cognitions. *Journal of Consulting and Clinical Psychology, 59,* 282–288.

Winfield, I., George, L.K., Swartz, M., & Blazer, D.G. (1990). Sexual assault and psychiatric disorders among a community sample of women. *American Journal of Psychiatry, 147,* 335–341.

Wing, J.K., Cooper, J.E., & Sartorius, N. (1974). *Measurement and classification of psychiatric symptoms: An instructional manual for the PSE and CATEGO program.* New York: Cambridge University Press.

Winokur, G. (1985). The validity of neurotic-reactive depression. *Archives of General Psychiatry, 42,* 1116–1122.

Winokur, G., Coryell, W., Keller, M.B., Endicott, J., & Akiskal, H.S. (1993). A prospective follow-up of patients with bipolar and primary unipolar affective disorder. *Archives of General Psychiatry, 50,* 457–465.

Winokur, G., Coryell, W., Keller, M.B., Endicott, J., & Leon, A.C. (1995). A family study of manic-depressive (bipolar I) disease: Is it a distinct illness separable from primary unipolar depression? *Archives of General Psychiatry, 52,* 367–373.

Wirz-Justice, A., Graw, P., Krauchi, K, Gisin, B., Jochum, A., Arendt, J., Fisch, H.U., Buddeberg, C., & Poldinger, W. (1993). Light therapy in seasonal affective disorder is independent of time of day or circadian phase. *Archives of General Psychiatry, 50,* 929–937.

World Health Organization. (1992). *International statistical classification of diseases and related health problems* (10th ed.) Geneva, Switzerland: WHO.

World Health Organization. (1993). *The ICD-10 classification of mental and behavioural disorders: Diagnostic criteria for research.* Geneva, Switzerland: WHO.

Wu, J.C., & Bunny, W.E. (1990). The biological basis of an antidepressant response to sleep deprivation and relapse: Review and hypothesis. *American Journal of Psychiatry, 147,* 14–21.

Youngren, M.A., & Lewinsohn, P.M. (1980). The functional relationship between depression and problematic behavior. *Journal of Abnormal Psychology, 89,* 333–341.

Zahn-Waxler, C., Cummings, E.M., Iannotti, R.J., & Radke-Yarrow, M. (1984). Young children of depressed parents: A population at risk for affective problems. In D. Cicchetti (Ed.), *Childhood depression.* (New directions for child development, no. 26, pp.81–105). San Francisco: Jossey-Bass.

Zahn-Waxler, C., Cummings, E.M., McKnew, D.H., & Radke-Yarrow, M. (1984). Altruism, aggression, and social interactions in young children with a manic-depressive parent. *Child Development, 55,* 112–122.

Zahn-Waxler, C., McKnew, D.H., Cummings, E.M., Davenport, Y., &

Radke-Yarrow, M. (1984). Problem behaviors and peer interactions of young children with a manic-depressive parent. *American Journal of Psychiatry, 141,* 236–240.

Zeiss, A.M., & Lewinsohn, P.M. (1988). Enduring deficits after remissions of depression: A test of the scar hypothesis. *Behavioral Research and Therapy, 26,* 151–158.

Zeiss, A.M., Lewinsohn, P.M., & Munoz, R.F. (1979). Nonspecific improvement effects in depression using interpersonal, cognitive, and pleasant events focused treatments. *Journal of Consulting and Clinical Psychology, 47,* 427–439.

Zimmerman, M., Coryell, W., Pfohl, B., & Stangl, D. (1986). Validity of the Hamilton Endogenous Subscale: An independent replication. *Psychiatry Research, 18,* 209–215.

Zimmerman, M., Coryell, W., Stangl, D., & Pfohl, B. (1987). Validity of an operational definition for neurotic unipolar major depression. *Journal of Affective Disorders, 12,* 29–40.

Zonderman, A.B., Herbst, J.H., Schmidt, C., Costa, P.T., & McCrae, R.R. (1993). Depressive symptoms as a nonspecific, graded risk for psychiatric diagnoses. *Journal of Abnormal Psychology, 102,* 544–552.

Zuroff, D.C., & Mongrain, M. (1987). Dependency and self-criticism: Vulnerability factors for depressive affective states. *Journal of Abnormal Psychology, 96,* 14–22.

Author index

Manson, S.M., 55
Manton, K.G., 19
Margolin, G., 112
Margolis, E.T., 115
Maris, R.W., 41
Markowitz, J.C.,
150, 157
Marks, T., 100, 120
Marstellar, F., 36,
110, 133
Martin, J., 94
Martinsen, E., 138
Marttunen, M.J., 41
Maser, J.D., 8, 17,
18, 30, 31, 38,
112, 113
Mason, B.J., 133
Mathews, A., 85
Matias, R., 114
Maurer, M., 127,
130, 133
Mayer L.S., 161
Mayol, A., 100, 120
McCabe, S.B., 24
McCann, C.D., 89
McCarley, T., 151
McCauley, E., 13,
14, 15, 35, 36,
106, 110
McClain, T., 138
McCrae, R.R., 21
McDonald, C., 100
McEachran, A.B.,
130, 156, 157
McGeary, J., 68, 88,
145, 148, 150, 151
McGlashan, T.H., 29
McGonagle, K.A.,
19, 44, 49, 55, 56
McGuffin, P., 61, 64
McIntosh, J.L., 48
McKeown, R.E.,
36, 110
McKnew, D.H., 114
McLeod, J.D., 121

McManus, C., 105
McNeal, E.T., 64,
65, 67, 129
McPherson, A.E.,
110
Meltzer, S.J., 117
Mendels, J., 96
Mendelsohn, M., 25
Mendelson, W.B.,
137
Merchant, A., 24
Meredith, K., 151
Merikangas, K.R.,
35, 60, 113, 115
Metalsky, G.I., 5,
16, 83
Miklowitz, D.J., 71,
72
Milburn, N.G., 56
Milden, R.S., 97
Miller, G.A., 22
Miller, I.W., 109,
112, 151, 154
Mills, M., 114
Minasian, G., 110
Mineka, S., 119
Mintz, J., 151
Miranda, J., 88, 89
Mirttznik, J., 94
Mitchell, J.R., 13,
14, 15, 35, 36,
106, 110
Mock, J., 25
Moeller, J.R., 136
Moilanen, D.L., 162
Mongrain, M., 100,
120
Monroe, S.M., 5,
33, 74, 85, 97,
101, 150
Monson, R.R., 42
Moos, R.H., 34, 93,
94, 109, 110, 115,
116, 121, 122
Moran, P.W., 24

Moreau, D., 110,
116, 161
Morphy, M.A., 146
Morrell, W., 35
Morrow, J., 53
Moss, S.J., 13, 14, 15
Motoike, P., 151
Mount, J.H., 18, 73,
108
Moyer, J., 150
Mueller, T., 17, 30,
31
Mufson, L., 161
Mukherjee, S., 136-
Munoz, R.F., 152
Murphy, G.E., 150,
152, 153
Murphy, J.M., 42
Murphy, M., 161
Murray, L., 114
Myers, J.K., 56
Myers, K., 35, 36

Najavits, L., 148, 150
Narrow, W., 125
Nasrallah, A., 41
Neale, M.C., 51,
61, 62, 63, 97
Neilson, M., 96
Neimeyer, R., 144,
146, 151
Nelson, B., 13, 14,
15, 36, 69, 110
Nelson, G., 106
Nestadt, G.R., 24
Neu, C., 156
Newman, J.R., 138
Newman, S.C., 28,
29
Nezu, A.M., 84, 122
Nezu, C.M., 84
Ni Bhrolchain, M.,
96
Nietzel, M.T., 100,
120, 144, 151

Nobler, M.S., 135
Nolen-Hoeksema,
S.N., 50, 51, 52,
53, 54, 73, 84, 85,
122
Norman, W.H.,
151, 154
Nurnberger, J., 61

Offord, D.R., 14, 50
O'Hara, M.W., 18,
47, 56, 73, 113
Olfson, M., 49, 73,
126
Oliveri, M.E., 150
Olivier, D.C., 42
Ollove, M., 87
Orley, J., 112
Ormel, J., 42, 126
Orn, H., 28, 29
Orvaschel, H., 14,
45, 115
Ouimette, P.C., 60,
108, 110

Padian, N., 156
Paley, B., 101, 106,
120, 123
Parashos, I.A., 71
Parker, L.E., 85
Parloff, M.B., 145,
146, 147, 156
Parrone, P.L., 13, 36
Parry, B.L., 137
Pasnau, R.O., 72
Paulauskas, S.L.,
29, 35, 36
Paykel, E.S., 6, 17,
91, 96, 121, 127,
132, 133
Perel, J.M., 32, 130,
133, 156, 157
Perri, M.G., 84
Persons, J.B., 88,
89, 151

Subject index

Cortisol 66-67, 68, 70, 73, 74, 107
Cultural factors 46, 48, 50, 55-56

Daily hassles 94
Decision-making 5-6, 10, 11
Delusions 7, 11, 15, 73, 74
Demographic factors 27, 32, 43-44, 45, 47, 55-57
Dependency 16, 108
  and depression vulnerability 120
  interpersonal relationships 39, 118-119, 120
Depression symptoms 1-7, 15, 21
  affective 4
  assessment 22-25
  behavioural 6
  cognitive 4-6
  dysthymic disorder 9, 10, 11
  endogenous 96
  gender differences 50
  major depressive episode 9, 10
  physical 7
Depressive distortion 86
Depressive neurosis *see* Dysthymia
Depressive personality 22, 117
Desipramine 128
Developmental problems 13, 28-29, 46, 104-105, 116
Dexamethasone suppression test (DST) 66-67, 74
Diagnosis of depression 7-25
  assessment methods 22-25, 43
  diagnostic criteria 10-11
  dysthymic disorder 9-12
  interview measures 22-24
  major depression 9, 10, 11
  subtypes 15-19
Diagnostic Interview Schedule for Children (DISC) 24
Diagnostic Interview Schedule (DIS) 23-24
Diagnostic specifiers 16-18
Diagnostic and Statistical Manual (DSM) 8, 9, 10-11, 22, 23
Diathesis-stress theories 76, 96, 97, 98-99
  genetic factors 63
  interpersonal relationships 119, 120

Differential Activation Hypothesis 90
DIS *see* Diagnostic Interview Schedule
Distraction response 52, 54, 84, 138
Diurnal variation 14, 17, 67, 70, 74
Dopamine 64, 70, 127, 128
Double depression 9, 32, 36
DSM *see* Diagnostic and Statistical Manual
Duration of depression 29, 30-31, 33, 35, 49
Dysfunctional attitudes 19
Dysfunctional Attitudes Scale (DAS) 87, 90, 91, 150, 152, 153, 154
Dysfunctional cognition
  causal role in depression 83, 84, 85, 87-88
  cognitive behavioural therapy 141-142, 154, 158, 159
  information processing models 90
  priming by dysphoric mood 88-90
Dysfunctional mate selection 113
Dysthymia 9-12
  antidepressant medication 130
  with anxiety disorders 19
  children/adolescents 13, 35, 36
  cognitive behavioural therapy 150
  diagnostic criteria 10, 11
  early-onset 9, 36, 108, 110
  genetic studies 60
  interpersonal psychotherapy 157
  with major depression 9, 12, 21, 32, 33, 36
  prevalence 44

Early morning awakening 7, 14, 17, 67, 68, 70, 97
Eating disorders 7, 14, 19, 23
Elderly people 6, 47-48, 151, 157
Electro-convulsive Therapy (ECT) 74, 133, 134-136
Endogenous depression 15-16, 96-98, 132, 133, 150
  biological factors 61, 68, 74-75
Energy
  children/adolescents 13
  diagnostic criteria 10, 11
  older people 48
  reduced 1-2, 7, 59, 132
  seasonal patterns 17, 70

Memory
  impairment 5, 6, 48
  negative representations 80, 81, 85, 90-91
Mental model theory 91
Mild depression 11, 21
  antidepressant medication 130
  genetic studies 60
  impairment effects 39-41
Minor depressive disorder 12, 21, 30, 34
Monoamine oxidase inhibitors (MAOIs)
  127, 128, 129, 131, 132
Mood
  children 12
  depression symptom 2, 3, 4, 7, 8, 18
  diagnostic criteria 10, 11
  diurnal variation 14, 67, 70, 74
  induction studies 88-90
  labile 18
  neurotransmitters 64, 65
  seasonal disorders 17, 70, 136-137
Mortality 41-42
Mothers
  see also Postpartum depression
  children with behaviour problems 114-
    115
  depressed 113-116
  insecure attachment of children 104,
    107, 108, 114
  loss impact 98, 99
  maternal responsiveness 107, 114
  mother–child relationship 38-39
  mother–infant attachment 104-105, 106-
    107
  negative interaction with child 108-109,
    114
  and school-age children 115
  stressful events 98, 99
  well-functioning children 104

Negative events 79, 83, 94, 98, 122
Negative self-schema 80, 81-82, 85
Negative thinking
  cognitive behavioural therapy 142, 143,
    151, 159, 161
  cognitive theories 79, 80, 85-88, 90, 92
  depression symptom 4, 5

Neuroendocrine dysfunction 65-67, 75, 76
Neurotic depression 15, 16, 96, 119
  see also Dysthymia
Neurotransmitters 64-67, 71-72, 75
  antidepressant medication 127, 128-
    129, 134
  electroconvulsive therapy 136
NIMH Treatment of Depression
  Collaborative Research Program
  (TDCRP) 20, 145, 146, 147, 148, 149, 150,
    152, 156
Non-recovery 31
Norepinephrine 64, 66, 70, 107, 127,
  128

Object-relations theories 104, 108
Onset of depression 27-29
Overprotection, parental 107, 108, 111

Parent–child relationships
  attachment 104-105, 106-107, 108
  interactions 105, 110
  negative effects 38-39, 108, 114
  quality 107-110
Parental discord 109, 110
Parental loss 98, 106, 110
Parenting
  see also Mothers
  dysfunctional 61, 105, 109
  involvement in child's treatment 159,
    160, 162
  quality 104, 105, 106, 107-110
  self-concept and stress 99
Parents, depressed
  psychosocial functioning of children
    105, 160
  risk to children 35, 38, 60-61, 113-116,
    162
Paroxetine 128
Patient–therapist relationship 151-152
Personality characteristics
  autonomous 82, 100, 132
  depressive personality 21, 22
  individual differences 82
  interpersonal relationships 117-119
  sociotropic 82, 108, 120, 132

SCID *see* Structured Clinical Interview for DSM-IV
Seasonal affective disorder (SAD) 17, 70, 136-137
Selective serotonin reuptake inhibitors (SSRIs) 128, 129, 130, 131, 132, 133
Self-concept 29
  cognitive theories 85, 90
  negative 4-5, 10, 11, 42, 81-84, 115
Self-control
  model 83-84
  therapy 158
Self-esteem 5, 7, 85
  children/adolescents 12, 14, 54, 158, 159
  diagnostic criteria 10, 11
  exercise therapy 138
  interpersonal psychotherapy 156
  stressful events 99, 100
Self-focus 19, 52
  increased 8, 19
  theories 84, 90
Self-modelling 159
Self-monitoring 24, 158, 160
Self-punishment 18, 84
Self-regulation 142
Self-reinforcement 84, 142, 160
Self-reporting 36, 39, 158
Self-schema 80, 81-82, 105
Self-worth 5, 10
  cognitive behavioural therapy 144
  cognitive models 82, 85
  dependency 119, 120
  insecure attachment 108
  stressful life events 99, 100
Serotonin 64, 66, 70, 127, 128, 129
Sertraline 128
Severity of depression 7, 11, 15, 29
  antidepressant medication 133, 135
  assessing 24-25
  cognitive behavioural therapy 147-148, 149-150
Sex differences *see* Gender differences
Sexual abuse 52, 54, 108, 109
Single parent families 52, 161
Situational depression 96

Sleep disturbances
  antidepressant medication 132
  biological aspects 59, 67, 68-71, 74, 75
  children/adolescents 13
  depression symptom 2, 7, 17, 18, 97
  diagnostic criteria 10, 11
  genetic studies 69-70
  sleep deprivation treatment 70, 137
Social behaviour 103
  childhood depression 13, 14
  depressed people 6, 11, 39, 116-123
Social dysfunction 103
  children of depressed parents 115
  of depressed people 4, 5, 6, 9, 11, 12
  interpersonal psychotherapy 155
  relationship with depression 29, 34
Social environment 15, 51, 52, 55, 56, 64, 93
Social isolation 48
Social mobility 46
Social skills
  deficits 118-119, 121, 142, 159
  of depressed individuals 103, 116
  problem-solving 122, 123
  therapy 159, 160
  training program 160
Social status 51, 56-57
Social support 21, 94, 99, 110, 121-122
Socioeconomic status 33, 38, 51, 52, 56
Sociotropic depression 16, 108
Sociotropic personality 82, 100, 120, 132-133
Sociotropy-Autonomy Scale 132
Stressful life events 42, 93-101
  and attributional style 98
  cognitive vulnerability 98, 150
  diathesis-stress model 98-99
  endogenous depression 16, 96-97
  generation of stress 101, 122-122
  genetic studies 61, 63, 64, 76
  interpersonal relationships 120-121
  measurement 94
  and social support 99, 121
  specific vulnerability 100, 120-121
  trigger for depression 93, 96, 98
  vulnerability 29, 97, 98, 99

Stressors
appraisal 98-99
association with depression 15, 16, 29, 34, 67, 76, 93-101
children/adolescents 54, 105, 109-110, 161
daily hassles 94
differential vulnerability 16, 75
environmental 21
family relationships 105
gender differences 51-52, 54
gene-environment interaction model 63-64
generation 101, 122-123
hormonal response 67
meaningful 98
measuring 94
role related 51, 54
Structured Clinical Interview for DSM-IV (SCID) 23
Substance abuse 9, 19, 20
children/adolescents 14, 15, 61, 114, 115
diagnosis 23
gender differences 50
Subtypes of depression 15-19, 74-75, 83, 96, 120, 150
Suicidal behaviour 2, 5, 20, 41-42
antidepressant medication 129, 131
children/adolescents 15, 21
diagnostic criteria 10, 11
elderly people 48
suicide ideation 10, 15
Symptoms of depression 1-7, 9-12

Talkativeness
increased 8
reduced 6, 11, 114, 116
Therapist–client relationship 151-152
Thought-catching 142, 143
Trazodone 128
Treatment of Depression Collaborative Research Program (TDCRP) 20, 145, 146, 147, 148, 149, 150, 152, 156
Treatment-resistant depression 135
Treatments
biological 125-139
psychological 141-163

Tricyclic antidepressant therapy 64, 65, 127, 128-129, 130, 132
children/adolescents 133
Twins, genetic studies 51, 61-62, 63, 76, 97
Tyramine 131

Unipolar depression 7, 9-12
age of onset 29
genetic studies 60, 62-63
impaired functioning 38
subtypes 74-75
Urban–rural differences 56

Vulnerability to depression 43-57
attachment quality 104-105, 106-107, 108
biological factors 50-51, 59-77, 97
brain structure 71-72
childhood experiences 105, 106, 109-110
cognitive theories 5, 85-93
and dependency 118-119
for depressive episodes 79
genetic factors 59-64, 69
interpersonal relationships 103, 118-119, 120, 122
parent–child experiences 105-110
parental care quality 105
personality characteristics 82
postpartum depression 18
relapse/recurrence 79
self-esteem 85
stress 16, 51, 98, 100

Weight 10, 11, 12, 14, 17, 59, 74
Women
see also Gender differences; Mothers
hormonal factors 72-73
postpartum depression 18-19, 50, 72, 73, 108
premenstrual syndrome 12, 51, 72
Work
depression impact on 29, 38, 39, 40, 51, 56
depression links 51, 56, 82-83, 98, 155